Studies in Sociology

Edited by
PROFESSOR W. M. WILLIAMS
University College, Swansea

13
THE FAMILY AND INDUSTRIAL SOCIETY

STUDIES IN SOCIOLOGY

By the same author:

The Family and Social Change (with Colin Rosser), Routledge
   & Kegan Paul, 1965
The Family, Allen & Unwin, 1969
Readings in Kinship in Urban Society (ed.), Pergamon, 1970
The Sociology of the Family (joint ed.), Sociological Review,
   1979
Fundamental Concepts and the Sociological Enterprise, Croom
   Helm, 1980

The Family and Industrial Society

C. C. Harris
University College, Swansea

London
GEORGE ALLEN & UNWIN
Boston   Sydney

**George Allen & Unwin (Publishers) Ltd,
40 Museum Street, London WC1A 1LU, UK**

George Allen & Unwin (Publishers) Ltd,
Park Lane, Hemel Hempstead, Herts HP2 4TE, UK

Allen & Unwin, Inc.,
9 Winchester Terrace, Winchester, Mass. 01890, USA

George Allen & Unwin Australia Pty Ltd,
8 Napier Street, North Sydney, NSW 2060, Australia

First published in 1983

British Library Cataloguing in Publication Data

Harris, C. C.
 The family and industrial society. – (Studies in sociology; 13)
1. Family – History 2. Family – Social aspects
I. Title II. Series
306.8'5'09 HQ503
ISBN 0–04–301155–1
ISBN 0–04–301156–X Pbk

Library of Congress Cataloging in Publication Data

Harris, C. C. (Christopher Charles)
 The family and industrial society.
(Studies in sociology; no. 13)
Bibliography: p.
Includes index.
1. Family – Great Britain. 2. Industry – Social
aspects – Great Britain.
I. Title II. Series:
Studies in sociology (Allen & Unwin); no. 13.
HQ614.H19 1983 306.8'5'0941 83–3833
ISBN 0–04–301155–1
ISBN 0–04–301156–X (pbk.)

Set in 10 on 11 point Times by Graphicraft Typesetters Limited
and printed in Great Britain
by Biddles Ltd, Guildford, Surrey

Contents

Acknowledgements

I wish to thank H. Stansworth and L. Morris for their very helpful comments on Chapters 9 and 10 respectively.

Getting manuscripts typed when secretarial resources have been halved as a result of university funding cuts is difficult for both authors and typists. I wish to record my thanks to Mrs H. C. Williams, who typed the first draft of Chapters 1 to 5; and Mrs S. Goodall, who typed Chapters 6 and 7, and finalised the whole typescript at extremely short notice. Above all I wish to express my gratitude to the secretary of my department, Pauline Dugmore who, in spite of multifarious and onerous academic duties, not to mention her domestic responsibilities, none the less typed the remaining five chapters.

C. C. H.

Introduction

This book is the successor to my earlier work *The Family: An Introduction* (1969). It is in no sense a revision of that book. Since *The Family* was written (1968), too much has happened in sociology, in the field of social studies and in family life itself, to make worthwhile the attempt to update it. Yet though changes in thought and family life together have rendered the original book hopelessly outdated, the period since 1968, particularly in Britain, has not been replete with family studies of an empirical or reflective kind. Indeed, though the study of the family has not been abandoned, the family as a topic has to a considerable extent been obscured by a new topic which, by almost universal consent, goes by the name 'sexual divisions in society'. So much is this the case that it is possible for Eldridge (1980) to review recent British sociology and include in his bibliography no section on the family, placing studies of the family which bear only indirectly on sexual divisions in a section entitled 'Sex, gender, generation'.

This perverse perspective is made even more absurd when the content of this new topic is examined. If we take a recent introductory textbook by Bilton, *et al.* (1981) as an example, we find that the section on 'sexual divisions' is not in fact about 'sexual divisions', but about the 'oppression of women'. This double confusion – of 'the family' with 'sexual divisions' with 'women's oppression' – is extremely unhelpful. For the importance of 'the family' as a topic derives in part from the family's being one of the major origins of sexual divisions in society, while any understanding of women's oppression requires a delineation of those familial characteristics which produce sexual divisions of such a kind that the oppression of women results. Conversely one of the benefits to be derived from a focus on the position of women is that it provides an illuminating new perspective on the family.

This book is premised on the assumption that 'the family' is still a sign which denotes on the one hand a distinct substantive area of social life, and on the other a complex of related issues, and that both are of fundamental importance to students of social life and to humankind in general. Such a judgement does not imply that other ways of abstracting from social existence which also draw from the area denoted by the term 'family' are in any way illegitimate or undesirable. It does imply that *by themselves* they are no more adequate than are family studies which ignore, for example, 'sexual divisions' or 'the oppression of women'.

The use of the term 'the family' in the title should not however mislead the reader. It is, perhaps, necessary to point out that use of a noun ('family') prefaced by the definite article ('the') does not presuppose that the author is therefore a Platonist who believes that actual families are in some sense only the expression of the (ideal) family, or that he adopts a position which holds that actual families or types of family are variations of a natural and necessary feature of human life. Nor should it be assumed that he is, therefore, a 'functionalist' who refers only to those minimal features common to all actual families within a population. 'The family' carries (except by association) no more methodological and theoretical baggage than does 'the English country house'.

The original book attempted to prevent any assumption on the reader's part that there was something called 'the family' which existed as an independent object of study by introducing at the very outset a comparative perspective, using anthropological work to discuss kinship and marriage before going on to attempt to define the meaning of the term 'family'. These three chapters, somewhat abbreviated, have been retained in the present work, one of whose aims is to provide a perspective by means of which contemporary transformations of family life may be better understood. There are, however, senses in which this sort of approach can hinder rather than assist our comprehension of contemporary family forms. For it may form the basis of what will be termed a great divide or contrast 'theory of history' in which something called 'the modern family' is seen as the result of the movement of social life from an ancient to a modern form. This is not only poor history; it enlarges our understanding of contemporary family life only by showing us what it is not, and not what it is. It results in the comparison of timeless forms and makes us insensitive to the complexities of the *process* of historical change.

These defects are amply illustrated by the structural-functionalist account of 'the family in industrial society'. Chapters 4 and 5 describe this approach, none the less, and they do so for three reasons. First, much of what is written about the family today is written in response to this approach, and some familiarity with it is necessary if contemporary work on the family is to be understood; as is familiarity with earlier family forms if contemporary family forms are to be understood. Secondly, theorising in the structural-functionalist tradition produced, in the 1950s and 1960s, a considerable amount of empirical work which added enormously to our knowledge of the family in industrial societies. Thirdly, it is not helpful (though currently fashionable) to divide the history of sociology into two periods: 'before 1965' and 'after 1965', and claim that sociology in the earlier period was dominated by an hypostatised entity called 'functionalism' or 'positivist organicism'. It is unhelpful because it obscures the diversity of what has gone before, and since the degree of consensus among sociological 'practitioners in that bygone era was in fact minimal, it makes it possible to identify 'functionalism' with whatever it is in the past you happen to dislike and then use this as an excuse for ignoring the past instead of learning from it. There are certain elements of any functionalist approach which are indispensable to sociology. If it is seen to denote a range of approaches, then we may say that 'functionalism' is by no means extinct and still exerts considerable influence over empirical research. In so far as it is mistaken, then it is as well to become acquainted with it in order to avoid similar errors oneself.

I am not and never have been a functionalist (or indeed anything else) but do not regard 'functionalism' as signifying an approach which is either wicked or erroneous. It appears to me, rather, to be inadequate, chiefly in its formal, ahistorical approach to the study of social life.

The defects of the functionalist approach to the understanding of the relation between 'the family' and 'industrial society' have to some extent been remedied in the last fifteen years not by sociology, but by the work of social historians. In Part 2 of the book, therefore, there is an account and discussion of some of the principle contributions of historians to our understanding of the nature of 'the family' in societies with industrial means of production. The history of the family emerges not as the story of what happened to an historical constant called 'the family' and its changing relation to 'the economy'; instead it is the story of the progressive differentiation of the social organisation of human activity which has resulted in the creation of what is now termed the family, that is, a nuclear child-rearing residential unit segregated from wider kin, the social life of the locality and the major forms of economic life. It is the history of a process which made it *possible* for functionalists to *regard* 'family' and 'economy' as separate subsystems and to *speak* of their relation as one of 'fit' or mutual functionality. But the 'isolated nuclear family', when seen as the product of an historical process, appears not as a structural feature of a stable societal system, but as a moment in a process not yet completed.

One of the difficulties in dealing with historical work is as follows. If, in delineating familial change, that change has to be specified in terms of the relation of domestic to other social activities or (to put it another way) the place or position of familial groups in a changing social structure, then it is necessary, simultaneously, to characterise that structure and the nature of those changes. It is not sufficient to develop theoretical categories adequate for grasping the character of 'the family' as if it were an isolated entity. An understanding of the family requires instead that it be grasped in categories devised for understanding the societal form in which it is found.

The functionalist approach cannot do this, since it understands any part as externally related to other parts which together form a synchronic whole. This makes it impossible to grasp the internal relations between elements and to analyse transition between structures. There is also another difficulty which is not distinctively functionalist. Most functionalists have attempted to characterise the modern societal form by reference to the *means* of production utilised. Hence, they refer to modern Western societies as *industrial* societies. I entirely agree that, if it is the case that 'modern' societies differ from past societies in any major way, then the historical moment that divides 'modern' societies from earlier societies is that period during which they adopted the industrial means of production. This book is concerned with modern societies, and chiefly with Britain. Hence, it is entitled *The Family and Industrial Society*.

However, it does not follow that 'industrial society' constitutes a coherent *theoretical* type. Indeed, it is difficult to see how it is possible at the theoretical level to derive a description of a societal form from a description of the means of production. 'Industrial' is, therefore, a descriptor which denotes an empirical class of societies. It has no theoretical weight. However, a theoretical basis for the analysis of societal forms is exactly what is required if we are to explain, rather than merely describe, the emergence of the modern family. Hence, Chapter 10 explores the contribution made by those (usually Marxists) working in the historical-materialist tradition. The adoption of Marxian categories requires, of course, that we see the *emergence* of modern societal and familial forms as occurring not in the nineteenth century during the process of industrialisation, but in the seventeenth century with the beginning of the rise of the capitalist mode of production and of the bourgeoisie. The nineteenth century, from this perspective, continues to be distinctive however: it is the period of the triumph of the bourgeoisie in which capitalism becomes the predominant mode of production, a victory to which the adoption of industrial means of production was vital.

Much of the work on the family in the materialist tradition is either feminist in provenance or orientation. However, Marxism stands in the same relation to feminism as functionalism does to historical materialism. For Marxism, even when it has turned its attention to the family, the family's relation to the labour process and the consequences of that relation for women, has taken for granted the relation it describes and has no more explained how this relation has come to be than functionalism has explained the 'fit' between the nuclear family and industrial society. However, while functionalism cannot provide such explanations, the materialist approach is not similarly disqualified. It has simply failed to produce them. In order to produce them, materialism must take its full title seriously and accept that, because all production takes place under determinate historical, social and cultural conditions, specific forms cannot be explained by reference alone to the mode of production of the social formation of which they are part. Their explanation always requires reference to conditions which are historically determined and incidental to the mode of production itself.

Anthropology and history provide perspectives. Functionalism and historical materialism attempt to explain. What? Contemporary family life. The final section of the book attempts to pull together what we know about contemporary family life, concentrating for reasons of brevity on contemporary Britain. An appropriate conclusion to this section might be that we know quite a lot, understand very little and can explain even less.

There is no conclusion, nor any discussion of future family forms or alternative families so much beloved of the 1960s. The future is limited but open, both for the family and sociology. Each section of Part Two is very much in the nature of *exploration*; a venture which is as yet incomplete. This is as it should be. For we are currently living through the beginning of a period of social change as profound in its consequences as the adoption of the means of industrial production which has provided this book with its title.

Rapid social change is frightening and exhilarating. In response some people cling desperately to disappearing social forms and confuse them with all that is good in family life. Others make the opposite identification and hail the disappearance of established forms as the dawn of a future utopia in which we shall miraculously escape the agonies and perplexities of the human condition. But both 'optimistic' and 'pessimistic' views are premised on the same error: a confusion of what is historically specific – a particular type of family – with something that is universal. It is the task of academic work to place what currently exists in a broader context, both socially and historically. That done, it then becomes possible to discern which features of what is commonsensically understood by the term 'family' are historically and culturally specific, and will therefore disappear as specific family forms disappear, and which are unalterable features of human existence. It is no business of sociology to advocate or deplore social change. It is its task to attempt to understand it and analyse it and, in so doing, serve those whose changing lives are part of that change. It is hoped that this book may constitute a contribution to that endeavour.

Part One

Introductory

Section I:

Basics

Chapter 1

Kinship

'I've just come back from visiting a relative in hospital.'
'What sort of relative?'
'Well, I'm not quite sure; she's connected with my parents, I
know that. I think she's some sort of cousin. She used to come and
visit Mum when we were kids. Auntie Florrie, we used to call her.
Of course, she wasn't our auntie, that is not really. But she's
definitely related – not close of course – but related.'
'Why did you go and see her?'
'Well, her being in hospital and that, you know, she could
probably do with cheering up.'
'But you don't visit everyone who is in hospital? Why did you
visit her?'
'Because she isn't just anyone, I suppose. I mean, when I was
over at Mum's on Tuesday – no wait a minute, it was Wednesday,
because that was the day the laundry came just as I was going out –
Mum said, "You remember Auntie Florrie – she's in the General".
"Well, I never did", I said. "What's wrong with her?" "It's for the
veins in her legs", she said. So seeing as how I had to pass so close, I
more or less had to pop in and see her, didn't I? I mean, she is
related, isn't she?'

We are all familiar with conversations of this type. They constitute
expressions not only of the feelings or sentiments of the individual
concerned, but also of beliefs as to what is socially demanded of
people who stand in that relation to one another, signified by the term
'related'. The last phrase 'she is related, isn't she?' is clearly not, in
this context, a plea for confirmation that the speaker is in fact related
to Auntie Florrie, but an appeal to a rule concerning the behaviour of
persons categorised as related to one another, which the speaker
expects her audience to share. She expects the other person to say:
'Ah, now I see why you went to see this person. She is a relative' (that
is, is a member of a socially recognised category of persons), 'and we
all know that people ought to visit their relatives, especially when in
trouble' (that is, she therefore has to be treated in the way laid down
by some rule specifying the behaviour of members of that category
towards one another).
If we examine this conversation further, it is possible to make

certain inferences about the system of rules which govern the behaviour of persons belonging to the same group as the speaker. In the first place, she is not at all clear how Florrie is related to her. Hence, Florrie's exact relationship to her is of small importance compared with the fact of her relationship. Secondly, she does make the distinction between close relatives and others (placing Florrie among the 'others'), even though she cannot be sure whether that relationship is through the mother or the father. Hence, we might guess that relationships through each parent are probably of equal importance. We might infer also that it is how 'far away' a person is that matters rather than who they're related through. That is, there may be more important differences between the way one is expected to behave to one's brother as opposed to one's father's brother or one's father's brother's son than between, say, your mother's brother and your father's brother. Or to put it more technically, we might say that the degree of *genealogical distance* is more important than differences in *filiation* (being the child of).

In the third place, we may note that the speaker uses the term 'aunt' of someone who is not her aunt according to the normal definition. It seems likely that she is expected to behave towards Florrie in the same way as to an aunt, which is why she is of course called 'aunt'. Her feeling that she has niecelike duties towards her (visiting her in hospital) tend to confirm this view. But both her verbal statement ('she wasn't our "Auntie"') and the fact that it is only because she is passing so close that makes her feel she has to visit, suggests that though using the title 'Aunt' for both 'real' and 'fictive' aunts, she is nevertheless very well aware of the difference.

Finally, it is clear from her account that she does not feel any particular affection for the person concerned, she has not been in frequent contact (she didn't know that she was ill until her mother told her – her mother said 'you remember . . .') but nevertheless feels some sort of obligation to 'pop in': 'I *had* to pop in and see her.' But no one was watching to see whether she went in (except God, who is not referred to). No sanctions on her behaviour are mentioned, no rewards or punishments offered or threatened by other persons. This suggests that the sense of obligation she feels to visit the 'aunt' (though only when passing) comes (at the point of time the speaker is referring to) from 'inside' herself.

Nevertheless, she does assume that others will understand and recognise this sense of obligation, which suggests that it has a public rather than private nature. This could be because people everywhere feel the same sense of obligation. The obligation depends on Florrie being categorised in a certain way, and on certain duties being accepted between members. But all men everywhere do not categorise people in the same way, nor consider the same duties appropriate. Her assumption depends in part on her expectation that we too associate the same duties with membership of the same categories. This feeling of obligation is, then, something that she shares with other members of the group (to which she thinks we also belong), *because* she belongs to that group. It is a feeling that she has acquired by virtue of being born into, and taught the values and ways of, the group. It is not a sentiment attached to Florrie as a person.

SOCIAL RELATIONSHIPS AND BIOLOGICAL RELATIONS

The study of behaviour of this kind is what the study of kinship is about. But behaviour of exactly what kind? Well, it is the study of how people feel they ought to behave to other people in different *genealogical* categories, that is to say, how they ought to behave to people who are related to them by ties of blood (*consanguineal* ties: father's father or mother's father's sister's daughter's son, for example) or by ties of marriage (*affinal* ties: wife, brother's wife, sister's husband, wife's sister's son, for example).

Taking a given individual as our starting-point or *Ego* we may distinguish relationships according to their *degree*. Mother, father, brother, sister, child, are *first-degree* consanguineal relationships; father's father, father's brother or sister, mother's father, mother's sibs, ('sib' is a useful shorthand for 'brother or sister') are *second-degree* consanguineal relations, and so on.

There is no standard way of classifying affines. Normally a distinction is made between spouses (husbands or wives) of Ego's consanguineal *kin* ('kin' is often used as a shorter word for 'relations') on the one hand, and the consanguineal kin of Ego's spouse on the other. Both types of affine can therefore be classified in the same way as consanguineal kin, that is, as the spouses of Ego's first-, second-, third-degree kin, or as the first-, second-, third-degree kin of Ego's spouse.

We can also distinguish between kin on the basis of the *generational distance* from Ego, Ego's father belonging to the *first-ascending* generation and his children to the *first-descending* generation; his grandparents to the *second-ascending* generation and his grand-children to the *second-descending* generation, and so on. We can then combine both classifications and refer, for example, to the Mo Bro (mother's brother) as Ego's second-degree consanguineal kin in the first-ascending generation.

For some purposes, it is sometimes useful to classify ascending kin through the parents of Ego. (All ascending kin must be related through Mo or Fa, since these are the only first-degree kin Ego has in the first-ascending generation.) These are usually referred to as Ego's *matrilateral* and *patrilateral* kin, these simply being Latin-derived shorthand forms for 'blood relatives on his mother's and father's side' respectively.

Basically, then, we have two types of kin – consanguineal and affinal; that is, people related by ties of blood and of marriage. These relations are basically biological. All that is meant by this statement is that they have reference to the biological activities of begetting and bearing children, being begotten by and born of the same person, and so on. But to refer to a kinship tie is not to refer to a biological relation, except indirectly. In the example with which we began this chapter we never discovered even what this relation was. What mattered was that, because a relation was *recognised*, this affected the behaviour to one another of the parties between whom the relation was recognised to exist. It affected it, however, because the group to which they belonged had rules which governed the behaviour between people recognised to be so related.

When two people or two categories of people share common expec-tations about the way they ought to behave to each other, then we may say that a *social relationship* exists between them. *A kin relationship is a social relationship and not a biological relation*. The term never refers except indirectly to such a relation. There are all sorts of problems which arise from this definition, as we shall see later (see p. 9), but this will do for the moment.

To say that a kinship relationship is a social relationship which refers to a biological relation is not to say that the one is always identical with the other. In our society the rights and duties of fatherhood are rights and duties towards a person which another person has, usually by virtue of their being the biological father (that is, the *genetic father*) of that person. But an illegitimate child's genetic father has not, even where his identity is known, the rights of a 'father'. That is to say, the child has no 'social father' or *pater*. A father is not necessarily the genetic father of a child. A father is a man who is recognised by the society as a whole as having the responsibi-lities and rights of a 'father'. These rights and duties are usually acquired by prior marriage to the genetic mother of the child.

To say that children have to have genetic parents is, of course, a tautology. The statement that in all societies children have to have social fathers is not self-evident. The universal social recognition of the necessity of a pater has been expressed by the British social anthro-pologist, Malinowski, as the *principle of legitimacy*. This declares that 'in all societies a father' (we should now say 'pater')

is regarded by law, custom and morals as an indispensable element of the procreative group. The woman has to be married before she is allowed legitimately to conceive, or else a subsequent marriage or an act of adoption gives the child full tribal or civil status. (Malinowski, 1930)

This is not the place to discuss this principle in detail. Here we need only note four points which arise. In the first place, the importance of this principle depends on the distinction between 'pater' and 'genetic father'. In the second place, whenever we consider a kinship relationship, we shall have to bring in other people than the parties actually involved, as Malinowski has to. The references to law, custom and morals and to tribal and civil *status* (social position) imply the existence of shared expectations by others, who constitute the group which shares the agreement on the way people ought to behave – which is expressed in legal, customary and moral rules. The fact that we have to bring in other people indicates that we are dealing with a *social institution*. A relationship or piece of behaviour can be said to be institutionalised when the relevant behaviour is known and expected throughout the group concerned. (Relationships or systems of relationships can only be institutionalised *within a group*. The statement that a piece of behaviour is 'institutionalised' is meaningless unless the group within which it is institutionalised is specified.)

In the third place, the reference to other people which is implied shows quite clearly that we are not dealing with the feelings of fathers: the 'natural' affection and concern of a man for his offspring. Fatherhood has public and not merely private characteristics.

Lastly, the fact that fatherhood is institutionalised suggests that it must be of importance not merely to the father and child, but to the whole group, and entails that the rules governing the determination of fatherhood and the behaviour of fathers are supported by legal, customary and moral sanctions.

However, we may feel that to describe fatherhood simply in terms of rights and duties is not enough. In our society a man has no specific duty to make model boats for his son or to take him fishing or play cricket with him in the back garden. But having a father around makes these things possible and there are certainly expectations shared among us that these sorts of thing will happen if the man is a 'good father'. This whole complex of social expectations as to what it is to be 'a good father' constitutes an example of what sociologists call a *social role* or simply a *role*. The word 'good' shows that these expectations involve some sort of moral evaluation and, hence, we can say that a role is a set of expectations which are *valued*. The role of father does not therefore only refer to the rights and duties, legal, customary, or moral, which are attached to the social position or status of 'father', but enables us to consider the expectations which apply to those occupying that position which do not result from the knowledge of specific rules.

Now, members of groups share not only expectations about the behaviour of other people; they also share expectations about the way in which such roles shall be allocated. In our society it is expected that the role of 'pater' will normally be played by the genetic father. This presupposes two things. First, that we are able to ascertain who the genetic father is; secondly, that we understand how children are generated. Hence, biological or genetic relations enter the picture through the process of allocation of kinship roles which depends on *beliefs* of the group about the biological facts of life.

Primitive societies have widely different beliefs concerning the relationship between copulation and birth, and these beliefs are related to the *structure* of their kinship system, that is, the pattern made by the types of relationship which constitute it. For example some societies have been thought only to recognise that intercourse is necessary to 'open the way' for birth. Hence, the child's filiation to the mother but not to the father is recognised. Alternatively the child may be thought of as being conceived by the father, the mother merely 'housing' the child. Here the child's filiation to the father and not the mother is recognised. These are extreme cases, but the beliefs mentioned may be seen to be consonant with the way that the societies concerned arrange the social relationships which are based on the recognition of kinship.

FILIATION AND DESCENT

Because the child is not considered related by blood to one or other parent, one parent is, in such a system, an affine and not a blood relative. Now, all kinship systems use the links of filiation as a means of transferring rights from one generation to another, though societies vary as to whether all types of right – to office, property and membership of social groups are inherited in this way. Sometimes these rights are transmitted through males and sometimes through females. When ties of filiation are recognised for the purposes of the transmission of rights to *group membership*, then we may speak of the members of the society concerned tracing *descent* through such ties. A descent system is a pattern of socially recognised relationships which are used for the transmission of such rights. Transmission may occur and descent may be traced through *males only* or through *females only*. In both cases we have a system of *unilineal* transmission. If the male principle is used, rights will be transmitted through the father; if the female principle is used, rights will be transmitted through the mother. Hence, we may speak of unilineal systems being either *patrilineal* or *matrilineal*, that is, transmitting rights through the male or female line. Of course, it can be more complicated than this. We find systems where one type of group membership or property is inherited through one line, and another type through another line. These are sometimes called *double unilineal* systems (nothing comes down both lines, different things come down different single lines).

We have to consider yet another possibility, that is, a *bilateral* or *omnilineal* system. In such a system rights are transmitted to Ego on *both* sides. Now, it may be thought that we have already dealt with this case. Is not Ego in a double unilineal system, a recipient of rights from both sides? He is not. Rights are transmitted through both parents (as in bilateral systems). But rights descend not from his father's mother, only from his father's father.

In a bilateral system he inherits not merely from the males or females on one side; nor one thing from the males on one side and another from the females on another side; but the same things from *both* males *and* females on *both* sides: hence 'omnilineal'.

This brief exposition will, it is hoped, give the reader some idea of the variety of ways in which filiation can be used as the basis for transmission of rights and for tracing descent. *But the recognition of ties of filiation is not the same as the recognition of descent.* The study of descent systems is a study of the principles adopted by groups who use ties of filiation as the basis for the transferring of rights and the allocation of statuses. It is the study of what different societies use kinship for and how they do it. The rightness of what they do may be expressed in terms of the beliefs they have about the biological facts of existence. Our two extreme examples of societies who recognised respectively the facts of biological maternity and paternity *only*, had, it will surprise no one to hear, systems of matrilineal and patrilineal descent.

In most societies, however, the facts of biological maternity and paternity are recognised if not understood, and even where this is not the case, the activities associated with the roles of motherhood and fatherhood are found and constitute the basis of social relationships. This fact may be expressed by saying that *the recognition of filiation as opposed to descent is universally bilateral.* The range of the recognition of filiation will however be affected by its descent significance, and by the other uses to which it is put. Similarly, if a kinship relationship is also a relationship which is recognised for the purposes of descent, it may acquire a societal or economic or political significance.

THE DEFINITION OF KINSHIP

We can now return to our problem of the definition of kinship. Kinship is a universal institution, hence the most likely place to find an explanation of its nature is not in other social institutions since their incidence and forms vary between societies, but in the conditions of action of all men everywhere. Whatever a society may be thought of as using kinship for, it is plain that what is being used is a set of ideas concerning the *biological* conditions of action of a society. This set of ideas – the sense which men make of their biological nature – must be such as to lead to social arrangements which make it possible for the members of the society to survive under these conditions. Hence, the study of kinship always involves a consideration of both these conditions of action and the sense made of them, and the way in which this sense is embodied in action.

This is the first sense in which it may be said that kinship is 'about' man's biological nature. Secondly, it can be argued that kinship relationships 'systematically overlap' biological relations. We have to say 'systematically overlap' because the people in the society concerned may not recognise biological relations that exist but 'biological relations' that do not exist. Our interest in the non-recognition of actually existent biological relations may be justified in terms of our interest in the biological conditions of action. In the second case we may say that the social relationships which are intelligible only in terms of an erroneous belief about biological relationships are kinship relationships precisely because they *do* have a biological reference, although it be erroneous.

The difficulty raised by the notion of overlap lies in the fact that not only do biological relations and the social relationships which we call kinship relationships sometimes fail to coincide – but even recognised *biological* relations do not always coincide with such social relationships. Societies where 'social paternity' is in no way dependent on genetic paternity are cases in point.

Let us pause and consider the implications of this argument. The question is: 'can kinship relationships be said systematically to overlap biological relations?' The question implies that we already know what kinship relationships are. If we leave out the word 'kinship', then the question isn't worth asking. If we know what kinship relationships are *before we have decided whether they have anything to do with biological relations*, then it would seem that their being kinship relationships cannot be dependent on their having something to do with biological relations.

There are two possible answers to the question 'how do we know what kinship relationships are'. The first is that they are relationships which we, the observers, would describe as kinship on the basis of the notions of kinship which exist in our society. The second answer is to be found by turning not to *our* ideas, nor directly to the ideas of the members of a number of different societies, but to the conditions of action common to all societies. Men everywhere must make sense of such conditions. Hence, all societies have a set of ideas about birth, procreation, and so on.

Social relationships are only possible because the people participating in them share common ideas which give the relationships meaning. *Those relationships which are intelligible only in terms of the ideas a society has about what we think of as its biological conditions of action may be regarded as constituting the class of relationships described as kinship relationships.*

By focusing on the conditions under which men everywhere act we have arrived not only at what is involved in the study of kinship, but also at a criterion for distinguishing a class of social relationships which is not determined by the ideas governing social relationships in one society.

We must conclude our consideration of this issue with a word of caution, however. Any type of social relationship derives its meaning not merely from the set of ideas which are constitutive of it. It derives its meaning also from the relation it has to other types of social relationship. Hence, any social relationship is not meaningful in terms of its constitutive ideas alone. Where relationships of two different types are regularly combined, it will not be possible to understand the meaning of the relationship to the actor without reference to the other type of relationship. Hence, the definition given above should not be taken as restricting the members of the class of kinship relationship to those relationships which are uniquely meaningful in terms of the sense made of biological conditions.

THE UNIVERSALITY OF KINSHIP

Why is it that kinship institutions are found in all known societies? This question could be put in two quite distinct ways. It could be rephrased to read 'why *is* it that man's understanding of his biological nature *leads* him to use the biological relations which he thus recognises as a basis for social relationships?' or 'why *has* man *been led* to do this ?'

As the different tenses used in the questions imply, the first demands an explanation in terms of the conditions that apply universally at all times. The second demands some sort of historical explanation.

Questions of this kind are questions about how society or aspects of society came into being. They start from an *initial situation* in which there is no society. They, therefore, refer to non-social conditions under which society exists; and the mechanisms by which such patterns arise, and in whose terms their existence must be explained, must be *non*-social mechanisms of some kind. The most obvious mechanism which would do the job is some sort of psychological mechanism.

We have to distinguish this type of answer from a third type, however. Instead of attempting a general historical explanation, or an explanation in terms of general conditions, we could try to explain the universality of kinship in terms of the characteristics which a society has to have for social life to be possible.

Now, the second type of explanation we distinguished was, at one time, very popular. It has one enormous drawback. Since human society emerged long before the date of the earliest written records, it is not possible to provide any but purely conjectural historical explanations of the existence of kinship institutions or the way in which they work.

The first type may appear more attractive. At a time when the feelings that people had towards kin were regarded as defining the nature of kinship relationships, it was tempting to use psychological explanations. Even if we accept the public rather than private nature of social relationships, it is still tempting to try and derive the recognition of kinship obligations from the psychological nature of man.

What is usually called the 'extension theory' of kinship was such an attempt. This theory, which has come to be associated with Malinowski and was at one time widely held, stated that kinship could be explained in terms of natural feelings of loyalty and affection which arose between members of the biological group of parents and offspring, which were 'extended' to more remote categories of related persons.

Let us now suppose that sentiments of loyalty and affection are generated by cohabitation and nurture, the activities which characterise the domestic domain. Can we go on to say that explanations of this type tell us anything about why men in the societies of which we have knowledge behave in the way they do? Obviously, they can. What they can explain is those regularities in behaviour which arise again in each generation as the same processes of cohabitation and nurture take place. This might well be plausible if all societies had the same type of kinship system. But although kinship institutions may be said to be universal, they are, as we have seen, of very different kinds. Malinowski thought of this difficulty, however. He saw the generation of sentiments as being bilateral, but this natural pattern being distorted by 'culture'. This, however, is exactly what we are trying to explain. If people in different societies behave in different ways in this matter of kinship, it is because the societies concerned have different rules governing kinship behaviour, or to put it another way, have different systems of kinship relationships, which exist prior to the arrival of each new generation. These cannot be accounted for in terms of sentiments which are continually created afresh.

We have not done with this argument. Even if kinship institutions were identical everywhere, the extension theory still would not do, because the argument which has just been put forward applies with equal force in this situation. Because I want to care for my mother in her old age does not explain why I feel I ought to do so. To recognise that an 'ought' is involved here implies the recognition of an obligation independent of sentiment.

Why, then, was the theory ever held? The answer may be found in regarding it not as a theory of the second type, but as a first-type theory in disguise. In other words, properly understood, the theory states that, because the activities of procreation and nurture create sentiments of attachment, then early in the history of mankind such sentiments were expressed in the form of rules which, though extended to serve other purposes and distorted in various ways by the weight of other types of relationships which have been built upon them, survive to the present day. Individuals are in the majority of cases motivated to follow them because of the natural creation of 'original' sentiments in each generation.

In this form the extension theory can be seen to be a plausible but unverifiable 'conjectural history'-type explanation. This does not mean that it is not of the greatest value to consider society from the standpoint of the way in which the psychological needs of its members are satisfied by their participation in the system of relationships that constitute it. But such a viewpoint does not enable us simply to derive culture from nature, nor, more specifically, a system of kinship relationships from psychological needs.

It may appear to some readers that what has just been said runs counter to the whole approach to kinship which is being followed here. This is not so. To say that kinship is only definable by reference to the sense that a society makes of the facts of biological relationship does not necessarily imply that that sense is necessarily reducible to it. We can learn two things from our criticism of the extension of sentiments theory. The first is that it is not possible to explain a kinship system in terms of the sentiments and activities which arise out of the co-operation of individuals in begetting and rearing children. The second is that it does not, therefore, follow that a kinship system is intelligible without reference to those sentiments and activities.

To account for the universality of kinship we must turn to the third type of explanation. If we stick to the biological group, we might be able to argue as follows. For social life to be possible, language and the rest of society's accumulated possessions must be transmitted to the next generation and arrangements for its nurture during infancy and childhood must be made. Then in the absence of any alternative arrangements, which are not likely under primitive conditions, these activities will be performed by the biological group. Unfortunately, what we have to explain is not the existence of relationships between members of the biological group, but the wider recognition of relationships. This can only be explained by relating the system of relationships to *other* systems of relationship in the society.

To put the point rather more crudely: if we find that a man distinguishes between somebody who is, say, his father's father's father's son's son's son and another person who has no recognised agnatic tie, instead of going away and puzzling about how it is that the feelings of duty and affection normally felt between father and son have become extended so that this man is a sort of brother, we ask rather rudely 'so what?' Hearing that all sorts of legal, political and economic consequences follow from this relationship the purpose of categorising people in this way becomes clear, and the significance of the relationship in the society becomes clear also. After all, it is only academics who make distinctions *for the sake of making distinctions*.

Now, admittedly this does not answer the question 'why should people use distinctions based on socially recognised biological relationships for this purpose?' Professor Fortes, in discussing a related problem, has pointed to the importance of this question and says that we cannot at the present time answer it. He himself suggests, however, that the answer lies in the homogeneous nature of those societies in which kinship is used as a basis for types of social relationship. By homogeneity he means the extent to which one person can replace another in a given social position. Where individuals are socially undifferentiated, 'there is nothing', he suggests, 'which could so precisely and incontrovertibly fix one's place in society as one's parentage' (Fortes, 1953).

We may note that this answer to the question is of a type which explains the cross-cultural regularity not in terms of an *initial historical situation* (all societies developed from kin groups), nor in terms of an *initial situation of the individual* (that is, because every individual grows up in a kin group, kin relationships are primary and form the basis of other types of relationship), but in terms of *conditions which are necessary for an ongoing society to be possible*. In other words, his explanation is a distinctively sociological explanation rather than an historical or psychological one. From this example, it can be seen that structural explanations can provide understanding of social regularities which are found not merely within societies, but between societies.

The example with which we began this chapter was chosen to illustrate the various problems, a discussion of which has formed its subject-matter. We began by examining the implications of that conversation and so started by pointing out the distinction between sentiments and obligations, between 'I want' and 'I ought', which was so important in evaluating explanations of the universality of kinship institutions. Now that we have looked at the meaning of kinship and its uses, we can get a little more juice from it.

To start with, the fact that the speaker did not know the exact relationship that Florrie had to herself suggests that, in the society concerned, kinship is not the chief means of 'placing' people in society. That is to imply statuses are not allocated in this society on the basis of kinship. Moreover, the fact that the speaker did not know whether Florrie was 'connected' through her mother or father suggests that either there is no system of intergenerational transmission of rights or if there is (which is likely), then this system is either omnilineal or patrilineal, since in other systems it would be vital to know through which parent the relationship was. Hence, we may guess both what type of system it might be and its importance to the society. From the way the speaker talks, it seems likely that in the society concerned the chief importance of the recognition of kinship relations is to 'define and sanction a personal field of social relationships for the individual'. There is nothing peculiar about a system being put to this use. However, if we are right in assuming that this is the *chief* use to which it is put, then this society differs markedly from most primitive societies. If it is the other uses to which a system is put which distorts the tendency to bilateral recognition, then this reinforces our guess that the system of transmission is omnilineal or at most weakly patrilineal.

The method of using an example has been deliberately adopted because when we are talking about 'a kinship system', 'a type of marriage', or 'a type of family', it is very easy to forget that this is simply a way of referring to the patterns of thought and behaviour which are shared by a group of people and are reflected in conversations such as the one described. In order to think straight about such matters, we need continually to translate what we are saying into patterns of thought and action in order to see if we really understand what we are talking about and whether what we are saying is sense.

The example given is, however, very brief and thin. Though we can see quite clearly that certain things are involved in behaviour of the kind which the conversation describes, we cannot make more than guesses about the nature of the kinship system in that society. To discover this we should have to ask more questions of the same person, observe the behaviour of the same person and extend our range of observation much beyond a single individual before we could produce an accurate description and arrive at a correct understanding of the sense which the members of the group – to which the speaker belongs –make of the biological facts of their existence and the way in which this sense is embodied in the rules governing their behaviour.

Chapter 2

Marriage

There was a right old to-do when our Jane got wed. The preparations went on for years, at any rate that's what it seemed like. You'd think with all that effort that on the day everything would have gone smoothly. Not a bit of it! In the first place, who should call in that very morning but Mrs Crawshaw 'to wish our Jane all the best'. What she'd really come for was to find out why the Crawshaws hadn't been invited to the wedding. You know, when we were sending out the invitations, Mum and me clean forgot that, though John came from down south, he'd still got relatives up here. Anyway, there she was, standing in the kitchen, dressed up to the nines, with people cutting sandwiches all round her, going on about how even second cousins had been invited on our side but on her side all Mr Crawshaw's relatives had been ignored ... And Jane was in hysterics and said she'd wanted a quiet wedding and it was nothing to do with all these people she didn't even know, and it was all Mum's fault – which upset Mum because Jane had been as keen on a proper wedding as any one – and she hadn't got anyone from the family to give her away – I mean, Bert looked very nice in his tails and all, but it's not like having your father or brother, is it?

Anyhow when we got to the church we went in and there was our side of the aisle filled to overflowing and scarcely three rows on John's side. I mean, we'd kept the numbers on each side equal – for the invitations, that is – but all sorts of people from around here dropped in to pay their respects, like. It was just the same at Uncle Arthur's funeral – you never saw such a crowd – and you know how many people Mum knows. Anyway, we got the ushers, though why they call them that I don't know, to shift some of our lot over on to their side to balance it up a bit. Anyhow, the service went off all right, though Mum was worried because she cried half the time and smudged her mascara – I *told* her not to wear any – but when it came to speeches after the buffet back at our house, and Bert ... he was deputising for our Dad, like ... came to that bit – you know, about not losing a daughter, but gaining a son – she started off all over again and couldn't stop – it must have been the Sauterne – and then they nearly missed the train. Well, what happened was ...

And so on.

In no society is marriage a relationship which is of purely personal concern to the persons thus joined together. In all societies it represents the creation of relationships between *groups* as well as individuals, a rearrangement of the relationships between persons (and hence of the rights and duties which are elements of these relationships) and it always involves a recognition of the changes that have taken place by the society as a whole as well as by the individuals and groups who are immediately concerned.

All these elements are indicated by the account of the wedding ceremony which prefaces this chapter. It is clear from the account that the ceremony is public: other people drop in at the church; a 'quiet' wedding isn't 'proper'. It is quite clear that two groups are involved: '*our* Jane wed'; there are references to 'our side' and 'their side', meaning 'our Jane's kin' and 'their John's kin'. Moreover, it is clear that there is a notion of balance between sides, symbolised by the segregation of the two sides in the church and the shifting over of people from one side to the other to make it 'look right'.

The rearrangement of relationships is clearly indicated. The girl's family experiences a sense of loss. The mother cries. One of the men of the girl's kin group '*gives* the bride *away*'. The old tag about 'losing a daughter' is trotted out and evokes more tears. The loss which is being thus recognised is clearly seen as a loss of a member of the kin group, however unrealistic that loss may be in terms of daily interaction. It is not a complete loss, however. Losing a daughter they gain, in a bilateral system, a son. They are gaining a father of the grandchildren who will be *theirs*. But still the mother cries. The loyalty of the daughter is now to her new husband, rather than to her mother. Whether, *in fact*, her mother's effective control (power) over her daughter is at an end, her *right* to it has been extinguished. She loses the right to her daughter's domestic services and to control her sexual behaviour. The rights to sexual access and to domestic services now pass to the husband, and the husband's kin acquire, like the wife's, rights in the grandchildren.

The bride, however, objects at the last minute to all these people who have quite clearly a legitimate interest in the proceedings. It is clear that, at that moment, she regards the whole thing as purely on the individual plane. For the 'happy couple', marriage is *not* concerned with intergroup relationships, but with individual relationships. They doubtless see themselves to have a personal relationship which exists independently of the marriage. The marriage itself merely constitutes the social recognition of that relationship. It is not seen as the creation of a social relationship within which a *new* personal relationship can grow.

The beliefs of both parents and children about this are probably not inconsistent. They both believe in love first and marriage afterwards, and not the other way round. There is only one snag in this doctrine.

The whole notion of romantic love presupposes that the lovers have a freedom of choice. Complete freedom of choice implies that the social groups into which the children are born have a corresponding lack of power to determine whom their children marry. Now, in no society known are such groups entirely uninterested in their children's choice of mate. They cannot be, because by virtue of the marriage they enter into relationship with the kin of their child-in-law. As we saw in Chapter 1 the significance of this varies enormously, depending on the use to which kinship systems are put, but the principle is clear. Moreover, depending on the nature of the system, the children produced by the marriage will be affected by their ties of filiation to the other group. Inheritance of different types of property and group membership are often involved, and in virtually all cases the children are evaluated by other people, at least initially, in terms of the evaluations made of *both* their parents.

Hence, we find in all societies either that marriage is hedged around by rules specifying which categories of people are eligible mates for the members of different groups or, at least, that the groups which constitute the society make strenuous efforts to control or influence their children's choice of marriage partner. It is a discussion of these themes that will be the concern of this chapter.

MARRIAGE AND THE TRANSMISSION OF RIGHTS

In Chapter 1 we were concerned primarily with the way in which relationships *between* generations were recognised and used. No mention was made of another very important principle which concerns relationships *within* generations. In all societies there is a recognition of the importance of ties of kinship between children of the same parents, and in many societies sibs act together with regard to other groups.

These regularities can, once again, be looked at in terms of both sentiments and rights. Sibs are likely to be reared by the same mother and, hence, their loyalties are likely to be in the first place to their mother and to their age mates. (We may note here that sibs are linked twice: directly to each other, and by loyalty to the same parent.) Hence, biological conditions are likely to lead to the formation of a cluster of individuals sharing common loyalties. This cluster will obviously occupy the same territory and share the income from any property. With the decease of any one of the members, their share of any income will be appropriated by the surviving members of the cluster. Hence, the members of the cluster will be held together both by common sentiments and by virtue of having common interests in the joint property of the cluster. Where such interests are socially recognised, they may be said to constitute rights.

With the decease of the parent(s), it will obviously be to the advantage of the siblings to prevent the dispersion of their inherited property. But if the group is to continue, they will have to produce a third generation. Ruling out for the moment an incestuous union between sibs, this means that they will have to bring in mates for the sisters or for the brothers. But other sibling groups will have the same problem. It is obvious, therefore, that the groups will not be able to. retain all their members. At the same time bringing in an outsider will create problems as to the entitlement of the children of such a union to the property, since they will not be full members of the group in whom the rights to the property were previously vested; two sibling groups will have claims on the children, and the children will have claims on two sibling groups. Some sort of *arrangement* will have to be arrived at, therefore, between the sibling groups concerning the distribution of rights to property and in children. This arrangement is usually called 'marriage'.

The solutions to the problem may be stated as follows:

(1)   Let the sisters take lovers to procreate the children who remain full members of the original sibling group of the mothers.
(2)   Let the sisters take husbands on the understanding that the husbands have no rights in the children.
(3)   Let the sisters take husbands and the men renounce rights in the children of the sisters and establish rights in the children of the wives.
(4)   as for 3, but let the men retain some rights in the sisters' children and establish some rights in those of the wives.

These arrangements imply matrilineal (1 and 2), patrilineal (3) and, according to the details of the arrangement, either double unilineal or omnilineal (4) systems of transmission. Artificially separated by the organisation of these two chapters though they are, types of marriage and types of transmission are now seen to be merely different ways of talking about the same thing. For marriage involves the transference of rights between groups which determines the pattern of inheritance and group membership (descent) of the children of the union thereby created.

PATTERNS OF RESIDENCE: DOMESTIC SERVICES AND. DOMESTIC AUTHORITY

Marriage is not merely concerned with a transference of rights in the children, however. It also involves a transfer of rights in the persons of the spouses, as we saw from the example taken from our own society. Here we can make distinctions of a kind which are related to (but not the same as) the distinctions which were made with regard to the children.

The first type of rights in the persons of the spouses that we will consider are those which arise from the composition of the *domestic group*. As far as the wife is concerned, the right to her domestic services is transferred by marriage to her husband. What this means in practice will depend on whether they set up house on their own or whether she finds herself living with her husband's parents and his brothers and their wives and, hence, under the authority of her husband's mother or in some other type of domestic group.

As far as the husband is concerned, the pattern of residence after marriage will determine whether he finds himself under the authority of his father, his wife's father, or on his own. Marriage, therefore, marks the reordering of domestic relationships as well as establishing those of descent and, if the domestic unit is an economic unit, of economic relationships as well.

There are only a limited number of possible patterns of residence. The wife may continue to reside with her brothers and the husband may merely visit her. Or the wife may continue to reside with her mother and her sisters and her husband may come to live with them. Or the wife may leave her natal group and live with her husband and his brothers. Or both husband and wife may leave their natal groups and set up a new domestic group of their own. These different solutions are termed nato-local, uxori-local, viri-local and neo-local respectively. They are, of course, related to the type of descent system. They are also related, however, to the type of property which is important, and its degree of partibility (whether it can be divided).

The way in which a given system of transmission will affect residence at marriage will depend on the uses to which that system is put. Often it is used to form exogamous groups whose members have to *act together* in economic or political matters. Such groups are usually described as *corporate* groups.

Since men have control in political and economic matters, priority is usually given to keeping the men together. A nato-local residence pattern keeps all the members together. A viri-local pattern keeps the men together, an uxori-local pattern keeps the women together and a neo-local pattern disperses the group. The only residence patterns that keep the men together are the nato-local and the viri-local. In patrilineal systems the viri-local pattern can be adopted. But in matrilineal systems, while this pattern keeps the men together, they lose control over the rearing of their heirs (the children of the sisters who have gone off to live with husbands in other groups). An uxori-local pattern can be an alternative here, provided that the geographical range of marriage is not too wide relative to the needs of the men of the group to meet together.

If the system of transmission is not used to form exclusive groups, but is primarily a means of transferring rights in property from one generation to another, then residence is no problem, provided the property is partible. If, however, it is not partible, then either only one of the siblings of the right sex can inherit or the siblings of the same sex will have to stay together and administer the property as a group.

When this is the case, the same problems arise as when the system is used to form corporate exogamous descent groups, since sibs cannot marry and they are forced to act together. Assuming that the men control the property and its effective control requires frequent contact, then a dispersion of the males by the adoption of uxori-local residence will, if the geographical range of marriage is large enough (and the available transport poor enough), prevent the exercise of such control.

If the property concerned is a farm whose economic viability depends on its *size*, then, in order to inherit, the children of the owner of that farm will have to stay together to work it. In such a case, in a patrilineal system (provided the farm is large enough), the pattern of residence of the sons after marriage is likely to be viri-local. Or the property may not be a farm, but a tenancy or the ownership of a dwelling-house. In such a case it will not be the control, but the utilisation of the property which demands co-residence. In a bilateral system the married couple would presumably have a choice as to the type of residence they adopted depending on the suitability of the accommodation available, and their ability to set up a neo-local household.

It is important to recognise that *different* residential groups may be formed in societies with the *same* type of descent either because the system is used for different purposes or the conditions under which the system operates (the type of property, the distance away of other groups who provide wives, the effectiveness of transport) varies between the societies.

It is equally important to recognise that descent-group membership is closely related to but quite distinct from membership of a residential or domestic group.

SEXUAL RIGHTS

The extent to which sibling groups act together is vividly exemplified in some societies which have forms of what is called *plural* or *polygamous* marriage. Plural marriage may be either the marriage of one man to several women, to which the name of polygyny is given, or it may be the marriage of one woman to several men, which is called polyandry. Where the several women are sisters, this is referred to as sororal polygyny; where the several men are brothers, this type of marriage is called fraternal polyandry. The latter type of marriage is, however, very rare, and sororal polygyny is the more frequently found. Different types of plural marriage are obviously related to the type of residence pattern and descent system.

Plural marriage should not be confused with *privileged mating*. The majority of known societies do not regard, as we do (officially), sex as something which is only allowable within marriage. In the first place, many societies allow premarital sexual intercourse with certain categories of people. In the second place, while the great majority of societies regard marriage as creating exclusive rights in the sexuality of the wife and, therefore, have strict rules which proscribe adultery, it must be remembered that marriage is primarily a transference of rights (even in the spouses) between *groups*. Hence, in a substantial minority of societies, sexual access to brothers' wives or wives' sisters, is not regarded as adultery. Here marriage transfers rights in the wife's sexuality not exclusively to the husband, but to the males of the husband's sibling group, or rights in the females of a sibling group to a husband of one of them. It does not follow, however, that such transfers therefore constitute a case of plural marriage. On the contrary, the rights in the child born of a woman to whom her husband's brothers have had privileged access will, in a patrilineal society, be regarded as belonging to her husband on the principle that the 'social father' of a child is the rightful husband of its mother, whoever the genetic father may be. That is to say, it is the marriage that establishes the *fatherhood* of the child, even though that same marriage may also have given rights of privileged *sexual* access to other members of the father's kin group.

We must take care, therefore, not to confuse the creation of rights in the children with the transfer of rights in the sexuality of the wife just because our society, stressing genetic paternity as the basis of social paternity, has to restrict access to the husband in order to ensure a 'proper' basis for social fatherhood.

LEGITIMACY AND PLACEMENT

So far we have considered three types of rights involved in marriage: rights in the children; rights in the spouses deriving from and reflected in patterns of residence; and sexual rights. We have not considered the first class of rights in any detail.

In Chapter 1 of this book we noted that it had been stated as a universal principle that a child must have a 'social father' or 'pater'. This 'principle of legitimacy' tied 'fatherhood' to 'membership of the procreative group' and to 'marriage'. We can now see why. Some agreement between the two kin groups of the man and the woman responsible for the generation of the child must be arrived at to reconcile otherwise conflicting claims in the child itself. However, the first solution to this problem that we put forward did not involve marriage, nor membership of the 'procreative group'. That solution was that the women take not husbands, but lovers, and retain all the rights in the children. Moreover, there is a society which approaches this situation.

Before we can deal with this problem, we need to be clear about the meaning of the term 'father' *as it is used in our own society*. First, it implies that the man would be recognised scientifically as the genetic father of the child. Secondly, it implies that the man is recognised by the society as the procreator of the child. Now, since different societies may have different beliefs about procreation and different ways of deciding difficult cases, we need, therefore, another term which means 'the man socially recognised as the genetic father (whether, according to our scientific ideas, he is or not)'. The term used for this purpose is *genitor*.

Thirdly, the father cannot be said to be a father unless the rights and duties are acknowledged and the appropriate behaviour expected by other people. This complex pattern of acknowledgement and expectation is partly what is meant by our describing a child born in marriage as legitimate. But equally, fatherhood can be regarded as being thus made legitimate. In, for example, a *consensual union* between a man and a woman (that is, where the two people consent privately to live together and produce children), the father is genetic father and genitor, and plays the role of father, but he is not thereby expected to play that role, nor has he any rights over his offspring or they to him over and above those they have in a genitor. The man in such a case is an illegitimate father.

To speak of a man being an 'illegitimate father' sounds very odd. Obviously, something more is involved in our notion of illegitimacy than 'lack of social expectations and of social recognition of rights and duties'. Now this 'something more' is apparently absent when we speak of 'illegitimate fathers' and, therefore, it must be something peculiar which follows from not having a legitimate father rather than from not having a legitimate child.

We can now see why in a patrilineal society it should be necessary for a child to have a 'pater'. Otherwise he may find himself belonging to none of the recognised social groups which go to make up the society, and eligible for none.

In societies with other types of descent system this is not the case. However, we have seen that most societies have rules governing mating and marriage. Failure to produce at least a genitor for the child makes it look as if these rules may have in fact been broken. Hence, there may be doubt as to whether the child in fact is a member of the society, or whether he is ritually unclean or something of the sort. Therefore, most societies withhold full social membership from children who cannot be 'placed' within the society or within a group within it.

The illegitimate father is not in this position. He may incur social opprobrium, but there is no doubt as to his rightful membership either of the society or to groups within it. We can now see a little more clearly what is involved in legitimacy. Legitimacy does not merely involve the recognition by others of rights and duties of parent and child. The 'third party' to any marriage, 'community' or 'state', is interested in the proceedings from 'its *own*' point of view, because in consequence of such proceedings, it will be possible to determine whether or not the children of the marriage belong to it

The concept of legitimacy involves, therefore, two distinct ideas: that of social recognition of relationship between parent and child (of importance chiefly to the individuals concerned), and that of the child as a full member of society. In our society both are achieved by marriage, the husband being both pater and genitor. We shall refer to the second idea as the 'attribution of societal membership'. The first will be referred to as 'the recognition of ties of filiation'.

In order that the child should be defined as properly belonging to the society, it will be necessary to arrange for some acknowledgement that he possesses the qualifications on which membership depends. If this depends on his having been engendered by a full member of the society, acknowledgement of genetic fatherhood by someone who thereby becomes genitor of the child will be enough. If, however, there is no notion of genetic fatherhood or it is not regarded as relevant to the qualifications for societal membership, the existence of a social father created by a marriage will be required.

In order that the child may have a proper set of kinship relationships, it will be necessary that someone should be recognised as the person through whom patrilateral ties may be traced. Once again, the acknowledgement by a genitor may suffice. It may be said, therefore, that both types of legitimacy do not need to be tied to marriage and can be independent of it. Nor must marriage necessarily ensure legitimacy. If acknowledgement of genetic fatherhood is necessary to obtain societal membership, then this will not be achieved by marriage where access to the wife is not restricted to the husband, though the husband may be regarded as father for kin purposes. If there is more than one husband, marriage will not determine the person through whom patrilateral ties may be traced, though the child will be legitimate for societal purposes. However we define marriage, therefore, it may be said that legitimacy is independent of it.

To say this is not, however, to deny that marriage usually has the effect of ensuring both types of legitimacy to the offspring. That does not mean that it has to be done this way. We have to recognise that we are dealing here with three sets of rules: rules concerning societal membership, rules concerning kinship relationships and rules concerning the rights established or transferred by marriage. It is only by examining the relations between these three sets of rules in particular cases that we can say anything about necessary relations between marriage and legitimacy.

To sum up: marriage frequently ensures the societal membership of children and the social recognition of their ties of filiation. It does not follow that marriage is the only way of doing either.

Now, it may have occurred to some readers that it is very odd that the stigma of illegitimacy should have been so long retained in our own society, where societal membership does not depend on parentage. When faced with a problem of this kind and we can find no logical connection between associated rules, there are two places to look. We can look to the consequences of following the rules for the following of other rules; or we can look at the beliefs and ideas which are embodied in the rules.

We know that societal membership was not always attributed in the way it is now. Before the coming of the 'nation state', societal membership, or at any rate social acceptance, seems to have been assured by the ability to produce genitors, and few disabilities attached to children born outside marriage. It was the advent of both church and state as centralising institutions that resulted in progressive legal disabilities being placed on bastards and, most important, made the parents not only criminals, but took the child away from them, raising it at public charge. Quite apart from beliefs which at first the church and later the Puritans inculcated concerning the iniquity of bastardy, the removal of the child from the parents made him unplaceable and destroyed the locally recognised and acceptable ties of filiation through a genitor. The legal requirement of the formal establishment of rights (which in a sense created bastardy) was reinforced by ideological sanctions (Pinchbeck, 1954).

In order to account for the persistence of the stigma of illegitimacy, we might argue as follows. People are placed in one or other of the various categories or groups which go to make up the society on the basis of the group membership of their parents, and such placements play an important part in determining behaviour towards them. When children are young, they belong to few groups and their memberships are determined by their parents. Children, therefore, 'inherit' group memberships in all societies whether or not the groups concerned are recruited on the basis of kinship. If you are born a Catholic, you can of course renounce your faith, but people will continue to say 'he is an *ex*-Catholic, you know'. There is no possible way of ceasing to be an *ex*-Catholic. Hence, when we are introduced to someone we have not previously met, we ask 'who is he?' and the answer almost always involves reference to his natal group. In a small community this may involve tracing connections between the subject of your interest and other persons who are known to you. It may involve merely placing the subject in a category. But the more categories, the better you can fix his 'position'. 'That was Lord X, chairman of So and So' is a pretty useful reply, but if it were to continue 'third son of a German-Jewish East End tailor' that would be generally regarded as even more satisfactory.

It follows from this that lack of knowledge of the memberships of one parent constitutes a severe drawback to the accurate placing of an individual. If we accept the currency of *ideas* which stress the importance of inheritance in determining character, then the lack of ability to place a person in terms of his parentage will arouse doubts as to one's ability to predict how he will behave. It is rather like buying secondhand furniture – 'you don't know where it's been'. What evidence one always has about the illegitimate is that their mothers

have been at best unwise and at worst immoral; undesirable characteristics which may well have been 'passed on' to the child. Discrimination against these unpredictable and dubious people naturally
follows.

Recognition of parentage then has the consequence of enabling the
child to be attributed not merely to the society, but to a *position
within* the society. Both of these attributions are quite properly called
placement. Placement within a society is always necessary but there is
no need for it to depend on the recognition of parentage. As long as
parentage is recognised, however, and parents given charge over their
children in their most formative years, it is highly unlikely that an
individual's parentage will not constitute one of the dimensions on
which he is 'placed'. The two senses of placement must be distinguished, however. The need for the attribution of societal membership
may be invoked to explain the origin of the universal human concern
to trace paternity. Its usefulness as a means of placement within a
society may be referred to in order to account for the persistence of
that concern.

It can now be seen why there is always a third party in any marriage.
The society as a whole is interested in what is going on because it will
thereby be enabled to determine the societal membership, and membership of groups and categories within the society, of the children
produced by the marriage. This last concern is, of course, shared by
the natal groups of the spouses whose arrangement as to rights in the
child has precisely the effect of determining his membership and hence
placement. Even where individuals are not recruited to social groups
on the basis of kinship qualifications (as in our own society), they
are, *in fact*, recruited in this way, though not uniquely so. Hence,
the establishment of relationships between parents and children
is of treble significance: to individuals, to kin groups and to the
society.

THE DEFINITION OF MARRIAGE

The definition of marriage may seem a trivial problem, and so in a
sense it is. More is involved than arguments about terms, however,
and the problems which underlie that of definition are of crucial
significance to our discussion of the family in Chapter 3.

Marriage has been defined traditionally in terms of legitimacy, and
we have seen what problems there are with *that*. Moreover, even if we
could arrive at a definition of legitimacy which was satisfactory, any
definition which made its defining characteristic the ability of the
mates to procreate legitimate offspring would run into trouble because
it would include cases which we might very well wish to distinguish.
The statement 'marriage is a universal social institution' would then
become no more than 'legitimacy is a universal institution', put in a
different way.

We have to be very clear about what we are doing here. We have to avoid the danger of thinking that, as Goldschmidt has put it, there is something called 'marriageness' which we could get at 'if only we could put it in a proper centrifuge and force out those extraneous substances that contaminate its cross-cultural purity' (Goldschmidt, 1966). The inhabitants of Europe and America have an idea which they call marriage. People in other cultures have other ideas which are similar to, but not the same as, our ideas. Traditionally the argument has been about how dissimilar the ideas have to get to force us to stop describing their ideas as 'marriage'. Simple-minded laymen who point out that *any* dissimilarity is usually sufficient to stop *them* describing an idea as 'marriage' have usually been jumped on very hard and told not to be ethnocentric. Now, the crime of ethnocentricity is indeed a grave one. It consists of explaining the concepts peculiar to one culture in terms of your own culture. This is, however, exactly what many of those who seek to produce a cross-cultural definition of marriage have in fact been doing since they use their own society's definition as a base. The correct question to ask is 'what concepts is it useful for students of society to devise in order to aid the understanding of different cultures'.

This precept still leaves us with serious problems. If you are not to be permitted to use your own society's concepts as a starting-point, how can you even define an area of social behaviour which you wish to consider? The answer to this difficulty that has been adopted so far in this book is to look at the sort of problems with which men everywhere have to deal and the sort of sense they make of them. One of those problems is, as we have seen, to make arrangements for biological reproduction and for the transmission of material goods and cultural possessions from one generation to another. What has been previously called marriage clearly is concerned with the performance of these tasks.

Towards an Adequate Definition

We need to ask, then: how do societies arrange for the orderly procreation and rearing of future generations and the transmission of material and cultural possessions?

This question may be further broken down into two sets of further questions. First, how does the society (1) arrange for the determination of the attribution of societal membership to the child? (2) Arrange for the determination of the recognition of the ties of filiation of the child? (3) Arrange for the child's allocation to social groups within society? (4) Arrange for the transmission of property? (5) Arrange for the acculturation of the child both with regard to the culture of society as a whole and to the culture of the group within it to which the child belongs? Questions 1 and 2 are what is meant by legitimising the child. Question 2 involves 3 if groups within the society are recruited on the basis of kinship. Question 2 involves 1 if societal membership is determined by kin-group membership. Question 5 is a corollary to 1 and 3.

Questions 1-5 are concerned with what is vaguely indicated by the term 'placement', though it refers in particular to 1 and 3. In some societies possession of property forms the basis of social-group membership. In all societies distinctions are made between individuals and groups according to the extent of their control over economic resources. Question 4, hence, is also covered by the term placement, except where groups or individuals within the society cannot transmit property to members in the next generation.

Secondly, how does society (1) delineate rights of sexual access? (2) Arrange for the economic support of immature children and pregnant and nursing mothers? (3) Arrange for their domestic care and support?

While it is true to say of almost any of these tasks, that in most societies it is performed as the result of an arrangement entered into by two kin groups and publicly acknowledged, in few societies are *all* of these tasks performed as a result of such an arrangement, and seldom is any task performed *entirely* as a result of such arrangements.

The variability of the 'bundle of tasks' that these arrangements are concerned with is, of course, directly related to the variability of the uses to which recognition of ties of filiation can be put, and the enormous variation in ideas about kinship which men have.

If we are to use the term marriage, it would seem to be *useful* to make it mean *the institutional means of providing for the performance of tasks concerned with procreation, rearing and transmission, where the means concerned involve a reordering of relationships of kin groups, and/or of the persons thought to be, already or potentially, the genetic parents of children.*

Such a definition has two elements. On the one hand it points out a class of tasks; and on the other it specifies that the type of arrangement we are concerned with is one between kin groups or between persons linked through actual or potential genetic parenthood, as it is understood by the society concerned.

It is necessary to add a warning here about the use of the term 'institutional'. We have already noted that we cannot speak of a role being institutionalised except in relation to a group. Some of the problems involved in the definition of marriage arise because the arrangement entered into is not recognised by some official body, or by some group wider than that to which the spouses belong, whose members do recognise the arrangement. *Any* marriage definition can run into trouble on these grounds.

It can now be seen that questions concerning 'the universality of marriage' are questions with no precise meaning. They are questions whose answer depends as much upon sorting out what we mean by marriage, as it does upon going and looking.

FATHERHOOD, LEGITIMA·CY, PLACEMENT AND MARRIAGE

It may be helpful to conclude this chapter by briefly considering the relationships between the various terms with which we have been struggling: fatherhood, legitimacy, placement and marriage. We have previously distinguished a 'pater' and a 'genitor'. There is no difficulty with the definition of genitor, but what exactly is a social father? We have answered so far: 'the man who has the rights and duties of a father as defined by the society concerned'. This will not do. Once again, it presupposes a prior notion of 'fatherhood'. By fatherhood we could mean: the man through whom ties of filiation are traced; the man through whom rights to property are traced; the man whose acknowledged relationship to the child establishes its societal membership; the man whose acknowledged relationship to the child establishes its social-group membership; or any combination of all these.

The notions of social fatherhood, marriage and legitimacy are systematically interrelated. The uses to which the recognition of ties of filiation are put will determine what marriage (the arrangement of rights between kin groups which provide for the recognition of filiation) involves and this, in turn, will determine the social identifications which are necessary in order to permit the ties of filiation to be used in that way. That is to say, it will determine what we mean by fatherhood. To speak of legitimacy is to speak of the recognition of ties of filiation by third parties. What actually follows from the recognition of a filiative tie as legitimate will depend on the uses to which such ties are put. Placement is a sort of catchall word which covers every conceivable use to which the recognition of ties of filiation can be put.

Chapter 3

Family

The discussion of what we mean by the family itself has been left extremely late in this book and for good reason. There is probably no other term with which we shall have to deal that is less clear than this one (except possibly 'placement'). If the reader looks back over the preceding pages, he will discover that we have been able to discuss a large number of topics usually covered or referred to in texts on the family without even mentioning the word. The reader may also have gained the impression that social anthropologists in general are not a great deal concerned with the family. Sociologists are very much concerned with it. The reason for this difference in focus of interest lies largely in the nature of the societies that members of the two disciplines study.

'Family' is a word which, unlike 'kinship', is much used by the inhabitants of the technologically advanced societies with which sociologists are concerned. It might be thought, therefore, that confusions might arise from differences between popular and academic uses of the term. But popular usage is itself extremely complex. We have already seen that people can refer to their relatives as 'the family'. 'All the family turned up for the funeral.' In the next breath they will say, 'Of course, I knew *my* family would come, but I never expected all *my husband's* family to show up'. Apparently we have one family which is simultaneously two families – his and hers. 'But, of course, my brother didn't bring his family along – they're much too young.' Here the reference is to offspring. 'The neighbours were very good, too. The Joneses came, and their two children. It was very nice the whole family turning up like that.' Here the usage is more restricted than 'relatives', or 'his relatives', but includes both parents *and* offspring. 'Of course, the children will be leaving home soon. It's always sad to see the family break up like that.' Here the reference is not only to parents and children, but to their co-residence, that is, to the household. 'Anyhow, they won't be living too far away – I always think it's nice if you can keep the family together.' So apparently the family hasn't 'broken up' after all. Even though the members are dispersed, they still do not cease to be members of the family – whatever that means.

Confused as it may appear to be, the usage of the term 'the family' and the patterns of social behaviour to which it refers are a distinctive part of our (Western) culture. To recognise this is to recognise that we cannot apply it without further definition to other cultures, and this is partly the reason why it is a confusing term to use in cross-cultural studies. (The reader may remember that we had similar trouble with 'father' and 'marriage'.) Yet it would be both pedantic and absurd to refuse to use the term in the study of those societies who have a concept of 'family' which closely approaches our own. Nevertheless any definition must be in terms of other, more general concepts. It is for this reason that a consideration of the family has been postponed for so long.

KINSHIP CATEGORIES

All social behaviour implies categorisation of some kind. All categorisation implies making distinctions: classifying people, for example, as the same as or different from one another in some way. Our interest in categorisation lies in the fact that it is necessary to classify people if we are to have expectations about how they are going to behave.

To claim that an item belongs to a particular category is to say nothing, unless it entails that the item does not belong to another category. Sets of categories which between them include all possible members may be termed *exhaustive* and the categories which belong to those sets may be termed *universal* categories. For example, the categories man and woman together exhaust the logical universe constituted by the category 'human-being'. Hence, the set: man and woman is exhaustive; 'man' and 'woman' are the names of universal categories.

'Man' and 'woman' are also *social* categories, that is, categories of people. Being universal logical categories they are also exclusive social categories. An exclusive social category is a category such that it is impossible for its members to be simultaneously members of another category belonging to the same set. A person cannot, simultaneously, be both a man and a woman. However, a person can simultaneously be both a mother and a daughter. Indeed, most women are both mothers and daughters. Kinship categories are not universal categories in the sense defined and do not yield exclusive social categories.

Now, it is, of course, impossible to be *both* Mrs X's daughter and Mrs X's mother. This example involves the introduction of a particular point of reference – Mrs X. *From her standpoint*, she is surrounded by categories of kin which *are* exclusive; her cousins are not her nephews and nieces, nor her parents her children. However, though a given population may be divided into exclusive categories (that is, categories with no common members, such as men and women), it cannot be divided into exclusive kinship categories, children, parents, siblings, and so on. This is because kinship categories distinguish between people in terms of their relation to particular individuals. They are not universal categories, but particular categories; not absolute categories, but relative categories – which is why we call their members 'relatives'.

When we refer to a kinship category, therefore, we are not distinguishing exclusive categories of people in the society as a whole. We are distinguishing categories of people which are exclusive only when seen from the point of view of the individual.

Kinship roles are allocated on the basis of the unique biological relation that one person has to another. Social relationships between members of different categories of kin are possible because the members share common expectations about how members are to behave to each other. But because of the way in which the roles are allocated, because they follow a pattern of unique biological relations, this allows me to infer only how I should behave to *my* father and not how I as a child should behave to all the members of an exclusive category of people called 'fathers'.

Because biological relations ramify bilaterally, each individual has a unique set of persons to whom he is biologically related. From this, it follows that however widely or narrowly these biological ties are recognised for the purpose of forming categories of recognised kin, no two persons will have the same set of persons to whom they recognise a kin relationship. Hence, the recognition of biological ties alone cannot form the basis of recruitment of individuals to an exclusive category of people whose members share the characteristic of recognising a kin relationship to one another. A kinship position has properties similar to that of a spatial position: no two points can ever have the same relation to *all* the other points on the same surface.

It is because of these properties that those societies who use kinship as a basis for the allocation of individuals to exclusive categories, have to cheat and ignore ties either through men or women. They then usually try and get the best of both worlds by distinguishing individuals in terms of bilateral filiation. From all this, it follows that whatever we mean by the term family it is not and cannot be an exclusive kin category of people.

CATEGORIES AND GROUPS

When we say that a plurality of people share expectations about the way in which different categories of people within that plurality behave, we imply that the members of the plurality concerned have some of the characteristics of a social group. We do not necessarily imply, however, that the categories within the group are themselves also groups. This is an important point because to say that a group exists is to imply some sort of categorisation. The notion of group is meaningless apart from the notions of member and non-member.

Such categorisation may occur before the formation of the group, or be based on the recognition of relationships between members of the group which distinguish them from non-members, but it must be there.

Now, we have already had cause to distinguish various types of group in our consideration of kinship. We have referred to the domestic group, the residential group, descent groups and the procreative or biological group. The first three types of group, if their membership is recruited on the basis of recognition of biological relations, must be recruited by ignoring (for the purposes of group formation) some ties of equal genealogical closeness. This may be done *in the same way throughout the society, that is, be governed by a societal rule, or it may be done as a result of agreements arrived at by the related persons concerned, which are peculiar to them,* but done it must be. The biological group is a special case, however.

It should be noted that the types of group distinguished are characterised by reference to the activities which they undertake rather than to their membership. They are terms which figure largely in any answer to the question: 'what do people use the system of kinship recognition for, and how do they use it?' Once again, however, the biological group is something of a special case.

It is true of the biological group but of no others that the activities which distinguish it prescribe its membership. Those activities demand a man, a woman and a sexual relationship between them. The biological necessity of care for offspring demands their presence also. Now, it does not follow from these biological considerations that these individuals must form a group. But such considerations do prescribe, in part, the way in which the different members of such a group must behave; that is to say, what may be expected of them the roles they must play. The terms 'father', 'mother' and 'child' are not merely the names of genealogical positions, the content of the roles attached to which may vary from society to society. They are also names of activities, and hence specify in part the content of roles. These roles do effectively determine the membership of the group if it is recognised that they do so by specifying universal activities, as well as certain types of biological relatedness.

It is to this set of roles that the term 'nuclear family', in part, refers. We should note, however, that it only succeeds in referring to an exclusive category of people by virtue of reference to the *activities* of the members.

When a set of people interact with one another over a period of time, they come to share expectations about the way in which *each other* will behave. When a set of people share expectations of this sort, we may describe them as a group. Obviously, procreation and rearing involve continuous interaction. Hence, by virtue of the activities which define the membership of this set, the members are likely to constitute a group whose ways of behaving both share elements in common with other sets of the same kind and differentiate one set from another.

To refer to a nuclear family, therefore, is to refer to a group which carries out certain activities which define its membership, and determine to some extent the content and distribution of the roles played. To speak of *the* family is to refer to the class of such groups; *a* family is any particular group which is a member of that class.

To ask 'is the nuclear family universal?' is to ask whether the biological activities, which occur in all societies, universally result in the creation of groups having the membership defined by those activities.

The nuclear family refers to the biological group. It is not a group based on a category of kin, but on a class of interrelated activities. The weak link in this group is, however, the man. There is no biological need to wait around for nine months for the birth of the children. The nuclear family has, in fact, at least two subgroups within it composed respectively of man and woman, and mother and children. The existence of these two subgroups need not necessarily overlap in time. If they do so overlap, this is because of the nature of the relationship between the man and the woman. The existence of the nuclear family as a group therefore depends on an arrangement being reached whereby the man helps the woman while she rears the children. Marriage as we have defined it is usually such an arrangement (see above, Chapter 2, p. 28). The relationships which characterise the nuclear family are, therefore, parent-child and mates.

KINSHIP AND THE FAMILY PROCESS

By defining the nuclear family in terms of its activities we have determined that it will be extinguished before the death of its members. Eventually the woman or women will become infertile. Eventually the children will be reared. Hence, the activities of the nuclear family will cease and its members will no longer constitute such a family. This does not mean they will no longer all be members of *a* nuclear family, however. The children will make arrangements with persons of the opposite sex and, in turn, produce children, thus becoming members of their own nuclear families. This process is illustrated in Figure 3.2 (p. 38). Each circle represents the members who at one time made up a nuclear family. It will be seen that each individual is a member of two such groups and that each group is connected to two groups in the ascending generation and with as many groups as there are children in the descending generation.

In the figure three or four generations are shown. The speed with which generations follow one another varies very considerably. If mating takes place as early as 16 and the average age of death is as late as the seventies, it is possible that there will be four generations alive at the same time. If on the other hand mating takes place later and the expectation of life is short, the parents are unlikely to survive sufficiently long to do more than see the infancy of their grandchildren. In either case parents will usually live to see the founding of at least their children's nuclear families. Hence, the extinction of the nuclear family with maturation of its children does not mean that its original members will no longer exist.

We noted earlier that we could call a nuclear family 'a group' because the performance of its characteristic activities involved the growth of shared expectations among its members. The shared values and expectations which have grown up as the result of nuclear family membership will not disappear because the activities cease to be performed. There will still be a sense in which the members of the defunct nuclear family can be called a group.

To refer to a *group* is to refer to the things that a set of people share. We distinguished the things that the members of a nuclear family share which make them a nuclear family, that is, the biologically necessary activities, and the other expectations, beliefs and values which they come to share as the result of a period of interaction. This last category of things shared is not, of course, destroyed by the cessation of the first activities. It is useful to have terms which distinguish these two sets of common properties. Unfortunately, there is no term which refers to families whose members no longer perform the activities which define the nuclear family.

There is, however, a term which refers to a kinship group made up of the relationships found within the nuclear family: spouse:spouse; parent:child; and sib:sib. Because these relations constitute the elements of any kinship system, such a family may be termed an *elementary family*. We may now say that a *nuclear family* is an elementary family in the first phase of its cycle of existence. In its nuclear phase the elementary family shares biologically based activities and consequently moves out of this phase after one generation. The non-nuclear elementary family shares those things which have become common to its members during the period of interaction involved in the performance of these biological activities. The members of both types of family are the same (they are both elementary): it is the sources of their solidarity that differ. In Figure 3.2 all the mother, father and children groups shown may be called elementary families, but only the lowest circle or circles are elementary families in their nuclear phase.

It is only fair to warn the reader that this distinction is often not clearly made, and the terms used are often used to mean exactly the same thing, namely, a set of persons playing the roles father, mother and children to one another. Such a set is also termed the *immediate family*. Some sociologists may regard this distinction as pedantic, but it is of fundamental importance because it makes clear the different types of solidarity which exist between the different members of a family group at different stages of its development.

To the reader who has dutifully waded through the chapter on kinship this may have a familiar ring. We seem to be coming back to the 'extension theory' of kinship. And so, in a way, we are. For Malinowski argued that he had witnessed with 'his own eyes' this process of extension. What he could only have witnessed, in fact, was this development of sentiments among the group which was performing biological activities, which outlasted the performance of those activities and persisted among the members even when the younger generation had founded nuclear families of their own.

We noted in Chapter 1, however, that we could not explain kinship in this way. Similarly, we cannot explain the behaviour of members of families entirely in this way, either. For their behaviour to one another is not determined solely by the activities they carry out. Nor is it determined solely by the values and expectations which they come to share which distinguish one family from another. It is also determined, in part, by the expectations as to the behaviour of people performing the biological activities of mates and parents which are shared by the society as a whole.

The behaviour of the Jones family (to put it another way) can be understood partly in terms of the biological conditions of their action, partly in terms of their social conditions of action (that is, the expectations of others which they have learnt and acquired through the membership of their society) and also in terms of the unique set of experiences which the members have come to share as a result of their acting together under those conditions.

To put it yet another way we could say that a nuclear family is a set of people who play biological roles, and institutionalised social roles to one another and, in so doing, develop beliefs and values which inform sets of expectations (roles) which are peculiar to them.

We cannot, therefore, explain the existence of these general expectations about the behaviour of family members in terms of the generation of sentiments among them through the performance of common biological activities. We can only explain their existence completely if we explicitly recognise that it is partly through the prior existence of kin roles that they come to have the relationships to each other that they do (see Chapter 1, pp. 11–14).

We are, then, dealing with a continuous process of family formation which we may call the *family process*: the creation and extinction of nuclear families; the creation of new members by birth; the loss of existing members by death; the establishment of affinal relationships by marriage; the supplementation of these ties by ties of filiation as the children are born and affines become kin's kin. It is by this process that the exact shape of the set of relations which constitute the web of kinship in any given society at a given time is determined. But at the same time it is only by virtue of the definition of kinship roles, and the rules governing marriage, and so on, that this process is regulated and controlled.

We may now use the terms which we have defined to help us understand the use of the term 'family' in popular speech. It appears, then, that such usage is less confused than highly complex, and it is so because of the complexity of the situation which it describes.

Each individual belongs, first, to one, and then to two, elementary families. He is born into one family, his *family of origin*, and creates his own *family of procreation* (Figure 3.1 (*a*)). (The family of origin is sometimes referred to as his *family of orientation*; the family of procreation is sometimes called his *family of marriage*.) Together Ego's families of origin and procreation constitute his *kinship core*; that is, all his first-degree kin (Figure 3.1 (*a*)). Ego's family of procreation is linked, however, not only to *his* family of origin, but also to *his wife's* family of origin. Hence, the overlapping kinship cores of Ego and spouse constitute a T-shaped cluster or core of three overlapping elementary families linked by his mating arrangement (Figure 3.1 (*b*)).

At birth Ego is a member of the T-core of his parents, all the members of which are his consanguineal kin (Figure 3.2 (*a*)). With his marriage and the birth of his children, Ego is a member of an additional T-core constituted by *his* families of origin and procreation and *his spouse's* family of origin (Figure 3.2 (*b*)). With the birth of his grandchildren, Ego now becomes a member of several new T-cores – as many as he has mated children (Figure 3.2 (*c*)). With the birth of his nephews and nieces, he becomes a member of as many new T-cores as he has married sibs (Figure 3.2 (*d*)).

At any given point in time we may think of a given Ego as occupying a position in a complex cluster of interlocking T-cores, each constituting the kinship core of a married couple. We may see Ego as moving throughout his life through the typical positions which constitute a T-core; starting off as grandchild, becoming a parent and ending up as a grandparent. Or we may think of Ego starting off as a grandchild in his parents' T-core (ABC), becoming a parent in his own

F_o, family of origin; F_p, family of procreation; •$_s$, spouse; C, Ego's F_o; R, Ego's spouse's F_o; D, Ego's and spouse's common F_p.

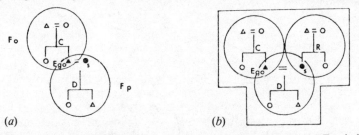

Figure 3.1 Families of origin and procreation: the kinship core. (*a*) Ego in his families of origin and procreation (Ego's kinship core); (*b*) the overlapping kinship cores of Ego and spouse (their T-core).

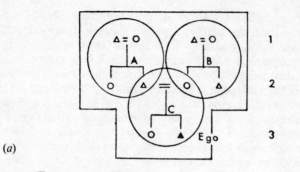

(a)

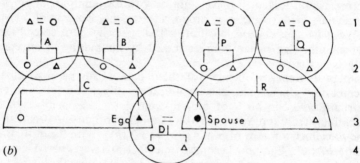

(b)

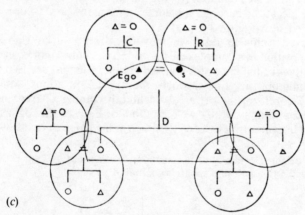

(c)

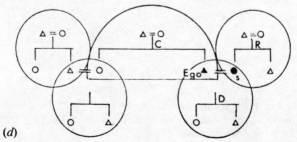

(d)

and mate's T-core (CRD) and an uncle in his sibs' T-cores (Figure 3.2 (d)), and ending up as a grandparent in his children's T-cores (Figure 3.2 (c)).

The behaviour of an individual is not, then, to be understood simply with reference to his membership of any one elementary family, nor simply with reference to his membership of categories of kin, but with reference to his position in an ongoing process through which both categories and groups are formed. As a consequence we need to regard the terms 'father', 'mother' and 'sibling' as each referring not to single roles, but to *role sequences* – which affect behaviour not merely within the elementary family, but also affect the pattern and content of interaction with other kin outside the elementary family or kinship core which is being considered.

We must stress again, however, that neither an elementary family nor a kinship core of an individual or couple constitutes an exclusive category of kin, except from the point of view of the individual or couple concerned. Ego's family of origin is first-degree kin to him but second-degree kin to his children. The second-degree matrilateral and patrilateral blood kin of Ego's children are not blood kin, but affines to each other, and so on. Moreover, Ego is simultaneously a member of two elementary families and may be a member of many more than two T-cores.

THE FAMILY PROCESS AND GROUP FORMATION

So far, we have been concerned simply to try to understand what is involved in the concept 'family'. And we have broken the notion down into other related concepts. We have not considered what types of family it is useful to distinguish. We have merely developed concepts which will be useful in distinguishing such types.

Any typology of the family will be concerned to distinguish the various uses to which what we have called the family process can be put either by whole societies or by pluralities of individuals within them. Before we can consider this further, we have to return to the composition of the biological group itself. The procreation and rearing of children is *not* a use to which the family process is put: rather to speak of the family is, we have seen, to speak of the consequences which these activities have for the formation of social groups. In contrast the formation of domestic, residential and descent groups depends either on the existence of the biological group or on the recognition of kinship relationships, or both.

As far as the biological group is concerned, we have noted that it

Figure 3.2 The family process (for key, see Figure 3.1). (*a*) Ego in his parents' T-core; (*b*) Ego in his parents' T-core and his own T-core (his spouse's parents' T-core shown also); (*c*) Ego in his own T-core and those of his children; (*d*) Ego and his own and his siblings' T-cores.

can be seen as composed of two subgroups: mates, and mother and children. Continued interaction between father and mother and children is not a biological necessity. The smallest biological group is, in fact, 'mother and children' rather than 'parents and children'. The conditions of survival of the mother and children are frequently such as to require a man to fend for them. There are two candidates for this task: the mother's brother or other male kin, and the mother's mate. In the Nayar case we find the mother's male kin performing this activity. We may find it shared between them as is the case where residence after marriage is nato-local, as it is among the majority of the Ashanti (Fortes, 1950). In the majority of societies these activities are performed by the husbands, except where their presence in the domestic group conflicts with the necessity to keep the men of the descent group together.

Fending for dependent females and children requires some measure of co-residence. Obviously, rearing is even more dependent on co-residence. A consideration of the membership of the *biological* group cannot, therefore, be divorced from the conditions which lead to the formation of the *domestic* group. This does not mean to say that the two types of group cannot be distinguished from one another. Because performance of the biological activities which characterise the biological group requires the performance of activities of the domestic group, it does not mean that members of a domestic group are necessarily restricted to the members of the biological group. Indeed, the nuclear family is frequently 'submerged' in a larger domestic group.

Where various types of plural marriage are practised, then the basis of the domestic group will not be a simple nuclear family, but a compound nuclear family composed of a man and his wives or a woman and her husbands. The polygynous family we may regard as a set of co-resident groups of mothers and children and a set of groups of mates, the groups of mates being linked by a common member, and each group of mates overlapping a group of mothers and children.

To describe a group as a 'domestic group' is to classify it according to the activities which it characteristically performs. This set of activities is not the same as those of the biological group, although they overlap. Characteristic of the domestic group is the provision of shelter, food and clothing for its members. Where these activities are provided separately for subgroups within the group, as in the case of a polygynous group where each wife cooks for herself and her children and is not under the authority of another wife, and each mother–child group has its own dwelling, the group is more properly a residential group rather than a domestic one.

Similarly, in our own society, where a married child, spouse and children live in the same *house* as the parents of the child, they are not said to be members of the same *household* unless they eat together and share a common housekeeping. To share a common housekeeping implies that the food is prepared by the same person or persons and purchased from a common fund. Even where they do form a common household, they cannot be said to be a domestic group in the full sense of the word unless the house is owned jointly or, if owned by one of the members, the other members share it as of right and without conditions as to tenure and payment. Because in many societies with which sociologists are concerned all the various characteristics of the domestic group are frequently not found together, they usually distinguish the 'composition of the household' from the 'ownership' and type of 'tenure' and do not use the term 'domestic group'. It is important to remember, however, that these two items do not exhaust the characteristics of the domestic group and that we need to know the terms on which the other members of the household participate in the occupancy of the dwelling.

Such pedantry has its purpose. When, as is frequently the case, members of the elementary family continue to form domestic groups after the extinction of the nuclear family, this may be explained in terms of the ability of the group to provide certain services for its members which they could not obtain elsewhere. At the same time the examination of the rights and duties which subsist between members of the group is essential to a complete understanding of the behaviour of its members.

Domestic groups and households may be classified according to their composition. They may be composed of a nuclear family alone. If this is the normal type of household, then it follows that there must also be found 'denuded elementary family' households composed of people whose children have formed their own nuclear family households, or siblings one or both of whose parents have died, or individuals who have lost parents by death and sibs (if any) by death or marriage. Conversely, we may find augmented elementary family households, where children's spouses and grandchildren are also brought into the household. Such households may be described as *composite* households.

If the members of the elementary family are kept together, we shall find that the household reflects the shape of the family process. Because it is not possible for all family households to retain all their members, some of the children must leave home at marriage (whether this is governed by residence rules or left to choice). Even so, there must be a rapid growth in the size of the household, except where the family size is two or less and there is an even balance between the sexes of the children. Depending on these factors, and the incidence of death, such composite households will grow too large for the dwelling and have to split up. In consequence of the large number of factors which are operative the actual incidence, size and number of composite households in any society will vary enormously, even where there are strict rules of residence. Where this is not the case, as in our own society, the variation may be even greater.

The crucial factor which appears to constitute a necessary condition of the dissolution of the composite household is the ability of the children to create households of their own. In order for this to be possible, it is necessary for them to be able to command economic resources such that they can acquire a separate dwelling. But they also have to constitute a viable social group which can perform without such aid from the parents or sibs as is dependent on co-residence, the characteristic activities of the biological and domestic groups, the performance of which are the necessary conditions of their children's and/or their own existence.

Their ability to do this will depend on the strength and stability of the marital relationship and the degree to which the spouses are able to perform the tasks allotted to them by the family system in which they participate. Where, for example, marriages are arranged by the kin of the spouses, the spouses having no previous relationship with one another, the establishment of such a relationship will be a condition of their nuclear family forming an independent household. Discussing the reasons why bilateral Sarakatsani shepherds of Greece continue to live after marriage in the households of their parents and do not until much later set up, with their wives, households of their own, Campbell remarks that, among other reasons, 'it requires the passage of time and the birth of children before it can be said in any real sense that an elementary family has been founded, (Campbell, 1963). Of course, the Sarakatsani, whose marriages are arranged, are an extreme case. Nevertheless, this example draws attention to the way in which in our own society co-residence after marriage may be related in part to the length of courtship and the extent to which marriage creates a relationship as opposed to merely ratifying an existing one.

The ability of the spouses to perform their domestic roles required by the formation of an independent household may be related to the definition and performance of the parental role itself. Where the role of the mother is extremely permissive, and stresses the provision of services for the children to the exclusion of their training through requiring their participation in household tasks, children of both sexes will be dependent on the mother, and the husband, deprived of his mother at marriage, dependent on his wife. Hence, the new wife will be faced with a situation in which she is formally responsible for the provision of domestic services to the husband, from whom she can expect no help. The apparent permissiveness of the mother has the effect of giving her power over the child by reducing her daughter's independence, and moreover, establishes an obligation on the child's part to repay the services which she has received. Such patterns of dependency have been described in Britain and may occur among some types of Italian family, and probably also in some parts of Spain (see Klein, 1965; Kenny, 1956; also Leonard, 1980).

It is important to recognise that the provision and exchange of domestic services is not dependent on residence in the same dwelling. A newly married couple may be enabled to take up separate residence at marriage even though they are not fully able to perform marital roles adequately, provided that they live near enough to the parents of one or other of the spouses to continue to receive services from them. Such arrangements may make the application of careful definitions of the household difficult to apply. Meals may be prepared and consumed alternately in different households, children may sleep in the grandparents' dwelling, and so on. Even where the arrangements made do not go as far as this, residence in the locality of one set of parents may lead to the development of *residential groups* sharing domestic services, their membership being determined by arrangements between the parties concerned. Since what is taking place is the continuance of a relationship of dependency between mother and daughter, the pattern of residence is likely to be uxori-local (see Young and Willmott, 1957).

Composite households and residential groups sharing domestic services may also come to benefit the parental generation by providing care and support for aged parents, though it would not seem that groups consisting of parents and more than one married child come into existence for that purpose. Hence, relations between the households and families in such groups are characterised by an exchange of services, though there may be considerable variation in the timing of the flow of services in different directions. In some cases the early flow of services from parents to children is reversed as the parents age; in others the flows overlap; and in others services flow in both directions right from the marriage of the children. The timing, content and direction of these flows are important in determining the nature of the relationships between family members (see Sussman, 1965; Stehower, 1965).

We have already had occasion to refer to the existence of property-holding groups. A domestic group is, of course, such a group, since it holds the occupation of its accommodation. All domestic groups are also *economic groups* in the sense that they purchase and *consume* goods as a unit. Where a group's members act together to exploit productive resources owned by all or one of them, then the group may be regarded as an economic group in the *productive* sense. In some societies most economic production is undertaken by groups of kinsmen recruited through the family process. Property and employment are obtainable primarily through one's membership of such a group. A kin group may own property without working it. In such a case it is a *proprietary group*. Alternatively, it may constitute a work group without owning the property required. In such a case it may be termed a *work* group.

If inheritable property is partible and is not worked by its owners, there will be no necessity for those who inherit it to constitute a group. However, in such a society they will be unable to support themselves until they inherit. In this situation the man must either postpone marriage (Williams, 1956; Rees, 1950; Park, 1962) until he inherits or must come to some arrangement whereby he receives a portion of his inheritance before his father's death or receives employment from him which enables him to support a family. If the size of the family property is small, this will not be possible. In such a case a man must obtain employment outside the family – which may be difficult – or work for his father – which will entail remaining under his authority. Here the elementary family will be an economic group, in the sense of the co-operative exploitation of resources, that is, a work group but not a proprietary *group*. If the property is not partible, but can support the son's nuclear family, a similar situation will obtain.

If there is more than one inheriting child, it will be frequently impossible for them all to be supported by the property, thus forcing one or more of the sons to 'travel', that is to say, to seek some other means of earning a living. Where both men and women can inherit, he may, of course, solve the problem by marrying an inheriting daughter.

The consequences of property inheritance have been related to the partibility of the property. This is, however, a vague notion. Land, for example, may be divided, and if as is frequently the case it is regarded as impartible, this is so because of the system of agriculture used, or because of beliefs concerning the undesirability or wrongness of dividing it. According to varying conditions and beliefs, therefore, the rules of inheritance may restrict inheritance to one of the children, thus preserving the property intact.

Where families are economic groups, marriage will take on an enormous economic significance, since it will become an alliance between economic interests. Where the daughter's inheritance takes the form of a dowry (a marriage payment by the bride's family to the groom), this may sometimes be in the form of land. Judicious alliances between families may, therefore, increase the size and profitability of the holdings and affinal ties may provide a source of important economic help in times of crisis and difficulty (see Williams, 1963; Stone, 1961).

The family process may, therefore, become a means whereby various elementary families become linked by common economic interests, thus leading to the creation of economic groupings wider than the elementary family itself. At the same time where the members of the family not only own, but together *work* the capital, the authority of senior members of the elementary family or cluster of families is also that of an employer. Control over the capital upon which the children depend gives senior members the power that the capitalist always has over the proletariat. Frequently, in rural communities, successful exploitation of economic resources requires co-residence and, hence, we may find overlapping elementary families together constituting residential and domestic as well as economic groups.

In the same way, therefore, that biological activities form the basis for the development of interpersonal relationships which outlast the performance of such activities, so those relationships may in turn provide the basis for the formation of groups concerned with the performance of other types of activities. Since such groups are formed through the 'family process' and constitute an extension of the elementary family, the formation of such wider groups has been described as extended families. It is to a discussion of the extended family that we next turn.

In the preceding discussion we have distinguished types of family groups according to their activities and shown the way in which such groups are formed through the family process. It is necessary to stress the need for one further distinction, however. Such groups may be formed *ad hoc* according to need, that is, according to the material conditions under which people act. They will also be affected, however, by the social conditions of action – that is to say, the rules governing kin recognition, inheritance, and so on. Such sets of rules will, of course, have to fit the non-social conditions of action. Given a certain type of agricultural technology and a certain type of soil and a certain birth rate, equal division of landed property may result in such fragmentation of holdings as to result in death through starvation for the population concerned. Such rules are, therefore, related to but not completely determined by the material conditions of action, and hence constitute a separate type of condition.

When we find that the members of a society form groups wider than the elementary family by means of the family process, we have to ask whether the type of group formed is *required* by the rules governing the family process or merely *permitted* by such rules. In many primitive societies unilineal systems of transmission make possible the existence of rules which require the formation of exclusive kin groups. In societies which have bilateral systems of recognition it is logically impossible to have rules which require the formation of such groups unless some non-kinship criterion is added. In such societies, therefore, groups wider than the nuclear family are permitted but are not necessarily required. Hence, when we find, for example, a tendency to uxori-locality, we need to ask whether it is the type of activity that demands such a pattern or whether it is required by the system of rules governing the family process. It is one of the 'advantages' of a bilateral system that it is extremely flexible, since it provides the means of group formation without specifying *either* the membership of the groups *or* the activities which they must perform. In a bilateral system where there is no rule based on a non-kin criterion prescribing the formation of exclusive kin groups, the activities of kin groups wider than the nuclear family must be explained in terms of their activities and the conditions of their action created either by *other* social institutions or by material conditions.

THE EXTENDED FAMILY

There is probably no other term, except 'family' itself, about which there is more confusion than the *extended family*. Throughout our discussion so far, we have seen the family not as a category of kin, but as a group. In a bilateral system it is not possible to define the membership of groups on the basis of the rules governing kinship alone. We must, therefore, define such groups both in terms of the family process *and* in terms of different types of activity.

The term 'extended family' has been used by sociologists in the study of bilateral kinship in Western society, to point out a particular type of family which had been found. The term has been used to describe European families in which inheritance was patrilineal, which were characterised by the formation of composite households, and which performed the activities of productive economic groups (see, for example, Litwak, 1960a). Such households were formed either of parents and one son or of all or some of the sons and their wives, living and working together as a joint domestic and economic unit. The first type of extended family was described by Le Play as the *stem family* (*famille souche*).

'Extended family' has also been used by anthropologists in connection with the *joint family*, which is found in Hindu India. The term 'joint family' refers to the co-residence in the *same dwelling* of lineally related persons of the same sex under the authority of a single head. This last additional criterion is, of course, implied in the sociological use of the term 'extended family' since the sharing of property owned by a senior member will entail that the senior male will hold authority over the other members of the group. In anthropological parlance the term 'extended family' is relatively seldom used, but has been defined as 'the dispersed form corresponding to the joint family'.

We have already noted that co-residence in the same dwelling may not be an absolutely necessary precondition of the co-operative exploitation of a common economic resource, even where that resource is land. Hence, the lineally linked nuclear and elementary families may form only a patrilocal group resident within a *locality*, or if they do not contribute labour but merely exercise control over the property, they may not even have to form a residential group of this kind. The term 'extended family' was developed to deal with such a situation.

The difficulty created by the above definition of the joint family is that it does not specify the types of solidarity which characterise it and, hence, does not define the type of social relationships, including authority relationships, which it exhibits. In consequence it becomes extremely difficult to know, once the criterion of co-residence in the same dwelling disappears, whether the linked elementary families concerned are dispersed *joint* families, that is, whether they are extended families or not (see Goode, 1963a).

Similar problems have confused the use of the term 'extended family' in the study of Western society. Sociologists speak of extended family relationships, extended kin relationships, extended family networks and extended kin networks, as well as of extended families. In Britain some students have restricted use of the term to the domestic group, or to a residential group performing domestic activities, or defined the extended family in terms of interaction (see Rosser and Harris, 1965, p. 29 ff.).

This confusion has arisen partly because sociologists rediscovered the existence of links between nuclear families which were previously thought to have atrophied in urban industrial societies. Hence, a great deal of time has been spent refuting the proposition that in such societies the nuclear family is isolated (see below, p. 54 ff.). There has been a great deal of discussion about what links are recognised and what they are used for, but little discussion of the different ways in which the family process can lead to their maintenance.

In their study of Swansea Rosser and Harris (1965) define the extended family as 'any grouping wider than the elementary family' (ibid., p. 32). The use of the term 'grouping' here is significant in that it does not make clear whether the extended family is a social group or a set of people who recognise relationships to another. Such vagueness of definition may be justifiable for delimiting a field of research interest, as was the purpose in this case. It is not, however, adequate for theoretical purposes.

The family process can be used by society as a whole to define the membership of groups by the use of various descent-type rules, or individuals themselves may form groups as a result of arrangements made between them for specific purposes. In the latter case the arrangement and the purposes will define the membership where the principles of descent and inheritance are not adequate. It would seem useful to describe such groups as 'extended families'. Extended families may be of different types according to the different activities they perform. They may vary in size and membership according to the length of generations and the principles of descent and inheritance even where the activities performed are the same.

Where we do not find social groups being formed through the family process, however, this does not mean that, because there is no extended family, the nuclear family is therefore isolated. In the first place, the universal family process will continue. Hence, we shall be able to discover overlapping elementary families. Hence, the spouses of a nuclear family will always be members of their elementary families of origin, all of whose other members are outside that nuclear family. The nuclear family will not be 'isolated', therefore, because it will overlap other family groups, even though, together with them, it does not constitute an extended family. Moreover, the children and spouse in the nuclear family will recognise relationships to Ego's parents and sibs, even though they do not share the common values, beliefs, expectations and activities which distinguish Ego's elementary family. Hence, nuclear families will always be linked to other elementary families both by ties of common group membership and by the recognition of blood or affinal relationship. If we were to describe such links as 'extended family ties' because they are the ties which are used to form the various types of grouping wider than the elementary family which we call the extended family, we should have no way of referring to *relationships within extended families*, for which this term is better reserved. Perhaps 'extended kin relationships' could be used to denote *ties between members of overlapping elementary families* when such families do not constitute extended families.

The notion of an 'extended kin network' is, however, important and useful and is one that is closely related to the formation of extended family groups. This term is vaguely used, often in a metaphorical sense, though there have been attempts to define it and related concepts with more precision. A network may be regarded as a set of interconnected points. The points are people and the connections social relationships. These relationships, however, are not necessarily of the same kind. A might be the friend of B who was the brother of C who was the workmate of D who was the husband of E who was the sister of A and the brother of B. Some but not all of the relationships in the network described are relationships which involve participation in a group. A and D are workmates and share work-group relationships with others who are, in turn, connected with the members of the network through C and D. Logically a network is unbounded; in other words, it goes on for ever. All the members do not recognise relationships with all the other members, but are all linked with varying degrees of closeness depending on the number of relationships involved. Taking any individual as our subject we can see the network from his point of view as being composed of individuals at one, two, or three removes from him. He will necessarily come into contact only with those people with whom he has direct relationships. Ego and his directly linked members are referred to as 'a set'. They are not necessarily a group. They are not even necessarily linked to each other; the only thing they necessarily have in common is a relationship to Ego.

In fact, of course, a network may not go on for ever, it may be 'bounded'. Similarly, it may not be true for a given Ego that the members of his set have no relation to one another except through him. They might all have relationships to every other member of the set. In such a case Ego's set would not only be a set, but also a 'close-knit' network. If in a network this is true of the sets of all the members of the network, then the *network* may be said to be close-knit.

It is obvious that the bilateral recognition of kinship produces a kinship network, since each individual has overlapping sets of recognised kin, and that this network will be unbounded. It also follows that because of the degree of overlap the network will be relatively close-knit. Not all but most of Ego's recognised kin will recognise relationships to most but not all of Ego's kin.

Whether or not it is true that many of the relationships which go to make up a network are group relationships, the fact that a plurality of individuals recognise relationships with one another means that they are well able to act together in certain situations, even where they do not constitute a group. Because a set of individuals act together, it does not imply that they are a group, unless that co-action is dependent upon their sharing established value-expectations governing that co-action. Frequent co-action on the part of the same individuals in similar situations will, of course, lead to the formation of such shared expectations. Hence, by virtue of their membership of groups (elementary families) which overlap one another, individuals come to be members of close-knit networks. Such networks may provide the opportunity of co-action, and repetitive co-action may lead to the establishment of groups wider than the elementary family, that is, to the establishment of extended families.

If this process has been seldom explicitly described, this is partly because clear distinctions have not been made between extended families of different types and extended kin networks. It is well recognised that the gatherings of kin, for example, at marriages, do not constitute the gathering of a kin *group*, since all the attending kin have in common is relationships (of different types) to a particular Ego. However, a succession of marriages will see a considerable overlap in the kin attending them, resulting in the same people meeting again and again in the same situation. Similarly, the mobilisation of kin resources in time of crisis by a succession of related Egos may have the effect of activating relationships between the kin so mobilised. How far and in what way the movement of information, sentiments and resources along a kin network have consequences for the formation of more permanent groups remains to be investigated.

The extended family is then a *group* formed through what has been described here as the family process, whose membership is defined by an arrangement of the members in relation to the activities of the group in the situation in which it has to act, and is not required by the rules governing the family process. It is not a category of kin. Types of extended family can be distinguished by the use that they make of the overlapping family cores which the family process creates and the nature of the activity undertaken by its members. The extended family is not necessarily a *corporate* group, that is a group whose members act as a unit in some way, though it may be. Such groups are usually domestic groups, household groups, property-controlling groups and economically productive groups, or any combination of them. Where their activities require co-residence, they may also constitute residential groups. The list of activities is not, however, exhaustive. If we do not know of other types, it is probably because we have not looked for them.

The Family and Industrial Society — the Functionalist Approach

Chapter 4

The 'Fit' between Family and Society

The 'functional theory' of the family seeks to explain the existence of the family by showing that it has certain *social functions*. To say that an institution has a social function is to say that the performance of the activities (governed by that set of expectations concerning the way people should behave to one another, to which we refer when we speak of the institution concerned) has certain *effects* on the other social institutions which go to make up the society. However, it says more than this. When functionalists speak of the social functions of an institution, they are not concerned with *any* effects the activities which it governs may have. They are concerned with those effects without which a society could not exist.

That isn't quite the end of the story, however. The expectations which govern the performance of those activities which are necessary to the existence of *any* society must not only ensure the adequate performance of such activities. They must also 'fit' the other sets of expectations which govern the performance of other necessary activities in the particular society concerned.

If he can show that the activities governed by a particular institution must be performed in any society and that, given the nature of the other institutions in that particular society, the institution he is interested in must be of the type that it is, then a functionalist claims to have explained the institution concerned. Frequently, if not always, he is unable to show that an institution must be of the form that it is in order to 'fit' other institutions. He may then speak of there being a range of 'functional alternatives', that is, different ways of performing the necessary activity, all of which fit other social institutions.

Because such explanations or partial explanations involve not only establishing that the activity of one part is necessary for all the other parts to exist, but establishing the *relations* of the parts to one another, such explanations are called *structural*-functional explanations.

Functional analysis requires that the analysis distinguishes carefully between the conditions which have to be fulfilled if the people and their descendants are to continue to *co-operate* together and the conditions which have to be fulfilled if the *individual members are to survive*. The fulfilment of one set of conditions is, however, a condition for the fulfilment of the other set; humans cannot survive as biological organisms or reproduce themselves as humans except through membership of a society, nor can a society survive unless its members survive or successfully reproduce. To distinguish between these two sets of conditions is important because it is not necessary to explain in distinctively *social* terms the existence of activities which are necessary to the survival of individual organisms.

We can now turn to the family. A functionalist would list the activities which must occur to ensure the survival of the society's members and the activities which must occur to ensure the survival of the society, and examine which of these the family universally performs and whether any other institutional group could perform such activities. Alternatively, he might look at the activities which the family in fact performs, and examine how far they are indispensable to the society.

Whichever way it is done, there has to be some list of activities which are necessary for the survival of a society and its members. Such lists are compiled by attempting to elaborate what is logically involved in the notion of 'a society'. Most theorists prefer to take the more modest course of describing the effects that family activities universally have. This is in fact very modest, since they are often able to get out of explicitly stating how they decide which of the activities that the family performs have effects which are 'functional'.

In his book *Social Structure* (1949) Murdock claimed that the family performs four characteristic functions: the sexual, the economic, the reproductive and the educational. He argues that the sexual drive is a powerful impulse and cannot be left without restraints, and that the nuclear family provides for its satisfaction and at the same time controls it.

He also claims that the nuclear family is everywhere characterised by economic co-operation between man and woman based on a sexual division of labour. By this he means that apart from childrearing the woman also produces goods and services for the family.

It is indisputable that it is a condition of the survival of the population of a society that it must reproduce. It is also true that the family universally controls reproduction.

In the term 'education' Murdock explicitly includes 'socialisation'. These two activities may be seen as satisfying two conditions: one that children develop psychologically in such a way as to make it possible for them to constitute members of *a* society, and the other that they should be made members of that *particular* society by virtue of their having acquired the values, beliefs, expectations and accumulated knowledge which constitute its culture.

If it is granted that the four activities specified are necessary conditions of the continued existence of either the society's members or of the society itself, it still does not follow that this amounts to an 'explanation of the family', because there is no reason why all these functions must be regulated by the same institution and performed by the same type of group.

This point is explicitly recognised by Davis (1948). Davis lists four functions of the family: reproduction, maintenance, socialisation and placement. The first three functions fulfil the conditions of the perpetuation of the *membership* of the society and on which the existence of the society *indirectly* depends. The last two functions serve to fulfil the conditions of transmission between the generations of both culture and social positions, upon which the continuance of the social life of a particular society *directly* depends. He claims that only the family could provide for the performance of this set of tasks, but 'all of these functions could be performed independently of each other'.

It becomes clear that the 'functional theory' neither claims to explain nor succeeds in explaining the existence of the family. What it does make clear is the way in which changes in the family, as functionally defined, will affect all other institutions in the society.

It could be argued that a more useful explanatory approach is to start with the biological and psychological conditions of the perpetuation of the members of the society, and then show that something very much like the family must emerge if members of the society are to reproduce, and that once established the family will inevitably start to perform the functions of cultural transmission and placement (see Parsons, 1952, pp. 160-1). Its biological activities determine its structure, and its structure determines its direct social functions.

It is significant that Davis starts with function and then goes on to discuss the way in which the structure is related to the function. In fact, one must start with the activities of the individuals and not the functions of an institution (intercourse and bearing and rearing children – not 'replacement'), show how these determine the structure of the group and only then start worrying about the effects on society. For though we cannot reduce society to its members (it's something more than a lot of people), the idea of society is only intelligible in terms of the individuals that go to make it up and their activities.

Our discussion of the functions of the family points to the way in which functionalists see family activities affecting other social institutions and processes. We have already noted that the particular form a social institution takes can be understood in terms of the necessity of its 'fitting' other social institutions.

In order to be clear about this, we need to specify the different ways in which institutions may in general be said *not* to 'fit' one another. We may distinguish two main types of lack of 'fit': logical inconsistencies between the rules governing two activities and practical inconsistencies arising from the fact that the performance of one activity constitutes necessary conditions of the performance of the other.

Rules are not only related to one another logically and practically, however, but also through more general beliefs and values which they embody. For example, an attempt to compel married women to work and to direct labour would be regarded in British society as an attack on the liberties of the individual and upon the sanctity of marriage. In other words, it would be rejected because it did not fit, not so much the precise pattern of expectations which governed activities of different kinds, but because it was inconsistent with general beliefs which those other expectations reflect.

When we turn from general considerations to examine the actual fit between different social institutions in particular societies, it becomes apparent that if we are to argue that the family has a particular form because no other form would fit the economic institutions with which it is associated, then we must specify in much greater detail the exact ways in which rules and beliefs may be said to 'fit'. While there have been many attempts to deal with this problem, few have been sufficiently precise as to enable us to determine what empirical evidence would support or falsify the hypotheses which derive from them.

PARSONS'S THEORY: THE CONFLICT OF VALUES

Parsons (1949) has argued that the isolated nuclear family is the type of family which is most adapted to (that is, 'fits best') the other institutions found in industrial societies. What Parsons means by 'isolated' is of crucial importance here, since it has been widely held that the work of students like Sussman (1959), Sussman and Burchinal (1966a, 1966b) and Litwak (1960a) in America, and of Young and Willmott (1957) in Britain, has shown that the nuclear family is not isolated.

Parsons writes:

> This relative absence of any structural bias in favour of solidarity with the ascendant and descendant families in any one line of descent has enormously increased the *structural* isolation of the individual conjugal family. This isolation . . . is the most distinctive feature of the American kinship system. (Parsons, 1943, pp. 184–5; emphasis added)

What Parsons means is quite clear. Because the American kinship system is in his words an 'open, multilineal, conjugal system' – that is to say, because there are no rules prescribing or favouring marriage with particular relatives or categories of relatives ('open'), and no single line of transmission is preferred ('multilineal') – there are no principles which *by themselves* can lead to the formation of kin groups wider than the nuclear family. Hence, the nuclear family is *structurally* isolated. In other words, the rules governing the behaviour of individuals provide for the formation of nuclear family groups only. This is the social situation in which people are placed in our society. What they do in this situation is another matter. They may use the family process to form all sorts of extended family groups, but they get no help from the rules which govern it. *Structurally* the nuclear family, based on the marriage bond between husband and wife ('conjugal'), is the basic unit, and *structurally* it is isolated (see Parsons in Anderson (ed.), 1980, pp. 223–4).

Similarly, if we look at what Parsons says in discussing kinship in industrial societies in general, we find him writing that the 'extent of kinship solidarities' and the 'most stringent kinship obligations' are limited 'to the conjugal family of procreation isolating this in a relative sense from wider kinship units' (Parsons, 1952, p. 186). Here he is referring both to the formation of groups and to the recognition of obligations (that is, to relationships). What he is implying with regard to the latter is less clear, however. If he means by 'conjugal family of procreation' a 'nuclear family', then his statement implies that Ego's most stringent obligations to his children become less stringent after the children's maturation. If he means by 'conjugal family' 'elementary family', then he specifically provides for the existence of stringent obligations between two elementary families, one of which is nuclear, and hence denies the isolation of the nuclear family (where isolation is taken to mean that obligations between its members are more stringent than obligations to kin outside it).

It is clear from the whole passage that by 'conjugal family' he means 'nuclear family'. In other words, what he is saying is that Ego's duties to his spouse and *immature* children are more stringent than his duties to his parents. Let us suppose that this is true when Ego's children are immature. What happens when they marry? It is clear that the *children's* obligations to Ego will be less stringent. But why should *Ego's* obligations to them be less stringent than before?

The confusion arises through not making a clear distinction between the phases of development of the elementary family. Our family system implies the *primacy* of obligations within the elementary family only in its nuclear phase. Since the nuclear family is extinguished before the death of its members by the maturation of the children, it follows that relationships between parent and child are not fully reciprocal throughout the whole family process, the duties of members of Ego's generation to the descendant generation having primacy over their duties to the ascendant generation. That does not mean to say that they have no duties to the ascendant generation, nor that they are not important, nor that they are not equally stringent. It merely points to the fact that neglect of duties to the ascendant generation can be justified if those duties are shown to conflict with Ego's duties to the descendant generation.

There is, therefore, another confusion – that between the *ranking* of obligations and their degree of 'stringency', if 'stringency' means 'their importance and the degree to which they are sanctioned'. Parsons is not so much wrong as unclear. What he seems to be claiming is that, in Western industrial societies, the kinship system makes no provision for the formation of kin groups wider than the nuclear family and that obligations between members of the nuclear family take *precedence* over those to kin outside it.

Let us now turn to the characteristics of the economic system which according to Parsons necessitates this type of family. The simplest one to deal with may be described as 'occupationally induced geographic mobility'. This is assumed by Parsons to be a characteristic of industrial societies. He confines his discussion to pointing out that membership of any kin group wider than the nuclear family would inhibit the geographic mobility of individuals and that, in industrial society, the nuclear family is the unit of mobility (Parsons, 1949, pp. 262–3).

If it can be shown: that an industrialised economy can only function if there is a considerable movement of people between jobs; and that such movement must involve frequent geographical mobility; and that the age at marriage is such and the age of retirement such that fathers and married sons are working at the same time, then it follows that in industrial societies the formation of extended family *households* will frequently be impossible. However, it would be very difficult to show that all these conditions *must* be fulfilled under any industrial system, and even if they were, this would not prevent the existence of *non-residential* extended family groups.

There is evidence, however, that 'restricted' family types are more frequently found in hunting and gathering societies than in societies which are non-mobile. The crucial factor here seems to be property-*ownership*, which is closely related to the *type of organisation of economic production* (Nimkoff and Middleton, 1960).

Industrial society is characterised by the existence of specific institutions set up to perform economic activities. From this, it follows that in such societies the family cannot in the majority of cases be a *productive economic unit*. This point, which Parsons makes repeatedly, is a reference to what he sees as the characteristic difference between industrial and pre-industrial societies. It is of the first importance to note that the use of kin groups to co-ordinate economic activity distinguishes the latter type of society (Parsons, 1952, p. 176). Where the kinship system is not used to form productive groups, because the productive function is assumed by other institutions, 'the individual' is 'not bound to a particular residential location by the occupational, property, or status interests of other members' (Parsons, 1949, p. 263). Nor in a conjugal family system are ties to ascendants and collaterals as 'stringent' as those to Ego's wife and immature children, as we have seen. There are, therefore, no rules which prevent individual mobility, nor domestic activities which restrict it. Moreover, Parsons assumes that the wife in a nuclear family (that is, where the children are immature) will not work, so that the demands of her employment will not conflict with those of the only member of the (nuclear) family to participate in the productive system. It is these three factors operating in conjunction with one another that leaves the adult male free to move at the behest of the economic system.

Parsons's main arguments, however, do not depend on inconsistencies between rules governing the activities of economic and kinship institutions and the way they condition each other. Rather, they centre on the *conflicts of value* which arise because of the difference in type of the much more general ideas upon which each institution depends, and which govern the way in which roles in the society are allocated.

Parsons sees the growth of successful industrial activity as associated with the adoption of values which he calls 'universalism' and 'achievement'. We have noticed that social relationships involve categorising people and that kinship categories are categories of a special sort – 'relational' categories. That is to say, one does not behave in the same way to all the people who are fathers, but distinguishes between fathers according to the relationship they have with particular other people. It is the relationship to the particular person that determines the behaviour, rather than the membership of the category alone. Bus conductors are treated *universally* in the same way irrespective of differences in their relations to *particular* others.

We would think it shocking if bus conductors distinguished between different sorts of passenger in the fares they charged – if, for example, a conductor let all his first-degree kin travel free but charged double to the man he'd had a row with in the pub on Saturday night. We would think it equally shocking, however, if he showed no more filial affection towards his mother than he did to anybody else's mother.

The belief that it is wrong to differentiate between people in the same category on the ground of their relation to you is what Parsons means by 'universalism'. The belief that we ought to differentiate between people in this way is its opposite, 'particularism'. It is obvious that the family constitutes a set of particularistic relationships, while the economic institutions reflect universalistic values.

By 'achievement' Parsons means the belief in the rightness of varying one's behaviour towards other people on *other* grounds than their possession of inherent qualities, which he calls in contrast 'ascription'. The landlady who says, 'I'm sorry, I don't care if you are the Secretary-General of the United Nations and Louis Armstrong's brother; I won't have no coloureds here', is behaving universalistically – she refuses to be influenced by the relationship of the man at the door to a particular person. Nevertheless she is also behaving 'ascriptively' because the way she chooses to categorise him depends on his inherent qualities and not upon what he has achieved.

Kin relationships depend on categorisation on the basis of inherent qualities (being born of . . .), and not upon achieved qualities. They are governed not by achievement values, but by ascriptive values. We have already shown that they are also governed by particularistic values. Modern industrial enterprises are governed by universalistic and achievement values. As a result individuals who are both members of families and workers in industrial enterprises will be required to hold two contradictory sets of values at the same time.

If they act in accordance with those values, further sets of problems arise. From time to time they will be confronted with difficulties in the economic sphere when a relative asks for help in getting a job, or comes in to the shop where they work and asks for special treatment. Within the family they may find that they have to suspend judgements on their kinsfolk which depend on the values which govern their behaviour at work.

Parsons wishes to argue that this makes life extremely difficult, but that if you restrict the family group to the nuclear family, you do not get these difficulties *within the family group* because the children are immature and the wife busy raising them. As a result there is only one occupationholder in the family and all the members share the same amount of prestige and economic power – that which derives from his position. If the most stringent family ties are those between members of the nuclear family, no two persons playing roles opposite each other in the same economic institution will be connected by such ties.

Major conflict is, therefore, avoided by *two* types of segregation. The nuclear family is cut off from *wider kin* in the sense that the most stringent ties are confined within it, and because its members do not perform economic roles opposite one another it is also segregated from the *economic system*, except for the husband. In this way intrusion of family values into the sphere of work is avoided and work values do not disrupt the solidarity of the family.

Parsons's argument has two parts. First, it argues that the two sets of values which he specifies are inconsistent, and that the two sets of values are held respectively by the two institutions concerned. Parsons is on fairly firm ground here. He is not saying that in industry no one is ever refused a job because of his colour or given one because of his particular relation to the foreman. He is drawing our attention rather to the fact that such behaviour is not *justified* in terms of dislike of 'the blacks' or the rightness of looking after one's own. It is *justified* rather, by saying 'he wasn't up to the job' or 'he's the best man I could get'. This is precisely why it is so difficult to establish how much discrimination and nepotism there is.

The second part of his argument also has two parts. First, it could be argued that 'strain' between the family and economic institutions could be avoided if the different sets of values are segregated, that is, if the occasions on which they apply are quite clearly demarcated. Parsons stifles this objection at birth by saying that the values of the economic institutions are the *dominant* values in industrial society.

Secondly, Parsons not only assumes that the values he specified characterise the economic sphere, he also assumes that people actually *act* upon them; in other words, he assumes that extended kin are differentiated from one another in occupational terms, and that people in industry act universalistically and promote and recruit on an achievement basis sufficiently often to make that differentiation a reality.

The American studies which show that help and aid are transmitted to married children are, as Pitts (1964) has pointed out, in no way inconsistent with Parsons's hypotheses, provided such aid does not intrude into the occupational sphere. Such aid is not inconsistent with the elementary family structure, since it flows from the senior to the junior generation, and is merely a continuation of a pattern established in the nuclear family. Pitts points out, however, that the aid is very often designed to *further the more speedy establishment of the independent nuclear family*, which is still structurally isolated in the sense that care is taken not to diminish its autonomy and subsume it into a wider kinship group. Financial aid in particular is not dependent on proximity, and in the middle classes, where this kind of aid is common, it has the effect of 'evening out' over time the incomes of families whose earnings increase progressively over the life cycle by transferring wealth from the 'rich' oldsters to the 'poor' youngsters (see Bell, 1968, p. 173).

On the other hand the widely reported reluctance of many working-class families to move when employment is no longer available in the area is evidence of the way in which ascriptive ties to neighbours and kin create problems in the economic sphere and is at the same time consistent with the evidence of the importance of the exchange of domestic services among working-class families.

Parsons's theory may then be criticised less because it assumes a single pattern of behaviour which has been shown to be false, than because it states *merely* that there must, in industrial societies, be an *absence* of rules determining extended family groupings and ties and, hence, gives us no means of explaining the wide variations in actual family groupings which are found.

A central place in Parsons's general sociological theory is occupied by the idea of socialisation, and this process, in which the family plays such an important part, is discussed at length in a collection of essays edited by Parsons (1956). In his introductory discussion Parsons stresses the importance of the family *not* being completely isolated from the occupational structure. It is obviously necessary that a family member should occupy a position and play roles in the economic sphere if there is to be an economic sphere outside the family. Such an overlap is also necessary, Parsons argues, because it makes it possible for a child within the family to learn and make part of himself or herself (internalise) the values which govern activity in the economic sphere. In a society where most activities are ordered with reference to values different from those of the family, the family has the job of transmitting the opposite values to those on which it itself is based, and it can only do this if at least some of its members take part in those activities.

This is not to say that the family is *exclusively* charged with the internalisation of such values, but it constitutes a major sphere of social life in which this takes place. For Parsons, therefore, the family must not be completely segregated from other social institutions because, if it were, new members of the society would not be socialised and, hence, could not take part in the activities which characterise other social institutions.

Parsons's writings on the family have recently been subject to criticism partly because of his analysis of the American family which is regarded as being biased empirically and normatively towards the *middle-class* American family (see Morgan, 1975, pp. 39–40). These criticisms have considerable force but they are irrelevant to the theoretical discussion concerning the family-industrial society relation presented here. There are, however, criticisms to be made of the Parsonian approach which are important and of direct relevance to the preceding discussion.

The first may be dealt with briefly. Functionalist attempts at explanation are thought to involve the attempt to show the necessity of existing social arrangements. If they are successful, they demonstrate the impossibility of any other way of organising social life, provided certain empirical assumptions hold. This position is clearly unattractive if you believe (as most contemporary sociologists seem to) that not only are all sorts of evils associated with the present organisation of social life in contemporary society, but also that it is possible to diminish the number of evils by changing the type of social organisation. The real source of the complaint against Parsons is that he appears to believe the opposite. The present writer agrees that much sociological work, including that of Parsons, is unjustifiably influenced by belief as well as determined by reason and evidence.

Secondly, the attempt to explain (that is, show the necessity of) 'the isolated nuclear family' involves the tacit acceptance of the inevitability of the association of the industrial means of production with the values and practice of economic individualism. That historically there has been that association is indisputable. Its necessity, however, is nowhere demonstrated in Parsons's work: it is uncritically assumed.

Thirdly, much of what Parsons has written about the sexual

division of labour has come under fire (Morgan, 1975; Oakley, 1976; Edgell, 1980). In this discussion we have merely mentioned in passing that Parsons assumes that the wife in the nuclear family will not work, and that a nuclear family with a domesticated wife and immature children is free to move in accordance with the demands of the market for labour. Nothing that Parsons's critics say counters this argument, and his comments on sex-role segregation in the two essays on kinship and age and sex in *Essays in Sociological Theory*, which seem to infuriate contemporary sociologists, make all the 'modern', 'feminist' points about the imprisonment of the wife in domestic tasks, her exclusion from the occupational sphere, the small amount of domestic assistance she receives from her husband and the negative effects on her psychic health. One discussion concludes:

> Hence it may be concluded that the feminine role is a conspicuous form of the strains inherent in our social structure, and not the least of the sources of these strains is to be found in the functional difficulties in the integration of our kinship system with the rest of the social structure. (Parsons, 1943, p. 194)

In other words, it is the woman that suffers from the cultural opposition between kinship and economy, particularism/ascription and universalism/achievement.

Why, then, has his writing attracted so much hostility? Because he is thought to dissent from the view that 'the sexual divisions that actually exist cannot be wholly or partially attributed to the "biological peculiarities of the two sexes" ' (Edgell, 1980, p. 18). The view that sexual divisions cannot be even partially attributed to biological differences is surely a very extraordinary one (though it does depend rather on what *exactly* is meant by 'attributed' and 'sexual divisions') and it is scarcely surprising that Parsons dissents from it. It must be frankly admitted however that Parsons does hold that, given the functional necessity of segregating the nuclear family from the economic system except for one link, participation in the economic system will be that of the husband, not the wife. Nowhere does Edgell actually *quote* any passage from Parsons in which he explains why he makes this assumption.

Parsons makes the assumption in the essays quoted by Edgell because he is there discussing the contemporary American family in which women usually perform domestic- and men work-oriented roles. In *Family, Socialisation and Interaction Process* (1956) Parsons attempts to explain this feature of the modern American family. His argument runs: *given* that social process in small groups differentiates them along two axes, leader:led, instrumental:expressive, we should expect to find the same differentiation in families and, of course, we do: parent:child and husband:wife. The allocation of leader/follower roles is determined by age and the allocation of instrumental/expressive roles is determined by sex: that is to say, that age and sexual differences are the criteria for the allocation of these roles. In the first case the actual role allocation is determined by functional capacities associated with age, and in the second by different procreative functions of the spouses. And of course, empirically, so they are. I find no evidence in Parsons's writings that he believes that it is impossible for men to perform expressive and women instrumental roles, or that it is impossible for a society to exist without sex-role differentiation and allocation of the expressive role to women. As Morgan notes, 'Parsons ... does not appear to be completely convinced of the necessity of this relation but merely notes that as a result of biology and (presumably) long centuries of cultural conditioning any alternative arrangements seem unlikely' (Morgan, 1975, p. 44).

Parsons has been misunderstood, once again, and this time because the logic of functionalist arguments has been misunderstood. Readers of Parsons have argued, in effect, as follows: Parsons is a functionalist; functionalism seeks to demonstrate the necessity of existing arrangements; Parsons claims that women are allocated 'expressive' roles on the basis of their distinctive biological characteristics, therefore Parsons must be claiming that this is necessary. Parsons is, of course, claiming that it is functional for the economic system, but so do many Marxist feminist writers (see Chapter 10, *passim*). But the establishment of functional relations between two items does not explain the existence of either. In order to explain the *existence* of sex-role differentiation and its allocation in a true functionalist manner, it is necessary to claim that such an arrangement has a greater *survival value* for societies and groups which adopt it. In other words, functionalist explanations only make sense in an *evolutionary* framework.

Parsons had always definite evolutionary views of a Spencerian kind, that is, that the evolutionary development of societies involved structural differentiation and functional specialisation, which develops to its highest power in industrial society. The family comes to specialise in socialisation and the personality stabilisation of its adult members. But specialisation occurs also within the family area. A family with a division of labour within it is more efficient than one without it. Since the woman must spend some of her time bearing and nursing children, it is more efficient for her to combine those tasks with others involving the same value-orientations and which can be carried on while performing her maternal function. In *industrial* society providing material support for the household requires leaving it and engaging in activities involving value-orientations opposed to those involved in childrearing. Hence, not merely segregation of roles, but allocation of the expressive role to women, is functional in industrial society. Families thus organised will do better than others; so will societies whose cultures prescribe this sexual division of labour. This is a perfectly plausible argument and does not deserve to be *lightly* dismissed.

LITWAK'S THEORY: PRIMARY GROUPS, BUREAUCRACY AND 'SHARED FUNCTIONS'

Before considering another 'theory of fit', we must pause to note briefly another sense in which the family in industrial society may be said to be isolated. In primitive societies it is frequently the case that the majority of roles and group memberships are allocated on the basis of kinship, and every type of co-operative activity undertaken by kin groups. Hence, at one time (particularly in the 1930s) sociologists were very fond of describing the family in industrial societies as having lost its functions (Ogburn, 1938; McIver and Page, 1957; Burgess and Locke, 1953). Here 'function' is used loosely to mean 'activities', though some of the lost activities are social functions in the strict sense. There are many splendid different lists to choose from but there is general agreement that kin groups have lost religious, political, economic and educational activities to specialised institutional *groups* called churches, political parties, businesses and schools.

We have already noted, however, that these institutions are dependent on the family and that Davis's four core functions can all be performed by other institutions either in whole or part. Litwak's (1965) argument runs as follows: there is no reason to suppose that there is a residual set of functions which only the family can perform, neither is it correct to assume that the family has lost in entirety its other functions.

In support of the first proposition he can cite the development of new social institutions such as day nurseries and child-welfare clinics who perform part of the activities of maintenance and socialisation, and the development of psychiatric agencies to take over the activity of 'tension management' which Parsons sees as a characteristic activity of the family. He can also point to the fact that placement is, in an 'achievement' society, no longer entirely determined by birth.

In support of the second proposition he can point to evidence which shows that without family support throughout the educational process, the child is likely to 'drop out'; that family type is an important factor affecting religious activity; that motivation to work is partly determined by family background; and so on. He wishes to argue, therefore, that the family in industrial societies is characterised less by a *loss* of functions than by a *sharing* of functions. The key process in whose terms this sharing by the family of the functions of other groups may be explained is, one might add, socialisation.

Who is doing the sharing? Litwak's answer is important because it makes clear what both he and Parsons regard as the distinguishing feature of industrial societies, an important point on which we have so far remained (deliberately) unclear. The sharing, says Litwak, is being done by the *primary group* on the one hand, and by various types of *bureaucratic* institutions on the other. The term primary group means 'groups characterized by intimate face to face association and co-operation' which 'are fundamental in forming the social nature and ideas of the individual' (Cooley, 1962, p. 23). The term bureaucracy is used in the sense of Max Weber's ideal type of rational bureaucracy. That definition cannot be dealt with here. It involves, however, an organisation composed of a number of social positions ('offices') hierarchically arranged in terms of authority, occupied by people appointed on the basis of their technical qualifications, who are promoted according to achievement, in which everyone is subjected to the same treatment; social relationships are impersonal – without affection or enthusiasm – in which the official's sphere of competence is strictly defined (Weber, 1964). It is an institution governed therefore by values of universalism, achievement, specificity and affective neutrality in Parsons's terms; the polar opposites of the values governing family relationships.

Stripped of its theoretical language, what Litwak says is that the family is a basic social institution upon whose activities all other social institutions depend, that all activities which go on in a society cannot be provided for by bureaucratic institutional groups and must, therefore, be performed by non-bureaucratic groups; and that the distinction between what the former can do and what the latter can do does not depend on the type of activity (political, religious, economic, and so on), but upon the extent to which the activity is sufficiently patterned, repetitive and predictable in its occurrence and the extent to which the need for it is recognisable.

'Shared functions', then, are really 'shared activities'. If the family was isolated or segregated from other institutions in society as Parsons has said it must be – Litwak goes on to argue – then neither type of institutional group would be able to perform its activities effectively and *such segregation depends on each type of institution having entirely separate activities.*

This would seem to be a gross misreading of Parsons. Parsons, we have seen, is concerned with the maintenance of the solidarity of the family group by the elimination of economic differentiation, and the segregation of particularistic and ascriptive behaviour within the family.

On the first count, the performance by the family of activities which contribute to the successful performance of activities by other institutions is quite different from the performance of roles in those institutions, that is, the membership of such groups. On the second count, Litwak's whole argument depends on the greater efficiency of the family in situations when a particularistic orientation is required. It is precisely because the family has a *monopoly* of particularistic roles that other institutions have to rely on it when their ways of behaving governed by universalistic values are inadequate.

The segregation of the family to which Parsons refers does not involve a complete loss of activities to other institutions, as Litwak rightly points out. What it refers to is the confinement of particularistic and ascriptive ways of behaving to persons playing kin roles to one another, the belief that it is wrong to give primacy to ties of kinship when playing any other institutionalised role and the ensuring that no two people in the same nuclear family play roles in bureaucratic institutions opposite each other, thus preventing them ever having to choose between loyalty to closest kin and the *im*personal standards demanded by their occupation.

What the family has lost is not religious and economic *activities*. It has lost the control and co-ordination of such activities. That is to say, that these activities are no longer performed by family members as a group.

Litwak has performed a valuable service in pointing out that the development of specialised bureaucratic institutionalised groups (which perform the activities which the family group once performed) does not imply that such bureaucratic groups have a monopoly of their characteristic activities, and that therefore the range of activities which family groups in such societies perform may still be very wide. But Litwak's confusion of 'function' and 'activity', and 'activity' with 'group membership', leads him to reject some of Parsons's arguments on which his own theory in fact depends. At the same time he fails to distinguish the sharing of an activity and the effect that the performance of that activity has on the activities of other institutions in society, a mistake which derives from the loose use of the term 'function' with which he begins his argument.

The unwillingness of bureaucratic institutions to accept in practice that they do share 'functions' with the family and that untrained and non-specialised individuals acting particularistically and ascriptively can be of assistance to them in the successful performance of their activities may be seen to be one of the sources of the belief that the family has lost its functions. The prevalence of such unwillingness would seem strongly to support Parsons's thesis that the two sets of values are extremely difficult to combine, and the 'loss of functions' theory may be seen to have the effect of making their non-combination legitimate.

GOODE'S THEORY: POWER, AUTHORITY AND LEGITIMATION

Goode's (1963a, 1963b) approach to the problem of fit between the family and other social institutions characteristic of industrial society involves an examination of the effects of industrialisation upon different economic categories ranked in order of their command over economic resources.

Goode argues that the new economic institutions in an industrialising society will be in the hands of those who control property and wealth in the society before industrialisation. As a consequence the upper economic categories will be able to control their children, because the children's membership of upper categories will depend on their inheriting property or jobs in the new economic institutions. At the bottom of the economic scale, however, the fact that the parents have nothing to offer their children will mean that the basis of the parents' power over the child, which previously depended on control of jobs and what property there was, will be gone. Because parents and kin generally have little to offer the child, the adventages of maintaining kin connections will be small and, in consequence, it will be lower-strata families that first begin to move towards the 'conjugal' family form.

Goode's emphasis is on the degree of 'fit' between the needs of the individual members of society, and the extent to which they satisfy them under any given system. The question he wishes to ask is: 'how far and in what way does any given family system satisfy the needs of individuals?', and he seeks to explain change in terms of the value to individuals of different family systems – or of the same system among different categories – in maximising the satisfaction of their needs.

Now, Goode is very well aware that though we may specify certain basic 'human needs', the way in which the satisfaction of these needs is to be achieved and the levels of achievement which are considered satisfactory will vary with the society or group within it, according to the beliefs, values and ideas that the members of the society or group share. However, because no system is entirely satisfactory and all systems require sacrifices of individual interest to that of the group, certain ideas such as equality and individualism have an almost universally popular appeal. Such ideas once evolved or introduced tend to favour *both* a family form where the subordination of the individual to the family group is reduced to a minimum *and* the development of other social institutions which promote free inquiry and freedom of economic activity on which the rapid changes involved in any industrial system depend.

Although Goode is too shrewd to take an extreme theoretical position on this issue, he seems to go some way towards a position which would hold that the 'conjugal' family and the industrial system of production fit each other not directly, but through the ideas and values built in to both systems and, *in addition*, that the development of such ideas are a necessary or even sufficient condition of the development of both types of system.

It must be stressed, however, that he explicitly lists the arguments that we have considered so far: geographical mobility makes it difficult to keep in touch with kin; occupational mobility leads to a differentiation of kin groups wider than the nuclear family; and the loss of control of important activities by kin groups diminishes the importance of such groups to their members. He also adds a new and important consideration. Industrialisation creates a large number of different jobs and occupationally differentiates kin. Hence, the chance of any individual being *able* to assist kinsmen is diminished, because in most cases they will be in different occupations.

Goode's theoretical approach may be explicitly linked with our discussion of different types of fit (pp. 53–4) by focusing on the notion of *power*. If we define power as 'the ability to affect the behaviour of another even against their will', and we define authority as 'power which is made legitimate in terms of beliefs and values held by the people concerned', then we may see the role of ideas which Goode stresses as affecting the basis of legitimation of family authority and the effects of changes in other institutions as attacking the bases of that authority (that is, the power of parents over children and men over women) which characterises most non-conjugal family systems.

To give a concrete example: when the children believe that each individual has a right to act in furtherance of his own happiness, they will no longer accept that their parents have a right to determine whom they shall marry. This may cause difficulties at home but the victory for the children will become complete when they can earn a perfectly satisfactory living, even if their parents cut them off with a shilling, because they can work in a factory. Whether beliefs as to the rightness of parental authority will hold an extended family group together, even though the children have the power to be independent, depends on how dissatisfied the children are, which in turn depends partly on their economic position and partly on the values they have. The values get in in two ways, therefore: they not only legitimise authority; they partly determine the level of dissatisfaction of those under authority. Since values which are likely to maximise their dissatisfactions are likely to be a prerequisite of industrialisation itself, dissatisfaction, the acquisition of economic power and the withdrawing of legitimation from parental authority, all go together.

The redistribution of economic power within the family is the result of changes in the material conditions of action of the children and, hence, Goode shows how the two types of fit – between conditions of action, and between ideas – *both* operate together *and* interaffect each other.

It is important to recognise that the process which Goode describes, attacks both the existence of groupings wider than the nuclear family in systems where the rules governing the family process *require* their formation and the existence of certain types of extended family in bilateral systems where such groupings are *permitted*. The existence of the first is undermined because the sources of legitimation of the rules are undermined, as well as the conditions of the groups carrying out their activities changed. The existence of extended families under the authority of a single head are undermined in bilateral systems not by withdrawing legitimation from the system of rules governing the family process *as a whole*, but by changing the ideas on which the authority of people occupying certain positions within it depend, as well as changing the material conditions of action.

DISCUSSION

If we may venture to criticise Goode's approach, which is elaborated here to a greater extent than he himself has attempted, it would be that like most students of the family he pays too little attention to the process of industrialisation itself. The factors which are implicitly assumed in the above discussions of the relationship between industrialisation and the family but are never explicitly mentioned are the degree of job differentiation and the increase in the level of skill. The more jobs are differentiated (that is, the more different types of job there are) and the higher the level of skill required, the less substitutable one worker will be for another. When substitutability is low, it will be difficult to 'fit' men to jobs. The more difficult it is, the more necessary it will be to appoint them purely on merit and the more moving of people around will be involved. It is upon this factor that Parsons's characterisation of industrial society depends.

Now, it is perfectly possible to conceive of a society in which a large number of the workforce are engaged in non-agricultural occupations, where the ratio of skilled to unskilled workers is very low and where the managerial skills required are of a rudimentary nature. In such a society, except in the case of the skilled tradesmen, members of the managerial classes and members of the working classes would be interchangeable within their class and, assuming a minimum level of education, even between classes.

In such a society it would be by no means necessary for the majority of the population to be mobile between jobs, nor would individuals in different jobs be very significantly differentiated in terms of economic power, except across class (propertyowning) lines. It would, therefore, be perfectly possible to transmit property and jobs on the basis of kinship (ascription) and for kin groups to form common households or residential groups of other kinds. The vast mass of the population, unable to amass enough wealth to enter the propertyowning classes, would be virtually immobile and, hence, tend to disvalue achievement and to value ascriptive solidarity with kin, neighbourhood and ethnic groups. The necessities of manufacturing would not require the performance of universalistically oriented roles. It may be argued that the existence of primarily economic relationships between individuals and groups which would characterise such a society implies the existence of universalistic categorisation. On the contrary, while it cannot be denied that people would be categorised in terms of ability to pay or deliver the goods, this does not mean to say that distinctions would not be made within categories (particularism) on the basis of kinship, friendship, membership of peer groups, and so on.

It may be suggested that Britain about 1850 bore a marked resemblance to this type of society, and that our present-day society at the very least bears strong signs of continuity with such a society. If this assertion is correct, it would seem to indicate that it is vital to make explicit wnat elements in 'industrialism' affect the family. The empirical evidence about the continued existence of extended kin relationships and groups in industrial societies may point less to the inadequacies of our theories in the family than to the inadequacy of the concept of industrialisation.

Let us very briefly try another approach. The basic requirements of industrialisation, it would be generally agreed, are a surplus of capital, the requisite financial institutions, willingness to employ capital in productive uses on the basis of maximising its return, enough people and/or good enough communications to constitute a mass market and provide a labourforce, an educated elite capable of technological innovation, a set of ideas which will legitimise the activities of control and co-ordination of productive processes, and a surplus of agricultural produce.

Successful industrialisation would not appear to require that, in all its stages, people act universalistically, and that roles are allocated in all cases on the basis of achievement rather than ascription. If universalistic and achievement values seem to be associated with industrialisation, then this is because of their effect in the *initial* stages of serving to legitimise the authority of the industrialising elite. It does not necessarily follow that people begin acting in the way approved by such an ideology.

The *first stage* of the industrialisation process requires primarily *a concentration of capital*, and the development of an *ideology to justify those who now control it*. This is the process with which Goode is chiefly concerned. Capital concentration destroys the economic base of the authority structure of the family while the new ideologies, which justify the concentration of capital and its control, remove its legitimation. It must, therefore, be inconsistent with the traditional kinship systems of descent-group societies (Moore, 1963). Historically the ideological and economic changes preceded the adoption of industrial means of production and seem to have been a precondition of autonomous industrial growth. It is not surprising, therefore, to discover that the 'conjugal' family also antedated industrialisation.

In the first stage of industrialisation we should expect to find wide differences between types of industry in the extent to which achievement and other values are adopted and even wide differences in the extent to which they are acted upon. At the same time we should expect to find considerable variation in the extent to which different groups within societies are proletarianised by the concentration of capital and variations between societies in the degree of concentration of capital related to the degree and mode of industrialisation.

Where industrialisation is induced from outside, then the importation of foreign capital may result in the coexistence of large kin groups and industrial production, since the basis of the economic power of the former (their property) will not have been removed to provide capital for industrialisation. Those actually working in industry may well establish extended family groupings in the towns created to provide labour for the new industries after the first disruption of kin ties created by the initial rural-urban migration has been overcome.

If the *next stage* of industrialisation demands *a more exact fit between work skills and job demands*, then a need to *act* in accordance with the values of universalism and achievement will result. Even if this is the case, there will still be large areas of industrial society (mainly service industries) where both level of skill and job differentiation are low, and the adoption of such values may not be required.

Whichever phase of industrialisation the society is in, therefore, we may expect to find great variation between different occupational areas in the degree of skill required and in the extent of job differentiation. Correspondingly we should expect to find wide differencies in family form between different occupational categories. As a consequence the sociologist may be faced with a baffling number of family forms all associated with 'industrial production' if that term is widely defined.

The Parsonian characterisation of industrial society may be regarded, therefore, as an analysis of a polar type of society. The form of family which Parsons sees as fitting 'industrial society' would only *necessarily* be dominant in a society of this type, and even the 'nuclear' type of family, it will be recalled, does not involve isolation from all kin in the simple-minded sense that Parsons's vulgarisers have assumed.

There is nothing surprising therefore, from the Parsonian standpoint, in the coexistence of extended family forms with the utilisation of industrial means of production. The inadequacy of the Parsonian approach does not derive from its putting forward hypotheses which have been falsified by empirical research, but in its failure to provide any way of analysing the variety of family types empirically found in industrial society and understanding their incidence and variation in terms of a theory of the social form of the societies in which they occur.

Chapter 5

The Family and Individual Mobility

The arguments about the 'fit' of the nuclear family form with the economy in industrial society have one thing in common. They assume that, whatever an industrial society is, it is a society in which there has been a functional differentiation of 'family' from 'economy', and that the family group has shrunk to its nuclear core. This 'shrinkage' is thought to be a consequence of, and functional for, the operation of an industrial economy. Central to the argument that it is a *consequence* of an industrial economy are two assumptions: that an industrial economy requires high rates of social and geographical mobility, and secondly, that such mobility necessarily weakens or destroys the solidarity of any kinship group. This chapter is concerned with the second of these assumptions.

DIFFERENTIAL MOBILITY IN THE NUCLEAR FAMILY

In societies where the kin group is wider than the nuclear family, and is a unit both of ownership and production, the individual's ranked position in the society will be determined by his group membership and he will be able to affect it only by affecting the position of the group he belongs to. In societies where property and economic activities are not shared by members of corporate kin groups, but belong to individuals, it will be logically possible for the membership of kin groups to be internally differentiated in terms of propertyownership and occupation.

The members of the nuclear family in any society are spouses and immature children. The children have neither power, authority nor prestige *in the society as a whole* apart from their parents. Their position in the society is ascribed on the basis of their parentage. Since the family is a unit of residence and consumption, young children can have no style of life independently of their parents. Where prestige is attributed on the basis of style of life, therefore, the child's prestige will be the same as the parents'. Changes in the parents' style of life and in their degree of power and prestige will mean changes of the same order for the children. As the parents move, whether it be geographically or socially, so must the children. Differential mobility between parents and children in the *nuclear* family is, therefore, an impossibility.

In contrast to parents and children neither *spouse* in the nuclear family is, by definition, dependent on the other. It will, therefore, be *theoretically* possible for both spouses to engage in different occupations and to occupy different positions in the system of stratification. Before discussing the consequences of the differential mobility of spouses, it is thus necessary to consider what determines whether or not both spouses participate in the labour market.

There are two ways of approaching this problem: diachronically and synchronically. The distinctive functionalist approach is to concentrate on synchronic explanation. That is to say, to forgo any attempt to show how differential participation in the labour market by the sexes has been historically determined and to seek to show how the allocation of the wage-earning role to males and the domestic role to females is necessitated by the differentiation of family and economy characteristic of industrial societies.

The standard functionalist argument is as follows. There are obvious advantages in a division of labour within the family: that is to say, in one partner specialising in childrearing and household management, and the other in providing the material means of support. Except where the earnings of the spouses are high, it will not be possible to employ someone to take over the childrearing and household management tasks, hence these must be performed by the spouses themselves. Since the wife must be periodically absent from employment through childbearing, she is the obvious candidate for the family-oriented role.

This argument needs to be treated with caution. It does not apply with equal force at all stages of the family cycle. The wife can work in the early stages of marriage if childbearing is postponed. The availability of the means of contraception and the fact that it is not effectively opposed by those religious bodies who object to it mean that in Western societies it increasingly is postponed. One of the results of this postponement is that it makes possible earlier marriage and reduces the necessity of parental support and, hence, consent. Nor does the argument apply during any time that may be left after the last child has been born and reared. If the age at marriage is low and the family size small (that is, four or under) and the expectation of life is long (that is, 60 or over at the age of marriage), then there will be a substantial period towards the end of the marriage when the wife's presence at home is not demanded by the cares of the *nuclear* family household and an even longer period where the wife's presence is not demanded by care for preschool children.

In modern industrial societies the age of marriage is low, the family size is relatively small, the expectation of life long and there are schools. The wife therefore, even if she plays the family-oriented role, will be able to work for a large part of her married life. However, her career will be interrupted by childbearing and this interruption will affect her chances of reaching a high position in her profession when she resumes work.

The separation of family and economy is seen by functionalists, therefore, to favour a division of labour within the family and the activities of the family to favour the adoption by the woman of the family-oriented role. The performance of this role would seem to militate against continuous employment of women and to diminish their career prospects. Moreover, where the woman's and the man's skill are both high, then *his* mobility to obtain employment may result in residence which prevents the pursuit of *her* career. As a result of these factors women have lower activity rates than men and fewer reach the higher level jobs.

This isn't the end of the story, however. Even if the woman works, the role which is most visible will be her domestic role. As a result the expectations which the children will acquire through being socialised in such a family will be that the family role of the wife is the dominant one. As a result they will regard working as an 'optional extra' for women, rather than as an integral part of a woman's adult status (see Parsons, 1942).

In the economic sphere the identification of the woman with the domestic role and men with the occupational role will favour the recruitment of women to jobs which are related to the domestic in some way – jobs which are connected with taking care of people, rather than involving the efficient manipulation of people and things. At the same time the periodic absence from work involved in pregnancies or domestic crises may give substance to beliefs as to the unreliability and expensiveness of female labour, while women's association with particular types of job tends to give rise to beliefs about their having specialised aptitudes and abilities.

If we now add to these considerations the fact that all known industrial societies *have developed from* societies where economic activity was controlled by men and where the superiority of men was taken for granted, we have a perfectly adequate explanation of the low female activity rates and women's lack of success in reaching the top jobs. How much of it can be attributed to the persistence of what are now termed sexist notions and how much to the incompatibility of the conditions for the successful performance of family activities and for the successful performance of career activities, it is impossible to say. It seems reasonable to suppose however that it cannot be explained entirely in terms of beliefs and values and that, even if there were no 'prejudice' on the part of either sex against the employment of women, women would still have a smaller proportion in the top jobs and have lower activity rates by virtue of their allocation of the family-oriented role.

Three further points must be noted. First, provision of communal care for children (for example, day nurseries) or the substitution of

communal for family care (as in the kibbutzim) are the precondition
of both spouses working on equal terms. Secondly, it does not follow
that, even when women are thus enabled to work, they will necessarily
take advantage of that opportunity. It is easy to suppose that women
must want to escape from the home into the outside world and that if
they do not use the opportunities this must be through prejudice or
ignorance. Goode, once again, has pointed out that the satisfaction
obtained from work by the poorly educated and low skilled is small.
In such cases the rewards from work are extrinsic rather than intrinsic,
that is, they work for the money. If they did not need the money, they
would not work. In this situation why should a married woman
consider the opportunity to work an inestimable boon? At the beginning of industrialisation women and children were forced into the
factories because low wages meant that if they did not work they all
would starve. It is not unreasonable to assume that the crucial factor
determining whether married women work is the degree which their
household's income provides what they consider a reasonable
standard of living. We must be careful not to suppose, because
middle-class women obtain satisfaction from their jobs apart from the
financial rewards, that this is true of everyone else.

The third point that must be considered is whether or not the activities of child care can be undertaken informally by people outside the
nuclear family or by an extended family. This depends, of course, on a
large number of factors. In the first place, proximity of residence is
required. Secondly, it will depend on the shape of the family cycle.
Where the parent is so old as to be retired when a woman's children
are young, then her mother or mother-in-law may be able to provide
help with the children and the house. In a society where the married
women work, if a woman's parent is under retiring age, this may not
be possible because the parent may also be at work. If the age at
marriage is low in both the woman's and her parent's generation, then
if the mother postpones her return to work in order to care for her
daughter's children while the daughter works, there will of course be
no net gain in female employment as a result.

Such services may, however, be of advantage to the family concerned. We have already noted that the middle-class family can 'even
out' its income over time by transferring income from rich oldsters to
poor youngsters (p. 59, above). The working-class family does not
enjoy a rise in real income over the life cycle and cannot provide help
to young married children of a financial kind. It can, however,
provide domestic services. When the children have married, the
parents' income may be the same but the expenditure has diminished.
Help can be provided to their married children either by the mother
returning to work and giving part of her earnings to the married child
or domestic services can be provided which enable the young couple to
go out to work. Since financial aid would be a denial of the autonomy
of the nuclear family, domestic services are likely to be a popular

choice. If the parent is, however, still raising children herself, it will be the only possible choice.

In industrial society therefore, though married women may work and frequently do work at different stages of the family cycle, few married women follow careers. It is highly unlikely that the woman is going to be *occupationally mobile* through employment outside the family, and certainly not on the nuclear stage of the cycle. The sexual division of labour, therefore, has the effect of minimising the likelihood of differential mobility between spouses. This is regarded as functional for the family, because it may be argued that differential mobility of the spouses has adverse effects upon the stability of the marriage, and makes difficult the placement of the children.

A sexual division of labour may be seen to contribute to the stability of marriage in the following way. Where there is a complete division the relationship can never be competitive. Each spouse has a clearly defined sphere of competence. Secondly, it is a relationship of exchange and complementarity. Obviously, in the sexual sphere there is an exchange. But in the domestic sphere there is equally an exchange relationship, in which one partner provides an income and the other domestic services. Where the wife successfully pursues a career, this interdependence is greatly diminished.

A marriage may be seen as being held together by both what the spouses have in common and by an exchange based on difference. Differential occupational mobility of the spouses, therefore, introduces an element of competition into the relationship which now depends much more on sexual exchange and shared values. However, if there is differential mobility in the full sense of the term, this will involve the mobile spouse in accepting the values and styles of life of a different occupational group. Hence, differential mobility may be seen to destroy the social basis of the marriage, since it socially differentiates the spouses (destroys what they share) and it destroys the basis of the exchange relationship. This means that the couple rely chiefly on sexual differences and personality similarities. This is not to say that it makes the marriage impossible, but it may place it under severe strain.

It must be made clear that this argument does *not* assert that if both spouses go out to work they will destroy their marriage. What is being asserted is that, if there is considerable differential occupational mobility after marriage, then this will produce grave strains in the marital relationship by diminishing the range of shared values and patterns of behaviour in which the marriage was founded. These strains are minimised by a family system involving a division of labour between the spouses.

DIFFERENTIAL MOBILITY IN THE ELEMENTARY FAMILY

So far, we have considered only mobility arising from the wife's employment. When the wife does not work however, if the husband is mobile after marriage and this involves his membership of a different status group from that to which husband and wife originally belonged, then, although this neither destroys the complementarity of the relationship nor introduces an element of competition into it, it still destroys the shared values with which the marriage began, *unless the wife can change her style of life along with her husband*. This, while not easy, is not as difficult as when both are working, since the unemployed wife does not occupy a position in a group whose status is different from that of her husband. She does not have to perform two different and inconsistent roles at the same time, which would be the case where husband and wife both had different occupational statuses thus requiring the wife to occupy two different occupationally defined statuses (for example, female company lawyer and butcher's wife).

The reader will be doubtless quick to spot the fact that the wife *does* belong to a group whose style of life will differ from that of her husband if he is mobile after marriage. She belongs to her kin group and at very least that means to her elementary family of origin. As a result she will have *either* to abandon the life style of her kin in favour of the new life style of her husband *or* retain the life style of her natal group and refuse to 'move' with her spouse. She has to choose, in other words, between her husband and her parents. This is a nice example of Parsonian 'strain' between the occupational system, which requires the husband's mobility and ascriptive loyalties to kin. A nuclear family system, therefore, even where only one spouse works, does not entirely solve the structural problem posed by the separate existence of family and economy.

This consideration directs our attention to the consequence of differential mobility between parents and adult children. Such mobility doesn't disrupt the nuclear family system but it does, according to Parsons, make impossible the formation of extended families, a position with which Litwak (1960a) has taken issue.

Parsons claims that

> The solidarity of the kinship unit is of such a character that if certain facilities and rewards are available to one member, they will have to be 'shared' with other members. In other words the two basic components of the reward system of the society, occupational approval ... and ... love and response in the kinship unit must go the same way (Parsons, 1952, pp. 160–1).

Parsons is arguing, therefore, that the prestige of family members in the society is pooled, so that Ego's mobility in prestige terms increases that of his parents, while his parents' stability diminishes the amount of mobility that would have been achieved by Ego through occupational ascent had Ego not had such parents. Hence, there cannot be superordinate–subordinate relationships between kin *based on prestige differences*.

Litwak argues that parents laud the success of the mobile son, who gains the satisfaction of being deferred to by his kin on account of his mobility. This is to make a very elementary confusion between the way a role is performed and its occupancy. Of course, parents may be proud of a mobile son – precisely because his prestige increases theirs; and of course, the parents hold the son in high esteem – precisely because he is such a 'good' son. Being mobile, in a society that values mobility, is a way of performing the role of son well. The esteem which derives from good *performance* of an existing role (son) Litwak confuses with the deference accorded because of the *occupancy* of a new role (the occupational one).

Within the family the recognition of social prestige differences is inconsistent with its sharing of social rewards, while ignoring such differences is difficult because of their wider social significance. For a parent not to defer to a mobile child is an effective denial of the mobility achieved, while to defer to the mobile member is in effect to deny his or her family membership.

If prestige of family members is pooled, the low prestige of the father diminishes that of the son. One of the functions of the family is supposed to be placement. 'A' places 'B' in terms either of his kin relationship to another known person, or in terms of his ascriptive category membership – *black, Welshman, son of* managing director, or whatever. We can see now why Parsons regards a social class as having an ascriptive membership. Class membership is kin determined twice over. First, the family into which one is born affects one's life chances, that is, the chance of becoming successful, and so on, because of the control over resources commanded by the family and wider kin. Secondly, because if family members share prestige, a social relationship with a member of a family group involves third parties in an obligation to treat the other members of the group in the same way.

If the elementary family is differentiated through differential occupational mobility, members of the occupational category into which a high-mobile family member has moved will be unwilling to treat him as an equal because so to do might involve treating his kin as equals which, in view of the kin's style of life and lower occupational prestige, they will be unwilling to do. Therefore they must keep their social distance from him, or not permit the approval they accord him because of his job to spill over into the diffuse esteem in which members of a ranked social category are held.

If, however, the occupational position of the 'mobile's' kin is unknown – or the chances of any contact being had are remote because of the distance between them and the 'mobile' then such consideration may have little effect, provided that the ideology of the group concerned does not involve justifying their superior position in terms of superior birth. Litwak is, therefore, correct to point out that the anonymity of a large city may make it possible for the 'mobile' to segregate kin and his new peers, and that geographical mobility may have the same effect.

Litwak also claims that a further assumption underlies the argument that kin groups wider than the elementary family are disrupted by social mobility. This is that there are 'extreme differences in socialisation among the various occupational strata'. By this Litwak means that there are differences in what is transmitted.

Litwak implies that he accepts that the resocialisation of individual members of an elementary family through mobility would constitute a real barrier to extended family communication. He argues as a matter of fact, first, that style of life differences are small and narrowing in contemporary American society, and secondly, that the degree of occupational mobility found is insufficient to involve crossing status category lines. These views can be questioned both on empirical and theoretical grounds, but to do so here would take us too far out of our way. We may note that he never mentions education in this respect, which would seem to be of some importance, and that he confines his attention to the white Americanised groups so as not to confuse ethnic differences with class differences. In a society where ethnic differences play an important part in determining class position this is an odd line of argument.

His last point however takes us back to ground covered in the previous chapter, namely, the frequency with which a high degree of mobility is required by an industrial economy. Here the Parsonian argument may not hold for all stages of industrialisation. Our concern here, however, is not with the amount of mobility *required*, but with whether it must disrupt the elementary family *if it occurs*.

It would appear that some types of mobility are possible without disrupting family relationships. Occupational mobility by itself need not be disruptive where it does not lead to social mobility. Where the approval which is accorded to an individual is prevented from spilling over into diffuse esteem either because of the refusal of the occupational category concerned to accord esteem, or because the job concerned has no clear implications for style of life or group membership, or because the mobile individual refuses to associate with members of the category to which his occupational mobility gives him access (except in the occupational sphere), a disruption of family relationships will not occur. The mobile individual will receive the praises of his family and they will enjoy enhanced prestige within their own category.

Where, however, the mobility is significant in so far as it involves movement between groups based on different styles of life and/or different economic or political interests, then it is likely to have a disruptive effect. If, however, the categories concerned do not conceptualise themselves as being differentiated in economic and political terms, but in terms of *standard* of living, then there is no reason why mobility should weaken the solidarity of the family group. In such a case the only meaning attached to the term social mobility will be occupational and income mobility, since the society or the area of the stratification system concerned will not be made up of groups or categories, but of positions ranked on an income and job-prestige scale.

Where social mobility in terms of group membership is possible, however, it still may not disrupt family relationships if they can be segregated from other relationships – provided the groups between which the mobile moves are not differentiated in terms of style of life rather than standard of living.

We may accept, then, that industrial society requires occupational mobility, and that where such mobility leads to social mobility in the full sense of the word, it will be disruptive of extended family groupings based on solidary ties between members of the elementary family. If different studies appear to provide different conclusions on this point, it is because they attempt to base their findings on measures of occupational mobility alone (compare Litwak, 1960a, and Stuckert, 1963). As Rosser and Harris (1965) have put it, 'the discrepancy between occupational achievement and social acceptance by another social group, by slowing down the rate of social mobility of individuals, enables the extended family to accommodate large changes in the occupational status on the part of its members because the consequent changes in social status are much smaller'.

Changes in social status are disruptive because of the way in which, as Parsons penetratingly shows, the ascriptive solidarities of kinship and of social classes and status groups intermesh. Parsons also points out, however, that both are articulated also with local community, since the family is a unit of residence as well as a unit of stratification. It is to a discussion of this relation which we now turn.

THE FAMILY AND GEOGRAPHICAL MOBILITY

Parsons stresses that the family is not only a unit of social mobility but also of geographical mobility, because it is not only the basic unit of stratification but also the basic unit of residence. As a consequence family membership determines the membership of territorial groups. Even where the 'normal' household's necessary membership is restricted to the nuclear family and no requirement concerning the co-residence of kin is made, the fact that the nuclear family is a household will nevertheless affect the formation of groups wider than the nuclear family.

In societies with advanced transport technologies the individual, once adult, can of course move literally anywhere. Nevertheless it would still be surprising if there was not some relationship between the geographical distribution of the overlapping elementary families, created by the family process, and the point of origin of such a cluster of families. For example, one would not expect that, at any given moment, the families of origin of an Aberdonian and his wife, and the families of procreation of their sibs, children and grandchildren, would be no closer to Aberdeen than the same cluster of families of a man who was born at the same time in Penzance. Of course, one's expectations might not be fulfilled in any given case, but the chances of two family clusters, having widely different points of origin, having the same geographical distribution relative to one another's points of origin would certainly be smaller than evens – although the effect of family ties in restricting mobility was not taken into account.

In other words, just because you have a high transport technology and an absence of rules of residence, it still does not follow that the distribution of family clusters is going to be random. As a result the individuals who inhabit a given geographical area are likely to be more connected by ties of kinship to other people within the area then they are to people outside it. Where transport is poor or the settlement relatively isolated from other settlements, this clustering of kin relationships is likely to be marked.

This is, of course, true not only of kinship relationships, but of other kinds of relationships as well. There is therefore, in every type of society, a tendency towards the geographical clustering of relationships whatever the transport is like, and whatever the settlement pattern. The transport, the settlement pattern and the degree of occupationally induced mobility may affect the size of the areas within which any given degree of clustering takes place, but can never eliminate it. The degree of clustering and the area over which it occurs will determine whether different types of activities involving the individuals in the area can take place. That is to say, it will determine whether the relationships within the area can be used to form groups through which the people concerned can co-operate to carry out different types of activities. In other words, the degree of clustering will constitute one of the necessary conditions of certain types of group formation. What groups are actually formed will, of course, depend on the beliefs and attitudes of the people and on the extent to which they vary among them.

All activities, however, are not dependent upon proximity for their performance. Nevertheless it is, as we have noted, difficult for group members to act together where they are widely separated. As a consequence it is unlikely that widely separated individuals will *form groups* for the performance of activities, as opposed to *maintaining relationships* with individuals, or continuing to recognise membership of dispersed groups whose solidarity does not depend on the performance of such activities.

If the members of a locality or an elementary family group are dispersed, they may still be members of the territorial or elementary family group but they will not be able to participate in group activities. Nor will members of an elementary family be able to form groups wider than the elementary family for the purpose of carrying out group activities. Members of dispersed groups may, however, be able to maintain interactive relationships with individuals. Where one member of the group only is physically separated from the rest, he may be able to act in concert with the rest of the group. As the proximate group members already act in concert, he has only to co-ordinate his activities with any one of them for the whole group to act together. Hence, if only one of the members of the group is dispersed, this will not prevent the co-action of the whole group unless that particular activity requires proximity.

Now, if we keep the preceding argument clearly in our minds, a large number of difficulties about the effect of geographical mobility on kin groups disappear. Litwak (1960b) has argued that modified extended families aid geographical mobility, and that extended family identification is retained in spite of breaks in face-to-face contact. He substantiates these propositions beyond the possibility of doubt as far as the population he studied is concerned. He is able to show in addition that the extended-family-oriented are more likely to live further away from kin in the early stages of their career and less likely to be geographically separated from kin towards the end of their career, and that the difference between the beginning and end of the career is greater among the higher than among the lower occupational groups. This he explains in terms of the greater requirement of mobility among those in higher-status bureaucratic occupations. Mobility is necessary to achieve success; hence when success is achieved, it is possible for Ego to move nearer relatives.

What Litwak is saying, then, is that contact between relatives can be maintained in spite of geographical distance. The existence of an extended family can aid mobility by providing emotional, social and economic aid to its mobile members. There is now ample evidence to support the contention that help is exchanged and relationships recog-nised between widely separated kin who are not members of the same nuclear family. Indeed, it is odd that it was ever questioned. The question we have to ask is what Litwak means by an extended family. He offers no evidence of the formation of extended family groups made up of dispersed kin and, indeed, no evidence of any sort as to what categories of kin his subjects were in touch with. We may assume that the 'relatives' with whom his sample were in touch, and who aided mobility, were in fact parents. To say that people retain the membership of dispersed elementary family groups and maintain rela-tionships with individuals is not to say that they form extended families in our sense or in Parsons's sense or, indeed, in any sense which uses the term 'family' to mean 'group'. Once this is understood, Litwak's work loses most of its theoretical importance. The data which he provides are consistent with two hypotheses put forward in this book, namely, that the degree of mobility required by the indus-trial society is related to the level of skill, and that relationships outside the nuclear family are of continued importance in assisting individuals to fulfil the demands made upon them by industrial society.

We may sum up Litwak's contribution to the study of the family as follows. Litwak has not, as he thinks, in any way undermined Parsons's theory. Whereas Parsons's contribution has been to argue that the maintenance of extended family *groups* is inconsistent with the requirements of social and geographical mobility likely to be made in advanced industrial societies, Litwak has shown that the existence of extranuclear family *relationships* can, in fact, be important in aiding this mobility.

It may be argued, however, that even the existence of extended family *groups* may be of assistance in providing some types of mobility. One of the reasons why it was at one time thought that urban society was characterised by the existence of nuclear families geographically isolated from all kin was that in a period of swift *urbanisation*, that is, when people were leaving the countryside for the towns, the towns must be full of nuclear families who had left their wider kin behind. We may note that this does not mean that *urban society* must necessarily be characterised by such a family type unless towns are only maintained in being by migration to them of a rural surplus population in each generation.

Even, however, in the stage of urbanisation it does not follow that urban nuclear families are necessarily isolated from wider kin. Both common-sense and later research suggest that kin ties may play an important part in determining the patterns of migration. For example, Brown (1952, 1963) has shown the way in which the migrants from a poor rural area in the Appalachian mountains tend to cluster in certain urban neighbourhoods. The inhabitants from this area, Beech Creek, live in families of a conjugal type but use the family process to form extended family groups. These family groups are ranked into strata and are endogamous within the strata and, hence, tend to be interconnected within strata by marriage. In consequence the ascriptive solidarities of 'class', locality and kinship overlap, though there are breaks in the local network of relationships at the boundaries of each stratum. This pattern is reflected in their migration pattern, members of both family groups and strata tending to cluster in the same urban area.

Brown then relates this pattern to the notion of the 'stem family' of Le Play. According to Le Play the advantage of the stem family is that it permits the migration of non-inheriting children without depriving them of the support of parents and sibs in times of difficulties. The maintenance of links with parents and sibs through parents, however tenuous they may appear at the moment at which they are observed, is important because they make possible the retention of a place of safety, as one of Brown's informants put it, 'should things get rough out there'. To Le Play's characterisation Brown wishes to add that sibling ties between the non-inheriting children aid migration by facilitating the adjustment of the migrant to the urban community and provide support and assistance in the initial phases of adjustment. The existence in modern industrial society of unemployment relief and other bureaucratic forms of aid precluded the necessity of actually returning to the area of the stem family when things get rough; but the knowledge that one has a place to go to and an ascriptive identity independent of that provided by one's achieved status is of considerable significance to the migrant.

Schwarzweller (1964) followed up this notion with a study of migrants and non-migrants in the urban area to which the Beech Creekers move. He is concerned to examine the other side of Brown's argument. If migrants retain an identification with their family of origin, and hence their place of origin, while this may be important in supporting immigrants in the initial phase of their residence in the city, it is likely to preclude their developing a sense of belonging to the locality to which they move because a large and important number of their ascriptive relationships will not cluster within their new locality. In other words, the retention of family ties with another locality will assist their *migration* but not their *assimilation* either by the group to which they have moved or of the values and attitudes of urban industrial society. He finds no evidence that the maintenance of ties 'with the folks back home' militates against the establishment of non-kin relationships in the new locality or retards upward occupational mobility, but finds that the feeling of residential stability is inversely related to frequency of interaction with the parental family. He is unable to say whether the people, who are dissatisfied with their urban situation and want to move, associate more with their stem family because they are dissatisfied, or are dissatisfied because they associate with their stem family.

Our chief concern here is less with the effect of the family on mobility than on the effect of mobility on the family. Brown and Schwarzweller's data seem to indicate that, by aiding migration, the maintenance of extended kin relationships remains of significance to migrants despite geographical separation, and Brown suggests that the process of migration may lead to the establishment of extended family groupings in the urban environment.

Although we have so far dealt separately with social and geographical mobility, it is important to recognise that they are usually explicitly related. The Beech Creek migrants are at least economically as well as geographically mobile. If the migrant belongs to a family group 'back home', then since the family group tends to pool its possessions whether of prestige or of economic resources, the migrant will feel it incumbent upon him to share his new prosperity with the family members. There are two ways in which this can be done: either he can send home money or he can save to bring other members of the family over to him. The existence of strong extended family groups in the migrants' area of origin may, therefore, stimulate rather than retard *migration*. That is not to say that it will facilitate differential *individual* mobility, economic or geographical.

Thus we find, among the migrant populations of urban America, and increasingly in Britain, that strong extended family ties tend to facilitate migration and lead to the formation of ethnic communities in the host country whose strong ascriptive ties of kinship and locality in their country of origin are recreated in the host country, to which are then added the other ascriptive ties of ethnic and 'class' membership, thus creating highly solidary communities which prevent assimilation into the host society (see, for example, Rex and Moore, 1967, pp. 84–132). The way in which extended family ties facilitate migration is vividly illustrated by the way in which attempts by the British government to control immigration have run into difficulty over trying to restrict entry to the dependants of existing immigrants. To the British 'dependants' meant nuclear family members; but to migrants from solidary local communities made up of clusters of extended families, patterns of dependency and economic obligation are infinitely more complex than anything ever dreamed of by either the British legislature or the average immigration officer.

It would appear, therefore, that the existence of extended-family groups inhibits differential mobility and adversely affects the assimilation of immigrants. When it occurs, individual mobility must destroy such *groups*, where their existence is contingent on the performance of an activity which depends on co-residence. The maintenance of extended kin *relationships* can aid mobility by providing services at a distance – money, information and advice – while high levels of mobility may produce a geographically dispersed extended kin network which may be supportive of the person who is highly mobile by providing 'instant' relationships in the various places where he or she spends short periods of residence.

THE FUNCTIONALIST APPROACH: A PERSPECTIVE

This chapter and Chapter 4 have considered the view that the nuclear family system is the most functional form of family system in an industrial society. This thesis has been discussed with frequent reference to the work of its most eminent exponent, Talcot Parsons. In spite of the attack which it has attracted from empirical family sociologists, it can be argued that it remains unchallenged, as these attacks are based on a number of fundamental misunderstandings of the Parsonian version of the thesis. Parsons's thesis does, however, depend critically upon certain assumptions about 'industrial society', namely, that such societies necessarily have universalistic and achievement-oriented cultures, and require significantly high rates of geographical and social mobility. The real weakness of the Parsonian thesis does not lie in its assertion of the inconsistency between the collectivistic values of 'the extended family' and those of economic individualism or the disintegrative effects of individual mobility on its ascriptive solidarity, but in its characterisation of industrial society itself.

The vast literature on industrial societies and industrialisation will not be discussed here – though such a discussion would not be out of place in a book entitled *The Family and Industrial Society* – because an attempt to formulate a type of society on the basis of a specification of the means of production alone is unlikely to succeed; while attempts to formulate either a type of industrial society or a typical process of industrialisation have been subjected to so much criticism, and have fallen into such disrepute, that an attempt to relate family forms to such type constructs does not seem worthwhile.

The reader will be aware that the functionalist approach in sociology is currently unfashionable and that Parsons is regarded as having been its leading exponent. In consequence it may be a matter of some surprise that two chapters have been devoted to expounding it. This would be to misconstrue the nature of these chapters, which could be more accurately described as a presentation of the debate between empirical sociologists and Parsons. Certainly, this debate concerns the effect of the demands of industrial production on the family and the effect of non-nuclear-family organisation on industrial production, but it could scarcely be claimed that any consideration of the effect of one activity on another necessarily requires the adoption of a functionalist approach to the study of society. Admittedly, we have discussed the loss and sharing of familial functions, but these matters could perfectly well be described as the loss and sharing of types of activity. The questions raised by the debate continue to be of importance irrespective of the terms in which they are couched.

That having been said, it must be admitted that the way the debate is organised and structured is in many senses inadequate and unsatisfactory in that it fails in a major way to enable us to grasp the nature of family life in industrial societies, the ways in which it differs from other classes of society and the reasons for those differences. In consequence the remainder of this book will attempt to exploit alternative approaches to our understanding of the family in industrial societies. Before we do so, however, it will be useful to locate more precisely the deficiencies of the approach which has formed the subject of the two chapters.

In the first place the approach lacks any serious historical dimension. Parsons is not arguing that industrialisation caused the demise of the extended family by means of an examination of the way in which family life changed in societies undergoing industrialisation. He simply compares the features of the nuclear family system with the requirements of industrial production, argues that they fit and that the extended family system would be inconsistent with such a system of production. This means that he is unable to discuss the differing ways in which the family was affected at different stages of the industrialisation process. He cannot show that its existence is the outcome of a process (industrialisation) which has taken place under certain historical (that is, non-necessary) conditions and results in part from those conditions, that it could be different if those conditions were changed and will be different as they change.

Secondly, Parsons's sociology is a sociology of forms. These forms are variable as between societies with different cultures. The content of these forms is, however, always the same: it is a universal human content. Hence, all sense of interplay between form and content is lost. There is no need for Parsons to examine the actual content of family life: it is adequately described for scientific purposes when its form has been specified, since its content is a universal human content. This, like the ahistorical nature of Parsons's approach, is one of the hallmarks of functionalism. For the essential explanatory strategy of functionalism is to show that an institution must be as it is not only because it 'fits' other institutions, but because it supplies universal human needs. So the argument runs: this need must be fulfilled in all societies, and given the other institutions of a particular society, then the institution fulfilling those needs must be of the form that it has in that society.

It would be very foolish indeed not to recognise the value of this type of explanation. It elegantly combines natural necessity in human affairs with the facts of cultural difference. Yet it is inadequate because the essential characteristic of human societies is that, unlike animal societies, they exhibit enormous diversity. Any explanatory strategy which relies so heavily on universals can only proceed at a level of abstraction which ignores the major part of the cultural and historical specifics of social life which constitutes that diversity. The result is an approach which relates forms at a high level of abstraction and relegates too much to the level of unexplained content.

Thirdly, Parsons's explanatory procedures involve two types of necessity: the logical necessity involved in the *agreement* of ideas, and the natural necessity deriving from mankind's material nature. This means, however, that the empirical consequence of acting in one social sphere, according to the ideas governing that sphere's activities for the performance of activities in another sphere, is left largely untheorised, to be filled in by empirical research operating on the basis of largely common-sense understandings.

Fourthly, except at this level there is no room for *disagreement*. The statements about the different parts of a social whole are restricted to statements which necessitate each other. Contradictory statements have no place in the theory. Hence, it is not possible within a functionalist framework to discuss at the theoretical level the contradictory demands made upon the family by the industrial system, or the lack of fit between the two spheres. Such statements have to remain always at the level of untheorised empirical observation.

Fifthly, differences between societies are seen to reside primarily at the level of ideas. For Parsons, man's relation to the world is mediated by ideas, and this relation is variable. Man's changing relation to nature is treated as fixed, and modifications of this relation by the transformation of the means of production are relegated to the status of an untheorised empirical condition.

Sixthly, this has a consequence which is of peculiar importance for the family. The family is seen as a natural group determined by its biological functions, to which (in human society) a cultural function has been added – the socialisation of the young. This is a cultural function, because the effect of interaction within the family is the children's internalisation of the culture of their parents. This function is, for. Parsons, absolutely vital to the maintenance of the social system of any society, since it ensures a fit between the values of the individual, and the values of the culture which are built into the prescriptions as to appropriate ways of behaving in different institutional spheres. No one can deny the importance of the family as an agent of socialisation and its pre-eminence in determining the social character of the individual. What is unsatisfactory about Parsons's approach is that he is only interested in explaining how it is possible to produce culturally conforming individuals. Culturally deviant children can only be explained in terms of a failure in the normal process attributable, once again, to untheorised conditions.

It is misleading to suppose that Parsons regards the human individual as some sort of robot programmed by socialisation to act in a culturally acceptable way. Rather, Parsons is only interested in the transmission of that minimum of common culture necessary to make society (that is, association) possible. But each human individual as a totality is a social product. While all explanation at the theoretical level depends on abstraction and necessarily does not explain any phenomenon in its totality, Parsons's abstraction leaves such an enormous residue behind that his theory is no more able to grasp and explain the different characters of individuals than to grasp the character of cultures and epochs.

The six points stated above are not intended to constitute an exhaustive or thoroughgoing criticism of either functionalism or Parsonianism. They constitute rather an attempt to specify those characteristics of Parsonian functionalism which render it, by itself, inadequate as a theoretical basis for understanding the family in societies utilising industrial means of production. A much more extended critique is to be found in Chapter 1 of D. H. J. Morgan's *The Social Theory and Family* (1975). For our purposes here, two criticisms stand out as of central importance: the formalism of Parsons's theorising, and its ahistorical character. The relation between form and content is a theme which will be further developed in Part 2, which will consider the light which recent developments in the historical study of the family have thrown on our understanding of its nature in industrial societies.

Part Two

Exploratory

Section I:

Historical Understandings

Chapter 6

The English Family before Industrialisation

The introductory discussion in Part 1 of this book embodies within it an argument concerning the relation between family form and social form. It may be helpful to the reader if this argument is disinterred from the accompanying exposition and subsidiary arguments. It has two parts: conceptual, and theoretical.

The conceptual part of the argument is as follows. There has been much confusion over the use of the term 'extended family'. This confusion can be dispelled and a number of issues clarified if the term 'family' is used to apply only to a social *group* in contradistinction to a social *network*. The *nuclear* family is a social group composed of spouses and *immature* children. Such groups are regularly formed in industrialised societies, and the vast majority of children in these societies are raised in nuclear-family *households*.

Because of the universal characteristics of biological kinship, any given individual stands at the centre of a network of biological relations which *extends* beyond the confines of the nuclear family group into which he/she was born. Equally this network *extends* beyond the nuclear family founded by his/her marriage. Moreover, some of these endlessly ramifying biological relations are socially recognised. Though the boundaries of the universe of recognition, and the obligations which exist between such socially related persons are highly variable, those boundaries always include relationships more *extensive* than those composing the elementary family (namely, hu wi, parent–child, sib–sib). There is overwhelming empirical evidence that the network of kin relationships which extends beyond a single nuclear family is of continued importance and retains some functionality in industrial societies. In other words, there is no question as to the continued importance of *extended kinship networks* in industrial societies.

These networks are the result of what we have termed the 'family process'. In contrast to the universalistic and impersonal relationships characteristic of the economic sphere, these networks comprise relations between people who either have experience of each other as persons or who have knowledge of each other as particular persons, as opposed to members of a general social category or class. They are, therefore, relations which are 'familial' in two senses: they are 'kin' relationships, and relationships between familiars. It is, therefore, perfectly proper to term the relationships constituting these *networks* 'extended family/familial' relations. It is perfectly proper but very confusing, because the relationships between the members of a kinship *group* comprising but larger than – a single nuclear family may *also*, with equal propriety, be termed 'extended family relationships'. To avoid this confusion the phrase 'extended *kinship* relations' can be used to refer to Ego's relationships outside the elementary family, and the phrase 'extended *family* relationships' can be reserved for relationships within a kinship *group* based on, but wider than, a single elementary family.

The confusion between extended kinship and family relationships (as defined above) is compounded by the fact that most of the empirical data concerning extended kinship relations derive from survey work which samples individuals and establishes the relations between individuals. It is admirably adapted for the study of Ego-centred *sets* of relationships which are the building-blocks of a *network*. This evidence is usually the only evidence available from which to infer the existence of *groups*.

The way is, therefore, open to confuse the empirical evidence for the continued existence of extended kinship networks as evidence for the persistence of extended family groups in industrial societies. There can be little doubt that while such *groups* are formed in industrial societies, their incidence is infinitely less frequent than that of nuclear family formation or of the existence of active, extended kinship *networks*.

The second, theoretical, part of the argument is as follows. It is characteristic of bilateral systems of kinship that it is impossible to devise rules which can utilise the recognition of kin relationships in order to divide the population into exclusive groups. It is impossible even to divide the population into exclusive *elementary* family groups, since each individual will typically belong through a substantial part of his or her life to two such groups: the elementary family of origin, and the elementary family of marriage. The division of the population into exclusive kin groups is only possible by the introduction of an additional rule which frees the young from their obligations to their *parents'* elementary family of marriage (*their* family of origin) and, thus, enables them to establish their own families of marriage. It is possible, in other words, to divide the population into exclusive *nuclear* family groups; for a nuclear family comprises parents and *immature* children, and the latter logically cease to be part of that group on social maturation, that is, at that point in their life when they are both full-grown and capable of shouldering such social and economic responsibilities as may be required by marriage. Any system which, at or before marriage, releases the young person from the authority of and duty to contribute to the family group in which he/she was born may be termed a *nuclear family system*. It should be noted, however, that this 'release' does not entail a severing of relationships with, and an end of obligations to, parents and siblings as *individuals*.

The opposite of a nuclear family system is an *extended family system*. Both are variant family forms found within bilateral systems of kinship. The key characteristic of the latter is that adult children continue to be members of, and subject to the authority of, the group in which they were born. In such a society the autonomous individual units which compose it are not adult people but families. Marriage in such a society, as in a descent-group society, involves the transference of rights in people between existing groups and is not merely a contract between the spouses as individuals. In a nuclear family system the kinship group is founded in the conjugal bond, and duties of spouses to each other are stressed over and against their ties of filiation. In an extended family system, in contrast, ties of filiation and siblinghood are stressed over and against the conjugal bond. In contrast to the families formed in societies with an extended family system, families formed in societies with a nuclear family system may be termed 'conjugal'.

It does not follow, however, that no nuclear family groups will be found in a population with an extended family system, or that no extended family groups will be found in a population with a nuclear family system.

The term 'family system' refers to the cluster of categories, rules and principles giving form to the practices (or governing the activities and relations) constituting or connected with domestic and reproductive activities. These are put into action under particular conditions which further determine the range of group types formed, their incidence and the nature of the relations within them. The formation of extended families may be impossible, or they may endure only for a short phase of the life cycle of the family if demographic conditions are unfavourable. The existence of an extended family *system* does not entail the predominance of the extended family as an empirical type within a given population.

Conversely, there is no feature of a nuclear family system which prevents the formation of kin groups larger than a nuclear family, but in such a system the formation of extended family groups, however frequent, must remain a matter of *private enterprise* on the part of the *individuals* concerned. Such groups are formed as the result of *negotiated* agreements between *autonomous* persons.

It will be immediately apparent that such a family system is consonant with social formations whose political and economic order requires that the society is seen as composed of a plurality of formally free, equal and independent individuals, under the authority of, and owing loyalty to no one other than, the state and, therefore, unimpeded in their response to the operation of the market as they seek their individual interest and profit. The question concerning the 'fit' between the 'nuclear family system'/'conjugal family form' and 'industrial society'/'capitalist social formations' is, however, distinct from several other, though related questions. The first is this. As a matter of historical fact, is it the case that the present British family system is the result of the processes of industrialisation and urbanisation or did the nuclear family system exist before those processes transformed the structure of the societies in which they occurred? If the latter is the case, a further question arises: what importance is to be attached to the pre-existence of the nuclear family system when attempting to explain the genesis of industrialism?

The argument of Part 1 of this book has no implication as to the answers to these questions. If within a bilateral kinship system the family system is nuclear, we should expect considerable variation in the incidence of extended family formation, which must be understood as a response to specific historic and regional conditions. There is no reason to suppose that the incidence of extended family formation will increase or decrease with the development of market relations, the expansion of manufacturing activity, the accumulation of capital and the eventual arrival of the factory system of production. If however the family system was extended, then whether or not these developments affected (not the rate of extended family formation but) the extended family system, will depend centrally on the economic functions of the family – or, to put it another way, its relation to or place in the mode of production. This is a matter of empirical historical inquiry, not of theoretical speculation.

Sociologically speaking of equal importance is the investigation of what historical study reveals of the *character* of family groups in the past, irrespective of the type of system within which they were formed and whether they were, in terms of composition, nuclear or extended. What is intended by the vague term 'character'? Since this will later become evident to the reader, no attempt to specify the connotation of the term will be made here. It is, however, appropriate to give some indication of the direction in which the term is used to point. In contemporary sociological work a number of different frames of reference are used to describe the family. Fundamental and indispensable are the frames of reference used in Part 1 of this book: those of anthropology and functionalism. The first is that of kinship theory. This derives from a minimal specification of the unchanging nature of human-beings and their reproduction at the biological level. This specification is a description of the raw material for cultural production, which is given different forms termed 'kinship systems'. The range of kinship systems may be seen as determined (that is, as having terms or limits set to it) by the nature of this universal material and its means of production, the human mind. Similarly, any attempt to specify a list of universal social functions, or a list of the functions of the family, must equally be grounded in the material nature of man and limited by the logical constraints imposed by the manner in which the theorist thinks the object of study: society. Both anthropological and functionalist approaches make a virtue of human limitation by the 'material' world and seize the opportunity it provides to specify a set of universal elements and the limited number of permutations in which they can occur. The result is a specification of social *forms*. What is necessarily and inevitably absent is any apparatus for describing the human *content* of these forms which, though limited by such forms, is not constant between different instances of the same form, and varies over space and time.

The superiority of *Parsonian* functionalism lies in its attempt (through the pattern variables) to devise a means for specifying the contents of social forms. These contents become however, in Parsons's schema, *ideal* contents, types of 'value' in terms of which *culture* may be further differentiated. Family sociologists also rely heavily on various psychological descriptive schemata to further specify variant contents within a given form of family life.

What is common to the anthropological and functionalist approach to understanding the family is the absence of history on the surface, and to the presence of a suppressed history beneath it. Typically this mode of analysis confines itself to tracing relations between elements co-present in a social whole; it is not concerned with large-scale processes which have produced the particular configuration under study. It is, therefore, ahistorical. However, this procedure is only possible because functionalism has its own suppressed theory of history which we may term the 'great divide' theory. Parsons's pattern variables derive directly from the work of Ferdinand Toennies and either directly or through him from other nineteenth-century social theorists, who saw history as the story of a transition between two poles – ancient and modern. 'Sociology' has been firmly located on the modern side of this great divide, since only the contemporary is available to experience, and experience is the touchstone of 'science'. Until recently family sociologists were little interested in the past. They were too busy studying the present *on the assumption that* the outlines of the past were already known and had been settled.

So it is that sociologists of the family speak quite happily about the contemporary family as having *lost* functions, of the Western kinship system being one in which the authority of the group *has shrunk* and the influence of the family *declined,* without ever questioning the implicit historical paradigm within which they are working: one which takes for granted that 'history records' the decline of collectivism and the rise of individualism, the shift from a society whose basic structure is determined by kinship and religion to one in which the structure is determined by economic activity and science. As a result contemporary kin and religious institutions appear as curious survivals which, while needing to be explained, are of little importance compared to distinctively modern phenomena such as class conflict, bureaucracy and science.

One of the many results of these assumptions has been an ignorance of the changing historical character or content of family life, which changes are concealed by continuities in the form of family life as defined by anthropological and functional categories. The study of the family needs an historical dimension for two reasons. The first is comparative. It has now become fashionable to compare our own domestic arrangements with those of exotic cultures. But since we cannot suddenly acquire a different culture, it is perhaps of more practical value to compare the character of our contemporary domestic life with that of our own past. The second reason concerns process. To understand our contemporary predicament we need to understand the process which produced it, remembering that the present is not its end product, but a moment in a continuous development. In Laslett's words (1977, p. 5): 'we do not understand ourselves because we do not yet know what we have been and hence what we may be becoming' (for expansion and illustration of this point, see Anderson, 1979).

It may be admitted that it is useful for certain purposes to think of 'a society' as composed of institutions, externally related to one another; and of changes in one institution thus 'causing' changes in another on analogy with the mode of relation of organs in an organism. It must always be borne in mind, however, that the deployment of analogical frameworks of this kind are heuristic devices: tools adopted for the purpose of getting to know and understand a certain range of phenomena. The proximate origin of the organic analogy in sociology is Durkheim, whose sociology derives from that of Comte and Spencer. It is worth noting however that, whereas Spencer claimed that *any* society is or is like an organism, Durkheim used this analogy to characterise an historically specific type of social formation which lay on the modern side of the great divide, and which was characterised by a high degree of social differentiation. It was used to characterise societies in which different human activities had become separated and distinguished from one another and were carried out by distinct social groups or categories, each of which was not subordinated to the control of others, but dependent upon the activity of other groups which vitally affected its own activities.

While the organic analogy may have some utility as a provisional orientation to the study of modern societies – and may constitute a way of expressing the difference between the structure of primitive (that is, first, or early) and modern social formations – it is totally inadequate as an orientation on the basis of which to trace the process of social differentiation itself. It is inadequate precisely because this process is one involving the emergence of differentiated activities and groups, a movement from a situation where the distinction between different activities exists only in the mind of the observer as the result of a process of abstraction, and a situation where these abstract distinctions have their counterpart in a concrete social reality.

The 'great divide' theory is only historically valid so long as one attaches the two characterisations which it involves to social formations separated by an actual or supposed great divide in *time*, or level of development, and contrasts, for example, Australian aborigine communities and contemporary industrial societies. This is the tradition wherein lies the origin of much of Parsons's writing on the family. On the one hand there are societies which are kin-based, and the population divided into exclusive kinship categories (tribes, lineages) which perform religious, political and economic functions within which are smaller domestic groups which perform the functions attributed to the modern family. On the other hand there are societies in which the kinship group has shrunk to its nuclear core, whose anatomical structure consists of economic relationships which have become freed from political and religious control.

What many sociological writers call the 'classical extended family' *does not, however, belong to either of these polar societal forms*. It implicitly refers, rather, to a family type believed to have existed in Europe in the mediaeval and early-modern periods and survived in Eastern Europe until a much later date. It is an empirical type which refers *neither* to the hypothesised primitive societies of the remote past *nor* to those contemporary societies with relatively undeveloped technologies and segmentary kinship systems studied by anthropologists. Its origins lie in the agrarian societies of Europe whose kinship systems were bilateral, not unilineal, and whose forms of production were infinitely more highly developed than those of 'primitive' societies, being literate, having a highly developed economic division of labour and a system of manufacturing production which was technologically advanced, though not yet industrialised.

It is improper to refer to the segments of a unilineal kinship system as 'extended families', since this is to impose a way of thinking derived from an implicit understanding of the character of domestic groups in a bilateral system on non-domestic groups formed by the operation of an entirely different kinship principle. It is permissible to describe the domestic arrangements of the inhabitants of such societies (in appropriate cases) as extended family households, so long as it is remembered that the rules governing the kinship system *in toto* make possible the operation of rules of residence which would be in conflict with the rules of a bilateral kinship system. Though permissible, it is therefore confusing and highly undesirable. It is much better to substitute the term 'composite' for 'extended family' households, when referring to descent-group societies, because it implies only that the household is composed of more than a single conjugal pair, and it has no historical or cultural reference.

We may now say that it is a mistake to confuse 'the classical extended family' (a term associated with the agrarian societies of preindustrial Europe) with the segments of unilineal kinship systems and the composite households found within them. When we contrast 'the family' in contemporary, advanced industrial societies with 'the family' as it existed at earlier periods *in those societies*, we are not making a contrast which spans the great divide which separates primitive communalism and capitalism, or military and industrial societies, or theological and positive (scientific) societies, or societies characterised by mechanical solidarity and segmentary structures, as opposed to 'organic' societies. We are contrasting the practice of family formation in societies with a bilateral kinship system in the period before and after their industrialisation.

It will be the purpose of this chapter to consider the referent of the term 'classical extended family', to examine the historical evidence as to when and where it was the case that domestic life was characterised by the regular formation of composite households.

THE PREINDUSTRIAL FAMILY: 'CLASSICAL EXTENDED' OR 'PEASANT'?

The belief in the existence, prior to industrialisation, of extended family households dates back at least to the 1920s in American sociology, but specific references to empirical studies attesting to its existence are rare. It is a term frequently used in the 1950s and 1960s in a way which presumes that the reader is familiar with its connotation. Probably its most celebrated usage and definition is by Litwak (1960a). Litwak attacks an article by Parsons (1949) and claims that Parsons identifies 'the extended family' with 'the "classical" type exemplified by the Polish and Irish peasant families and marked by geographical propinquity, occupational integration, strict authority of extended over nuclear family and stress on extended rather than nuclear family relations'. In fact, Parsons does not use the term 'extended family' at all; there are only two references to non-American ethnography (Homans, 1941; Arensberg and Kimball, 1940) and these concern only inheritance.

Litwak's article makes it clear, however, that 'the classical extended family' is defined in behavioural rather than normative or functional terms, and that its reference is to a family form characteristic of *peasant* societies. To claim that a society is a peasant society is, however, to say something about the mode of production in that society. The logic of the argument concerning industrialisation and the 'classical extended family' now becomes clear. 'Industrialisation', that is, the destruction of the peasant mode of production, changes the family type. But why must the family type necessarily change? The answer is quite simply that the peasant mode of production cannot be specified without reference to the family: a peasant mode of production is one in which the *family* is the productive unit, and industrialisation involves a shift to the *factory* system of production.

It will be immediately obvious that if industrialisation was accompanied by a shift in family behaviour away from the pattern described by Litwak, this shift did not result from changing circumstances which influenced individuals to behave differently. If industrialisation was accompanied by the destruction of the peasant family, its destruction did not result from changes in production relations distinct from the family. We are concerned rather with a process which involved the differentiation of productive and reproductive-domestic activities. The transformation of the family must be understood not as a transformation of domestic behavioural patterns induced by external economic conditions, but as a transformation of the activities jointly performed by its members. Such a change in activities would, however, inevitably have consequences for the composition and structure of the domestic group. Individual families, or aggregates of families, may exhibit the behavioural characteristics listed by Litwak, irrespective of the type of kinship system, family system and mode of production of the society of which they are part. Purely behavioural criteria are as inadequate as compositional criteria to distinguish family systems, which must be defined rather in terms of the categories and principles governing the activities jointly performed by the domestic group.

It will be helpful, therefore, to cease to refer to 'the classical extended family' and refer instead to the peasant family, and to consider, first, the proposition that the change in the mode of production which is termed 'industrialisation' destroyed the peasant family.

Peasant Social Formations and the Peasant Family

The term 'peasant' has been loosely used to refer to any system of agrarian production in which the producers are independent smallholders. To define a form of production in terms merely of the size of the units that compose it is about as helpful as attempting to define a family form in terms of the size of the household. Further criteria have, therefore, been added. These attempts to specify further the notion of a peasant society have moved in two directions: towards the specification of the characteristic structure of peasant societies, and the peasant mode of production.

The first of these movements is associated with Robert Redfield's writings about peasants, particularly *Peasant Society and Culture* (1956) and *The Primitive World and Its Transformations* (1953). His thesis is that peasant communities constitute part-societies with part-cultures: they are 'folk societies' (such as anthropologists study) whose social life has been modified by their articulation with a town and, through it, with other like communities. They are segments of a mechanically solidary society (in Durkheim's terms) whose undifferentiated and independent character has been modified by their articulation with a market, physically located in a town, to which they are usually politically subservient.

The second of these movements is exemplified by the work of Shanin (1972). He writes: 'the peasant may be defined as a small producer on the land who, with the help of their own labour and that of their families, produce mainly for their own consumption and for meeting obligations to the holders of political and economic power and reach nearly total self sufficiency within the framework of the village community' (ibid., p. 39). Of the peasant household, he writes: 'the nature of the peasant household seems to constitute the most significant single characteristic of the peasantry ... . A peasant household is characterised by the nearly total integration of the peasant family's life with its farming enterprise' (ibid., p. 28).

Thorner (1971) has put the products of these two definitional movements together to produce five criteria of peasant societies. Two of these define the system of production as agricultural and assert the necessity of a state, towns and markets. The fifth, which Thorner deems the most important, repeats Shanin's definition of the peasant household which is itself a definition of the peasant form of production (ibid., pp. 202–5). Shanin (1971, p. 241) takes this further: 'The *family farm* is the basic unit of peasant ownership, production, consumption and social life. The individual, the family and the farm appear as an indivisible whole. It should be noted immediately that the definition of the peasant family is simultaneously a definition of a mode of production, and because it is a definition of a mode of production, it simultaneously defines certain characteristics of the society as a social formation.

It is easy to see that the definition of the peasant family clearly entails those behavioural characteristics used as a criterion of the classical extended family by Litwak, at least as far as geographical propinquity and occupational integration are concerned. To see the connection between his other two criteria – the subordination of the nuclear to the extended family and the stress on extended as opposed to nuclear relations – it is necessary to elaborate further the characteristics cited by Shanin and Thorner. What is crucial is the claim that the family (not the individual) is the basic unit of ownership, production and social life, and that the farm, the family and the individuals that compose it 'appear as an indivisible whole'. If (as Shanin claims for the Russian peasantry) it is the family as a collectivity (not its most senior member) that owns the property, and land is the chief means of production, then family membership in a peasant society is a necessary condition of production and existence for most of the members of that society. Outside of the family agricultural production is impossible. In such a society families will have as much generational depth as demographic factors allow, for to leave the family is to forgo access to the means of primary production, to forfeit one's very subsistence. There will be no question of the individual leaving his/her family of origin on attaining economic independence and founding 'his own' family, since economic independence, for individuals, is unattainable. The nuclear family can only come into existence within the family of origin of one of its members, and its members will be totally dependent on the collectivity of which they are part. Such a society will be characterised by family *continuation*, rather than by family *formation*. Hence, Litwak's second pair of criteria.

This point may be put in a more general way. To speak of a mode of production is to speak of man's relation to nature. Because human-beings live in groups, that relation is always socially mediated. There would seem to be two possible modes of such mediation. In the first mode, it is only in and through their membership of a productive collectivity that men and women are able to produce and, therefore, to subsist. In the second mode, it is only through exchange in a market that production and subsistence is possible. In the first case, member-ship of a *collectivity* is a precondition of production. In the second, it is only through activity in a market that the *individual* is able to produce and is accepted as a member of that *society*. This distinction is closely related to that between production for use and production for exchange. The shift to a market economy is clearly impossible while the system of production is primarily that of subsistence, and the individual is not so much under the control and domination of the group, as has not differentiated him/herself from it.

The characteristics of a peasant family have so far been presented in the form of a pure type. Unfortunately, it is impossible to construct a pure type of a peasant *society*, precisely because peasant societies are by definition mixed types and may be transitional societal forms. The economy of a peasant society is not entirely a subsistence economy: there are markets; there is production for exchange as well as for use; there are towns. All the family groups in a peasant society will not, therefore, be peasant families. Equally peasant families will produce for exchange as well as consumption; imbalances between land and population will result in migration to towns, thus introducing occupa-tional differentiation, geographical dispersion and social individua-tion into the otherwise occupationally homogeneous, clustered collec-tivity of the peasant family. To put this another way: the shift from a folk society to a peasant society will involve (in Litwak's terms) some 'modification' of 'the classical extended family', which in its pure form must be characteristic of folk rather than of peasant societies. The local community and the family in a peasant society are no longer independent collectivities, but are articulated with other settlements with whom they are connected both by ties of kinship and relations of economic exchange. They are collectivities embedded in a network of such relationships. This modification of the 'classical extended family' necessarily predated industrialisation itself: necessarily because no society has moved directly from a folk society to an industrial society, and because in default of the development of markets and production for profit it is difficult to see how the capital accumulation necessary to industrialisation could occur.

Once it is admitted that the very nature of a peasant society is such that it involves some modification of that type of family which stands as the opposite of that characteristic of a nuclear family system, and that some such modification is a precondition of the emergence of industrialism, then there is no reason to suppose that the family type found most frequently in the period immediately preceding the industrial transformation of society was itself closer to the collectivistic than to the nuclear family type. Indeed, it is most likely that industrialisation would first occur in a society where the development of towns, markets and production for exchange rather than use, had already eroded the peasant mode of production and, hence, severely weakened if not transformed the peasant or collectivistic family system associated with it.

A careful definition of the peasant mode of production makes it possible to recognise that it does not follow that because a society is agrarian it is, therefore, necessarily a peasant society. It is *logically* possible for an agrarian society to have a capitalist mode of production. In such a society a landless rural proletariat would sell its labour power to the owners of the means of production (land) in return for wages, and the landowners would produce agricultural products for sale for profit in the market rather than for their own consumption or that of their workers. Provided productive property is concentrated in the hands of a few and products and labour are commoditised (bought and sold under open-market conditions, and production is for exchange not use), we are entitled to describe the mode of production as 'capitalist'. It does not follow therefore that because pre-industrial society was agrarian, its form of production was 'peasant'. Hence, it does not follow either that the family system which existed before the industrial revolution was necessarily even a modified form of the peasant family.

New Historical Evidence Concerning the Household in Preindustrial England

The reader should understand at the outset that the attempt to make statements about family types in past periods is fraught with difficulties. It is not merely a question of collecting facts which prove or disprove hypotheses. Facts about behaviour – statements, that is to say, about what people do, couched not in their terms, but in our terms have to be interpreted in the light of the way the people themselves conceptualised their activities, and in terms of activities other than domestic activities in which they engage and the activities of other collectivities to which they do not belong which constitute the conditions of their action. It is not possible when studying the past to observe the flow of events which constitute family life, nor to generate systematic data relevant to the hypothesis you wish to investigate. There are five main types of source for historical work on the family:

lists of households and their members; data from national Censuses and other similar types of investigation; documentary evidence concerning the meaning attached to their actions by the agents diaries for example; documentary evidence of a literary kind concerning the beliefs about and attitudes towards family behaviour; and lastly, legal evidence involving both the laws themselves and reports of legal processes concerned with or related to family life.

The most basic type of evidence is that concerning household composition. There are difficulties in interpreting even what appears at first sight to be unambiguous evidence (see Berkner, 1975, pp. 724–6), but even if these are resolved, difficulties still attach to the attempt to make inferences from statements about household composition as to the type of family and type of system. For example, a shortage of suitable accommodation within a settlement may require that dwellings are multioccupied. It is highly unlikely that parent–child relations will not be utilised to determine who, in such a situation, lives with whom. If the available accommodation cannot be subdivided, composite households will be formed. If the accommodation shortage is severe, then the proportion of composite households may be high. It is in no way to deny the importance of this information for our understanding of the day-to-day family life of the population studied if it is asserted that it tells little about the family system of that population, which may well be nuclear in the sense that composite-household formation is neither desired, expected, nor necessitated in that society except by the shortage of accommodation peculiar to that place or time. It certainly does not follow that a population with a high proportion of composite households must by virtue of that fact have a family system which approximates to that of the peasantry or the classical extended family.

Conversely, the existence of a peasant family system is perfectly consistent with a small proportion of composite households. If the age at marriage is 20 and the expectation of life at 20 is only twenty years, then in the typical case the parental generation will die before it is possible for them to become grandparents. In consequence the type of household predominant in such a population will be nuclear in composition, even though the family system is a peasant one.

It has to be recognised that the family is, as we have pointed out, a *process*, not a static structure, and as such the residential group formed by that process will vary according to the stage in the development of the family cycle to which they correspond. Extended family *households* are unlikely to constitute the majority of the households in a settlement even within a culture where the formation of such groups is prescribed.

Whether or not in the past people lived in large or small households, is none the less an important question. It is one piece of evidence concerning the type of family system. It is also a vital piece of evidence if the size of the domestic group affects relations within it and, hence, is relevant to the question as to how far the character of contemporary family life is the product of the small size of modern households.

It has been the self-appointed task of Peter Laslett and his colleagues to explode the myth that industrialisation in England was accompanied by any decrease in the average size of household. He writes:

> there is no sign of the large, extended co-residential group of the traditional peasant world giving way to the small nuclear conjugal household of modern industrial society ... the large joint or extended family seems never to have existed (in England) as a domestic group at any point in time covered by known numerical records. (Laslett, 1969, p. 200)

In the same article based on listings of inhabitants from 100 communities at points in time between 1574 and 1821 (revised as Laslett, 1972), he presents the evidence for this claim. Only 6 per cent of households had a depth of more than two generations and only 626 out of 5,843 households included extra nuclear kin. He claims that his figures 'dispose by themselves of any supposition that the traditional English household usually, or even often, contained resident kin'. Household size was small, 4.8 persons, and did not begin to fall according to the national Census (the first Census was taken in 1801) until after 1911. There is no evidence that household size was affected by industrialisation, therefore.

There is, however, one major difference in household type between the preindustrial world we have lost and contemporary England:

> although the mean and median household size were well below five, a majority of all persons lived in households of six or more. This is certainly not true today where the proportions in these larger households is only about $17\frac{1}{2}$%. (Laslett, 1969, p. 207).

The reason for this is that, in the preindustrial past, large households were not composed (as today) of families of low economic status with several children, but of families of high economic status with few children but large numbers of 'servants'.

In evaluating Laslett's work on household size it is necessary to distinguish the inferences which can be legitimately made from the data and the construction he tends to place upon them. After Laslett, it is impossible to assume (if anyone ever has) that before the Industrial Revolution people in England typically lived in large households, composed predominantly of kin. In this regard Laslett has performed a valuable service. However, that said, it must be noted that he tends to assume that his data for England support the hypothesis that the family system in preindustrial England was nuclear. Most historians, sociologists and anthropologists would claim that (whether or not this hypothesis is correct – and it may well be correct) it cannot be substantiated by this type of evidence. In Berkner's words (1975), 'valid statements about family structure require an analysis based on the function of kinship ties, the developmental process, and rules of behaviour, not on the composition of narrowly defined *residential* groups' (ibid., p. 738; emphasis added). Indeed, it is arguable (and has been argued – see Levy, 1965) that for demographic reasons the nuclear family household is likely to predominate, whatever the family form in the society concerned. It is possible so to argue precisely because so many factors other than family form determine the pattern of household composition.

Laslett has not, however, been concerned simply with proving by statistical means that the existence of 'the extended family' in the past is a myth, but also with the significance of the one statistic which does seem to distinguish contemporary domestic life from that of preindustrial society – the existence of households of large size containing substantial numbers of others besides kin. For Laslett has a thesis concerning the transformation of family forms which (some would say) can never be substantiated by purely statistical investigations of the type that he favours. This thesis is presented in his first book on this subject, *The World We Have Lost* (1971) and constitutes his personal attack on traditional 'great divide' theories of history. (It is necessary to add 'traditional' because Laslett immediately establishes a new great divide theory of his own.) The traditional great divide theory involves the classical contrast of British political thought between collectivism and individualism, which in sociological terms may be seen to involve the emergence of individuated persons from the collectivity of the group. Now, Laslett (rightly in the view of many, including the present author) does not believe that, in England at least, industrialisation effected that transition. He does believe, however, that it effected *a* transition, which will be termed here the transition to individual autonomy, to a society composed of autonomous individuals. This society which industrialisation brought into existence is contrasted with a society where the majority of the population were not, at any given moment, free and independent individuals, but the dependants of some senior or more powerful person, usually of the male gender.

High rates of mortality meant that a large proportion of the population (over 40 per cent) were children, legal minors under the authority of their parents. A further 30 per cent were adult females under the authority of their fathers or husbands. A further proportion, more difficult to estimate, were adult servants or apprentices living in the household of their master wherein they had the status of minors, since such relations were modelled on filial relations, hence the indiscriminate use, in the past, of terms 'household' and 'family'. 'England' as a society, was made up therefore of household heads and the dependants subsumed by the household. Such a domestic system

Laslett terms 'patriarchal', since the domestic group was under the rule or governance of a *pater* (social father), whether or not he was the *genitor* (biological father) of his dependants.

Laslett's thesis is that it is the patriarchal family/household that was destroyed by industrialisation. Laslett's implicit distinction between (in sociological terms) individuation and autonomy makes it possible for us to envisage a society in which individuation, resultant on the extension of the division of labour prepared the way for the emergence of industrialism but, at the same time, had not conferred upon the individual that autonomy which is associated with competitative free-market capitalism in its pure form. It also makes it possible to understand the existence of present-day dependency relations within family forms, in political life in rural areas and within traditional industries (usually termed 'paternalism' see Newby, *et al.*, 1978) not as the modification of an ancient collectivism, but as survival of a much more recent form of social organisation, which immediately preceded the industrial era.

In this early and stimulating work Laslett has also performed another great service to sociologists by considering the relation between the domestic group and the system of stratification. The high proportion of people living in large households meant that *a* major system of stratification was to be found within the domestic group. As a result a substantial section of the subordinate in the society did not constitute a class in the social sense, at the national level, being incorporated into small units (households) each with its own hierarchy, interaction and communication being vertical and not lateral. Lateral communication took place chiefly between heads of households, *paters*, who were able to constitute classes in the social sense.

It was common in the nineteenth century to regard the emergent proletariat as a class outside 'society'. The section of the subordinate referred to above may be regarded as incorporated into the little societies constituted by the households, but they remained outside the great society constituted by the association of household heads.

This point must not be pushed too far. It must be reiterated that only a minority of households were large households, and that households themselves were stratified according to their position in different types of political, honorific and economic order. However, it is of vital importance that sociologists be reminded that it is a mistake to assume that it is true of early epochs that the 'family'/household necessarily constituted the unit of the stratification system, and to be reminded that domestic groups can have their own internal systems of stratification. This recognition makes it possible to see contemporary household organisation as exhibiting hierarchical features, and suggests that more attention be paid by sociologists to the patterns of differential consumption and authority allocation even within domestic groups which do not perform co-operative productive functions.

The necessity of considering stratification within the household in the past derives from the fact that many of the large households were units of production as well as consumption. This is, of course, well recognised in the case of societies having a peasant or domestic mode of production. Laslett has drawn our attention to the fact that in England where, prior to industrialisation, the peasant mode of production did not prevail, there were none the less large households not composed entirely of kin, but of an elementary family and its paid servants. Wage labour is to be found, in other words, not in a pure, but in embryonic form, within the domestic group in preindustrial England. Hence, large households do not attest to the presence of the extended family, or to the persistence of peasant modes of production, but represent mixed types of domestic and economic organisation. The members of the nuclear group are related and recruited by kinship; the peripheral members are incorporated by contract whereby their labour power is exchanged for agreed payment both in money and kind. However, once members, the relations between the servants incorporated into the group and their employer are regulated by normative expectations concerning age and gender roles within the family. That is to say, that their status within the group is that of young and/or female dependants of a father, rather than that of employees of an employer in any contemporary sense.

This assimilation is possible, because the servants tend to be young persons whose parents occupy an inferior status to that of their pater/ employer. They are, in Laslett's useful term, 'life-cycle servants' – people from a class of persons who regularly spend a specific part of the life cycle as servants, rather than members of a servant class which spend their lives in the occupation 'servant'. This has an importance out of proportion to the actual number of households with servants at any given moment. Laslett (1977, p. 43) calculates that 20 per cent of all children were raised in households *with* servants, and a further 40 per cent themselves spent some of their life *as* servants. In other words, the majority of the population spent a substantial part of their youth in domestic groups containing or founded by non-kin. It follows that domestic relations in these households could not have been characterised by the same degree of intimacy and affect as that associated with the small closed nuclear family household whose incidence seems to have increased after industrialisation.

Laslett also wishes to claim however that, compared with other societies of Eastern Europe, immediate kin (universally the most important influence on young children) were of more importance in the West, because of the lower incidence of large households, and the small proportion of such households constituted by extended or multiple families (ibid., p. 37).

We may conclude, therefore, that Laslett sees industrialisation or 'modernisation' as having two chief effects on the household: the steady decline in the number of households with servants, and the physical removal from the household of the father and other earners for all of every working day. It is these two movements which involve the decline of 'patriarchalism' not merely as an element in a family system, but also as a more general principle of societal organisation. Laslett, however, wishes to insist that the domestic group in England, and possibly also in Northern and Western Europe, was already before industrialisation – different from that in other parts of the world for which data is available. Now, the distinctiveness of Northern and Western Europe is a theme not unfamiliar to socio-logists, for it is precisely in this part of the globe that capitalism/ industrial society originated, and the relation between these events and other distinctive predisposing factors, notably the Protestant Ethic (Weber, 1930) has long been a matter of sociological and historical debate. Laslett's distinctive contribution has been to suggest that one of the chief distinctive characteristics of Western and Northern Europe is its 'unique' demographic pattern and household structure and that this 'has had considerable effects on European economic, social, political, cultural and even industrial life' (Laslett, 1977, p. 10).

The distinctiveness of the West and North was first noted by a demographer (Hajnal, 1965). The thesis he puts forward is that in 'Europe' there was at the end of the nineteenth century a high age at marriage and a high proportion of people who never married at all. By 'Europe' he means those lands to the west of a line running from Leningrad to Trieste. The area thus delimited constitutes the whole of non-communist Europe, except Greece and Turkey. It also includes what is now East Germany. In spite of a number of difficulties with his sources, his work is now generally recognised to have established a significant difference between Western and Eastern Europe. He reviews the evidence, then available, in an attempt to determine when this pattern originated, and succeeds in establishing that it existed as far back as the beginning of the eighteenth century. He is able, therefore, to remark: 'the suggestion has occasionally been made that late marriage is characteristic of urban industrial societies while agricultural countries have early marriage. The suggestion is clearly unfounded' (Hajnal, 1965, p. 106). In his concluding discussion he notes:

> There was a widespread conviction among eighteenth century authors that European conditions were fundamentally different not only in marriage, birth and death rates, but above all in standards of living, from those obtaining elsewhere in the world ... This uniqueness of Europe, so evident to contemporaries, has been largely ignored in recent discussions of economic development; all that is pre-industrial, including eighteenth century Europe, is often lumped together in generalisations about 'agricultural' or 'peasant' or 'underdeveloped' societies. (ibid., p. 131)

He goes on to imply that the absence of partible inheritance, and of the classical peasant family in the West, may be the significant factor in differentiating Eastern and Western Europe.

Laslett's work may be seen as an attempt to investigate this hypothesis, by drawing on the work of the Cambridge Group for the History of Population and Social Structure which, by developing techniques for reconstructing the demography of historical communities, has brought to light much new evidence relating to the problem posed by Hajnal. Laslett claims to have discovered the Western European *family* pattern which underlay Hajnal's *marriage* pattern. The familial group is nuclear in form; the age of mother at childbearing is late; spouses are of similar ages, or the woman is older than the man; a significant proportion of households have 'life-cycle servants'. Like Hajnal he is at pains to show, where possible, that these features distinguished Western Europe from other parts of the world. His distinctive contribution is to connect late age at marriage with both the composition of the familial group and with 'life-cycle servanthood'. Composite households will be rare when the age at marriage is late. The age of marriage will be late if young people leave their natal family to act as servants in the households of others, and do not, while working in that capacity, have the autonomy required for marriage – at least this appears to be Laslett's implicit argument.

So far, we have deliberately abstained from criticism of Laslett's work and have avoided his less temperate statements and, thus, the necessity of citing the many critics of his approach, lest the great value of his contribution should be obscured. It should now be evident to the reader, however, that Laslett's work is somehow failing to live up to the high expectations he aroused in his first book (Laslett, 1971). As Medick (1976, p. 292) has pointed out, Laslett's claim that

> the new direction of research should be above all 'social structural history' (Laslett, 1971, pp. 241–53), oriented toward entire societies, examining the essential 'structural function of the family in the pre-industrial world' (ibid., p. 20), remains fundamentally unfulfilled ... theory formation and empirical research drifted apart ... [and] began increasingly to impede and hinder one another.

Medick notes (as we have already done) that the same type of household composition may result from radically different family systems, but goes on to point out a defect even more important when considering the relation between type of family system and type of economy: 'The structurally relevant "basic processes" of household and family, as they appear in production, reproduction and consumption, cannot be grasped by using Laslett's structural criteria, neither can the function of this familial unit within the larger socio-economic context of the entire society' (ibid., p. 295).

The reader who has dutifully worked through Part 1 of the present book should have been struck by a glaring omission in the account of Laslett's work as presented here: the absence of any reference to systems of propertyownership and the mode of transmission of that property between the generations. 'Inheritance' is a concept which occurs hardly at all in Laslett's writings, in spite of its centrality to what has been termed above their implicit argument. For if the inferior class of persons who live by their own labour, produce by applying it to their own property, and their product is inadequate to support them, and their mature children, spouses and grandchildren, then their mature children will be unable to subsist on the parental property and must perforce either sell their labour or enter the service of other more affluent households until such time as they inherit. If the family is not a propertyowning unit as well as a productive one, why should young adults become *life-cycle* servants rather than servants *tout court* or wage labourers? If the family even among the lower social strata is a propertyowning unit, then the great change brought by the Industrial Revolution will not merely be the decline in households with servants and the daily absence of the *paterfamilias*: it will involve the loss by the family group of the ownership and control of the means of production.

Laslett makes much play with the fact that, in England, his statistical indices show markedly little variation when compared with other countries. If the implication is correct that there was little variation in household structure (as defined by Laslett) in England, then this must be because the wide variety of forms of production which we know existed in England in the preindustrial era must have thrown up structurally similar family forms, whereas in other societies they resulted in variations detectable by Laslett's methods. This then raises the question, central to Laslett's tradition, as to what was distinctive about England? The answer to this question must refer to the categories and rules governing both the productive and 'family' processes. It must refer, that is to say, to 'culture' rather than 'structure' in Laslett's empiricist sense of the term. Laslett's statistical regularities constitute 'social facts' whose explanation requires that they be related to other social facts ways of thinking, feeling and acting which are general throughout a society whose properties they are.

It is not, however, desirable to oppose structure and culture in this way, since the opposition is not between two theoretical categories which denote two different ways of abstracting from the material, but is rather between two different types of evidence that concerning household composition, and that concerning laws, customs and practices. The central category absent from Laslett's work is that of 'mode of production'. This category refers to a set of relations of production specified in terms of the different relations to the means of production, and this specification in turn involves reference to relations of possession and the legal categories which give these relations form. The two types of evidence contrasted above are both indices of the existence of modes of production, since this category is defined in terms of the referents of these two types of evidence.

'Mode of production' is itself however a dangerous term, since it functions in Marxian thought as a means of periodising history, of establishing differences between periods, and can tend to blind us, just as much as the over-reliance on simple numerical indices of household structure, to the differences existing within an historical period. That is, the same mode of production may be associated with a variety of family forms, each having different consequences for the character of kinship and family relationships. Even if we concentrate solely on areas with peasant modes of production, we find an enormous variety of inheritance patterns, as the articles on inheritance in a recent collection amply testify (Goody *et al.*, 1976). If however we are concerned with a transitional period, such as the centuries between the 'feudal' and the 'capitalist' periods, then we will find even greater variation between settlements in the extent to which a form of production associated with the agrarian past is modified or has given way to new forms of production which may be termed proto-industrial.

None the less, the use of the category 'mode of production' does at least ensure that we conceive of the family and household as the site of productive and reproductive processes variation in which over time constituted a transformation of the productive relations of the society as a whole.

The Problem of the English Peasantry

The work of Hajnal, Laslett and others has, however, established a broad difference in gross terms between Western and Eastern Europe, and between England and other West European countries; and it is Eastern Europe that has provided the material which has resulted in the definition of the peasant family and seems to be the basis of the sociological conception of 'the extended family'. In Chapter 7 we shall consider the evidence concerning the family prior to and during the industrialisation process. Before we do so, however, we shall – as a conclusion to this chapter – consider more closely the arguments for the hypothesis that, in contrast to continental Europe, England did not undergo a transition – however long-drawn-out – from the peasant to the capitalist mode of production, for the good reason that the peasant mode of production never established itself in England in the first place.

This view, probably more startling to sociologists than to historians, has recently been put forward by the Cambridge anthropologist and historian, Alan Macfarlane (1978). His work is distinctive because it is informed by an anthropological training and experience and a familiarity with the anthropological and sociological literature on contemporary peasantries. This leads him to be more precise about the characteristics of peasant societies than some historians have been, and not to use the term to refer to any agrarian society, but to question whether the historical evidence points to the existence of a distinctively peasant form of domestic and economic organisation.

Historians as well as sociologists necessarily operate with assumptions about what is already historically established, and these assumptions determine the ordering and interpretation of their material. Macfarlane's chief aim is less to establish a new thesis, 'England was never a peasant society', than to challenge the assumption, 'England was once a peasant society', and to put forward the first proposition as a null-hypothesis. His argument is (1) that the existing historical evidence is not adequate to refute the hypothesis that England was never a peasant society; (2) that the reason the belief that it is has been so widely held is that evidence has been employed to illustrate this belief, rather than to test it; and (3) that the illustrative use of evidence has lead to a misinterpretation of that evidence which can now be seen to be misinterpretation in the light of *new* evidence which is now becoming available.

The conventional view is succinctly put by Medick. The proximate origins of nineteenth-century industrialisation lie in a period of protoindustrialisation (Mendels, 1972):

> Proto-industrialisation appeared as the combined outcome of the destabilisation and decomposition of traditional European peasant societies. Demographic growth and socio-economic polarisation of the rural population led, above all in the high middle ages and in the sixteenth and eighteenth centuries, to the emergence of a numerous under-employed class of small peasants or landless rural dwellers. This process formed an essential precondition for the penetration of industrial production into the countryside. (Medick, 1976, p. 297)

What Macfarlane questions is whether *England* experienced the destabilisation of a traditional, European-type, peasant society.

Medick, a German, can write as he does, because serfdom existed in Europe well into the nineteenth century, emancipation of serfs occurring between 1770 and 1860 (see Blum, 1978 – for a list of decrees of emancipation, see p. 356). The transition from a feudal to a capitalist social order was accomplished, *in continental Europe*, in a relatively short space of time. England is scarcely mentioned in Blum's magisterial work *The End of the Old Order in Rural Europe*, since it was not a 'servile land', and those few mentions it does get stress its difference. The uniqueness of England has long been recognised, not least as Macfarlane notes, by Marx and Weber. Indeed, the assumption he questions can be attributed in part to their influence. It is that **England was originally a traditional European peasant society, and** 'then by some strange accident, that has never been satisfactorily explained, some time between the later sixteenth and mid eighteenth century, it took a different course from its neighbours' (Macfarlane, 1978, p. 61).

It is not possible here to summarise Macfarlane's wide-ranging, stimulating and sometimes contentious discussion. It will suffice for our purposes merely to bring out a small number of central points. The first and most important concerns inheritance. 'Inheritance' is an institution whereby rights in property are transmitted between generations. This may be contrasted with a set of rules governing succession to property. 'Succession' involves the existence of a previously determined set of social positions and parcels of land, and the movement of the rising generation into those positions, into the occupancy of those estates. In the case of inheritance the identity of the property is determined by that of the owner. In the case of succession the identity of the owner is determined by that of the property. A further distinction may now be made between collective ownership and individual ownership, between a situation where the owner is a group and that where the owner is an individual. The peasant or domestic mode of production clearly involves both collective ownership and succession, and this mode of intergenerational transmission is therefore the opposite of what we term inheritance. Both involve forms of exclusive possession, but only inheritance is predicated on the existence of 'private property', that is, exclusive possession by individuals (cf. Harris, 1980, p. 59).

We may now state the first of the points arising out of Macfarlane's work in the terms we have specified. Macfarlane wishes to claim that as far back as the availability of historical evidence makes it possible for us to go, we find that English family life is characterised by inheritance and private property, rather than by succession and collective property. His evidence for these statements concerns law, testamentary practice, the existence of a substantial market in land and the existence of sales of land even between family members (Macfarlane, 1978, chs 4 and 5). Macfarlane's use of a model of the peasant mode of production leads him to regard the distinctions defined above as more important than distinctions between different types of inheritance around which discussion has previously centred (see, for example, Habbakuk 1955).

This is not to say that Macfarlane ignores distinctions between types of inheritance. On the contrary he wishes to argue (ibid., p. 87) that 'in essence, primogeniture and a peasant joint ownership unit are diametrically opposed'. It would perhaps be wise to translate this statement into the claim that unigeniture and joint ownership are opposed, which is then to claim that impartible inheritance and joint ownership are opposed. Macfarlane claims that primogeniture and individual property are linked and seems to use primogeniture as an index of impartible inheritance and individual ownership. While it is well recognised that the English nobility employed primogeniture more widely, and probably in a more extreme form than elsewhere in Europe, he is not able to show – only to surmise – that primogeniture was more important among those at lower levels in society.

More important, therefore, is his distinction between rules governing the disposition of property in cases of intestacy, and the existence of testamentary freedom, on the part of individuals, to bequeath their property at will. This freedom is certainly antipathetic to any notion of joint ownership, and Macfarlane makes out a strong case for claiming that this legal freedom existed as far back as the thirteenth century. He is thus able to conclude that '*Individualism* predates the sixteenth century changes and shapes them all'.

Whether or not Macfarlane's null-hypothesis 'England was never a peasant society' is falsified as a result of future historical research and debate, he has none the less made it difficult to claim that the present evidence is an adequate basis of its falsification. His work is of importance for sociologists who are concerned, as we are here, with the relation between family and industrial society, because he establishes beyond doubt that 'individualism' did not arise, in England, out of industrialisation, and casts doubt as to whether its birth is to be located in the seventeenth century or associated with the development of Protestantism or the economic changes which accompanied that development in the sixteenth century. In this sense his work complements that of Laslett: neither 'modern' individualism (as opposed to peasant collectivism) nor the nuclear family household (as opposed to the composite household associated with the peasant mode of production) are, in England, part of that transformation of society associated with industrialisation or protoindustrialisation.

His work may be seen to be concerned to establish the principles of the operation of a family system, rather than to establish the frequency of different types of household or kin group. Precisely for this reason he pays particular attention to the work of legal historians, as well as to the evidence provided by historical community studies, and to literary evidence. It is in this regard that his work is distinctively sociological in method, and shows most clearly the Durkheimian influence mediated by his anthropological training and contrasts markedly, in this respect, from that of Laslett. Neither Laslett's work nor Macfarlane's study provides us, however, with any way of categorising the undoubted changes that took place in the English family during the six centuries preceding the Industrial Revolution; in our terms it provides us with an argument concerning the persistence of the same family system, the persistence of the same form throughout the period, but is devoid of any suggestions about the transformation of the content of family life.

How, then, are we to understand the development of the English family? The sociologist must look in two directions. It is necessary, first, to consider the way in which the domestic group is articulated with other groups within the society and to relate changes in that mode of articulation to changes in its internal organisation. This is to employ the structural principle utilised by Elizabeth Bott (1971) in her study of the organisation of marital roles.

It is necessary, secondly, to consider the changing place of the domestic group in the mode of production. Macfarlane's study has made it impossible for us to attempt to explain those changes in the content of family life in England which are associated with industrialisation, by reference to the destruction of the peasant mode of production. Instead we shall be concerned with two processes: the protoindustrialisation of the English countryside, and the replacement of the productive forms generated by that development with the factory system of production and the consequent urbanisation of society. It is these themes that will concern us in Chapter 7.

Chapter 7

Family and Industrialisation

We have pointed out in Chapter 6 that much sociological writing about the contemporary family is premissed, albeit implicitly, on a 'great divide' theory of history – which sees history in terms of a polar opposition between ancient societies whose basic structural elements are kinship relations, and modern societies whose basic structure consists of market relations. Clearly, such a model is totally inadequate for historical work and makes impossible any understanding of contemporary family forms, which include remnants of forms which originated in social formations immediately preceding our own. Hence, the necessity of a concept like 'the classical extended family', which refers (we have claimed) to the family form characteristic of that transitional type of society which has been termed 'peasant'. However, an historical model which provides us with three lineally related stages 'folk', 'peasant' and 'urban' only constitutes a marginal improvement on a 'great divide' model. Certainly, it is an inadequate basis for any attempt to understand the relation between the movement to an industrial system of production and the emergence of modern family forms. Whether or not one accepts Macfarlane's (1978) contentious claim that the hypothesis 'England was never a peasant society' has not been disproved, it is beyond dispute that the industrialisation process in England destroyed neither a peasant society, nor the peasant family form; hence, contemporary survivals from the preindustrial period are not survivals of the peasant family, but of family forms that are associated with transitional forms of production which came into existence in the period between the demise of mediaeval and rise of industrial society.

To argue against the use of *simplistic* models – which are inadequate to interpret the evidence – is not however to argue against models as such. The function of a model is to provide a set of categories through which the complexities of social reality can be understood. As such, a model is necessarily more simple than the data which it is used to interpret. Models are not in themselves 'simplistic' or 'simplifications' unless the user of the model claims that it adequately represents the reality, rather than that it constitutes a device for its interpretation. The model that we propose here is not to be regarded as a description or representation of preindustrial family forms, but as an attempt – and a first attempt at that – to construct a set of categories through which the data can be interpreted.

Models have, however, to be constructed upon the basis of some theoretical principle, however simple. The principle that we shall adopt is, quite simply, that family forms must be understood in terms of the part that they play in a system of production, either directly or indirectly.

One source of empirical inadequacy in models is that they are constructed on the basis of simplistic empirical assumptions, such as, for example, that each social formation or epoch is characterised by *a* mode of production, and that there is *a* family form which corresponds to each mode of production. Even if it is *theoretically* justifiable to characterise social formations in terms of their dominant or predominant mode of production and associated family form, enormous empirical variation will none the less be found within formations of the same type, and formations in transition between one mode of production and another will necessarily exhibit even greater variation.

AGRARIAN FAMILY FORMS

Three family forms may be found within an agrarian economy. The first two are family forms in which the family owns or has access to land and works it with predominantly family labour. Clearly, the peasant family (as defined in Chapter 6) falls into this class, but constitutes the opposite of that family form which, following Howell (1975), we shall term 'smallholding'. The distinction between them is that between 'collectivistic', and 'individualistic' family forms. The smallholding family is characterised by inheritance rather than succession, which mode of transmission symbolises the emergence of family members as individuals, though not necessarily autonomous individuals, from the collectivity of the family. Both these forms are to be contrasted with the family of an agrarian proletariat, which subsists by selling the labour power of its members to the owners of the means of production, land. The exact relation between the family group and the land, and the character of the relationships between its members, will vary according to the mode of articulation of families with one another and with other types of group within the population, which will in turn be determined by the jural, political and economic institutions of the population concerned, and the exact relation (or absence of any relation) of the family group to the market.

Significant in this regard are variations in the extent to which levels of production are controlled by the market and in the degree to which they are oriented to the satisfaction of traditional consumption needs as opposed to the maximisation of profit.

THE PROTOINDUSTRIAL FAMILY

In contrast to these distinctively agrarian forms of production and family are those characteristic of 'protoindustrialisation', which term has been used to refer to the movement of manufacturing industry into the countryside during the seventeenth and eighteenth centuries. This process was already underway in England at the beginning of the sixteenth century, though in many parts of continental Europe it was not found on any large scale until the eighteenth century itself. The social as distinct from the economic consequences of protoindustrialisation have only been explored by historians in the last fifteen years. Consequently the picture of those consequences is far from complete. However, it is now possible to construct an outline of this process, and this has been attempted by Medick (1976) whose identification of protoindustrialisation draws on Mendels's (1972) work.

What follows is based largely on Medick's account. The reader who is not even minimally acquainted with European economic history during this period could do no better than to study the introduction to David S. Landes's *The Rise of Capitalism* (1966) and the essays constituting the rest of that volume.

For one reason or another, at different times and in different places in Europe, population growth led to the growth of a class of landless rural dwellers, and gravely impaired the viability of whole sections of the agrarian economy where the mode of production was based on the family group. There came into being, therefore, a rural population characterised by unemployment and underemployment which provided a supply of labour for manufacturing. The expansion of world trade associated with the discovery of the new world in the sixteenth century led to an increased demand for manufactured goods supplied for an increasingly international market. In this situation, as Landes has pointed out, the urban artisan was in no position to know and exploit the needs of distant consumers. Only the merchant could respond to the ebb and flow of demand. As a result the urban artisan came to depend more on the merchant not only for orders, but for credit and materials. The result, in Landes's words, was that the urban artisan became 'in fact if not in principle, a proletarian selling not a commodity, but labour'. Urban manufacturing began to move towards a situation where the principal was not the craftsman, but the merchant, the latter virtually employing the former to work on his materials and taking the greatest share of the profit.

There were obvious advantages in extending this system to the countryside. Rural labour was free of guild restrictions on the nature of the product, the techniques of manufacture and the size of the enterprise. The fact that it was also largely unskilled could be overcome by a judicious use of the division of labour. It was also cheap, for obvious reasons: the labour was not free labour selling to the highest bidder, but settled labour attempting to maintain subsistence within a traditional social structure by engaging in non-traditional forms of commodity production. In consequence rural labour was dependent on the patronage of the merchant. Moreover, the supply of labour was virtually unlimited. In this situation the bargaining power of rural labour was weak. The rural population came to constitute the first members of that 'reserve army of labour', which Marx associated with capitalism proper, which is recruited to work in times of prosperity and thrown into destitution with every downturn of the trade cycle.

At first rural industrial production was a welcome additional source of income to the population of rural settlements even if not on the borders of subsistence (cf. Levine, 1977, ch. 3 *passim*). With the further growth of population, however, a new class of cottage workers was brought into existence who were solely dependent on this type of employment and whose livelihoods were destroyed when it became possible to cut production costs even further, by the introduction of modern machinery into the productive process.

This crude outline of events will be familiar to most readers. What is important, however, is to understand the connection between the character of the protoindustrial family economy and the forms of production that preceded it in Europe, and those industrial forms that succeeded it. Medick argues that protoindustrialisation preserved and did not dissolve the family-based forms of production which had pre-existed it. Drawing on the work of Chayanov (1966) on the peasant family he characterises the family-based economy as follows:

> its productive activity was not governed by the objective of accu-mulating a monetary surplus or net profit. 'The family could not maximise what it could not measure.' (Millar, 1969) The object of its productive labour, rather, was to bring into equilibrium, into a 'labour–consumer balance', the basic necessities of economic, social and cultural subsistence on the one side, and the expenditure of labour by the family on the other. Consequently the family tried to maximise the gross product, not the net profit. (Medick, 1976, p. 298)

The economic logic characteristic of family-based forms of produc-tion involved a system whereby in Engels's words capitalists are enabled 'to subtract from the price of labour what the family produces in its own garden and small plots'. The existence of family labour oriented to traditional consumption goals constituted a factor, additional to the obvious factors mentioned above, which made rural manufacturing, through an alliance of merchant capital and traditional household economies, infinitely more profitable than urban manufacturing. Simultaneously it made possible the expansion of manufacturing but delayed the arrival of the factory system of production. This was eventually adopted, however, because the needs of the capitalist market could no longer be met through rural manufacture, again because of the traditional orientation of family labour. When traditional consumption needs were met, families took advantage of the opportunity for leisure forcing the merchant-manufacturer to extend his operations over an even wider geographical area, involving increased organisational and transport costs. These difficulties arising from the very productive form upon which merchant capital had previously depended, meant that the adoption of a new form of production was in its interest and resulted in the shift to the factory system of production when that became technically possible.

Protoindustrialisation depended on the continued existence of families as productive units oriented to the maintenance of traditionally determined life styles and consumption patterns. Protoindustrialisation worked, Medick argues, to preserve the family as a productive group, and at the same time created the conditions for the emergence of the factory system of production which destroyed that family type. However, protoindustrialisation threw up family forms which, though still based on the family as an economic collectivity, none the less differed markedly from peasant, smallholding and proletarian family forms.

We have already noted in our discussion of Laslett's work that, although simple wage labour was to be found from the mediaeval period onward, it was also found in embryonic form within the household in the shape of 'servants'. Servants expanded the labour resource of both rural propertyholding and urban artisan families. When protoindustrialisation simply involved the substitution, within the peasant family, of the production of manufactured for agricultural commodities to provide an income to supplement consumption of the family unit's own products, no change in family form necessarily resulted. Where, however, commodity production became the determinant of and not merely ancillary to families' consumption, a new family form emerged. The peasant and smallholding family forms were based on ownership of or access to land. The protoindustrial family, in contrast, depended entirely or almost entirely on its labour. But the labour resources of the protoindustrial family were not sold in individualised 'packets' to outside employers as in the case of a proletarian family; the family worked, rather, as a labour collective. The protoindustrial family is the site, in other words, of the shift in the function of the family from that of a propertyowning unit to a unit of labour supply for capitalist production. It is, therefore, a genuinely transitional form: as a collective it retains one of the features of an earlier mode of production: in terms of its function it is able to occupy a place in an emergent (capitalist) system of productive relations. Whether at any given point the preceding family form was of the peasant (collectivistic) or smallholding (individualistic) type, the protoindustrial family operated as a collectivity for the purpose of production, since in many cases subsistence could only be maintained by the participation of all the members of the household in productive activities. However, whatever the preceding form, the dependence of the family on manufacturing activity for subsistence entailed a transformation of both its internal authority structure and the shape of the domestic life cycle.

In a peasant family members are dependent upon family membership for access to the means of production controlled by senior males; in a smallholding family they are dependent directly on the senior male who owns the property. In both cases the control of productive property constitutes the source of power which supports the authority of the family head. In the case of the protoindustrial family that source of power is destroyed. As a result, in Medick's words, 'marriage and family formation slipped beyond the grasp of patriarchal domination; they were no longer "tangibly" determined by property relationships'.

This has important demographic consequences: the age at marriage fell and the number of children increased in response to the need to expand the household's supply of labour. Wages were such that an adult male could not support himself, let alone a wife and family. On the contrary a wife and children as co-workers were a necessity if he was to achieve subsistence. Once again, the individual is unable to produce, except as a member of a family group, but the economic viability of the male comes to be dependent on his 'dependants' rather than vice versa.

It is obvious, however, that there are two drawbacks to early marriage and large numbers of children as a survival strategy. The first is that the result in the long term is to vastly overexpand the supply of labour. The second is that it creates a cycle of family poverty, since infants increase consumption and their care reduces the production capacities of the spouses. Hence, the first part of the procreative stage of the family cycle is likely to be associated with extreme poverty. When, however, the children are adult, they can better themselves if they set up a household independent of their parents. 'With the birth of children the parents become poor; with their maturation they become rich; and with their marriage they fall back into misery' (Green, 1944, quoted in Medick, 1976). There was, therefore, ample motivation for parents to attempt to retain their adult children and to incorporate their spouses into the household unit, thus creating 'an extended family'. There is evidence that this sometimes occurred (see Levine, 1977, pp. 51–7; Berkner, 1972) creating households with a structure which was formally parallel to that of the peasant household. The similarity of household composition should not lead us to confuse the two types of family system, however. In Medick's words, the two types differed fundamentally in material, legal and institutional determinants. The extended family among the rural (manufacturing) workers was formed as the result of growing pauperisation ... The classical stem family, on the contrary, was formed essentially to conserve peasant family property ... The extended family of the rural artisans was much more the forerunner of the corresponding proletarian household configuration than a variation of the peasant stem family ... [It functioned] as a private means to re-distribute the poverty of the nuclear family by way of the family and kinship system. (Medick, 1976, p. 308)

In spite of this very clear distinction, Medick none the less wishes to claim that the protoindustrial family, like the peasant family, constituted a self-regulating unity of labour, consumption and production, which social formation a German scholar has termed *Das Ganze Haus* (the whole house) (Brunner, 1968, pp. 103–27). This claim is not however central to Medick's thesis, for it is still possible to make sense of the data which he cites in the way we have described if all that is assumed is that the family forms which preceded protoindustrialisation were oriented towards traditional consumption goals, rather than profit maximisation, and were concerned to maintain the family's position in a traditional local social structure. The cohesion of the protoindustrial family group need not be a residue of a collectivistic (peasant) family form, but could equally well arise out of the conditions of protoindustrial production themselves. In other words, the type of family Medick described could have been called into being even where preceding family forms were of the smallholding or rural proletarian type.

THE PROTOINDUSTRIAL FAMILY IN ENGLAND

It is necessary to raise this point not in order to question the validity of Medick's interpretation of the continental and particularly German evidence, but to enable us to take account, as Medick totally fails to do, of the fact of 'English difference'. This difference is to be found not in the character of protoindustrial production, but in that of agricultural production prior to protoindustrialisation. With the resumption of economic expansion, interrupted by years of stagnation after the Black Death, the British agricultural economy developed in a way different from its neighbours. In contrast to continental Europe agricultural holdings in England became increasingly consolidated, and either rented to tenants who farmed them with wage labour or to 'commercial' family farmers who produced for profit. The result was a rise in agricultural productivity which freed England from the crises of subsistence which characterised the peasant economies of continental Europe. This development continued apace in the seventeenth century with the abolition of feudal tenures and the general weakening of the legal positions of customary landholders, culminating in the Enclosure Acts of the eighteenth century which deprived the smallholder of access to common land. (For a brief account, see Lis and Soly, 1979, ch. 4, s. 1, ch. 5, s. 1; Howell, 1975.)

The result of these processes has been a matter of some dispute. What is indisputable is that wage labour came to form an increasing part of the agrarian economy. That is to say, wage labour as a factor of production became of increasing importance. It does not follow that a rural proletarian class was thereby created, however. The demand for agricultural labour is highly seasonal. Hence, in addition to the traditional source of wage labour, the truly landless rural poor, 'the sturdy rogues and vagabonds' whose increasing numbers caused so much concern from the Elizabethan period onward (see Lis and Soly, 1979, ch. 3, s. 4, ch. 4, s. 3; Wallerstein, 1974, pp. 117–18, 139–43) smallholding families increasingly sold their labour to supplement their incomes from their landholdings. The demand for labour came from large estates whose existence limited the supply of land available and resulted in the subdivision of smallholdings rendering them more dependent on wage labour as a source of income or the necessity that non-inheriting sons 'travel', that is, become rural craftsmen or rural proletarians proper. By the end of the seventeenth century cottagers, labourers and paupers were said to comprise as much as 47 per cent of the entire population (Coleman, 1955–6, p. 283). During the two centuries 1500–1700, in Evereitt's words (Thirsk, 1967, p. 399), 'a growing army of landless, or almost landless, labourers appeared, dependent on wages for their livelihood'.

It follows that whatever may have been the case when rural manufacture first began to make its appearance in England several centuries before, the protoindustrial stage of economic development in the eighteenth century could not have been chiefly dependent on the adaptation, in England, of the peasant family form involving a 'ganzes Haus' type of household economy to the needs of rural manufacture. The types of family drawn into this activity must have been substantially those of agricultural labourers seeking a remedy for unemployment and low wages, and smallholding families forced off the land by a combination of high rents and the enclosure of commons, together with artisan families whose skills were rendered unnecessary by the deskilling of traditional trades. In England it was these family forms which were modified, by market pressures, to approximate to the protoindustrial family as described by Medick. On the other hand the smallholding families that were recruited to rural industry were certainly not as 'individualistic' as their definition as such would imply. While it may be accepted that they did not include peasant families in the strong collectivistic sense favoured by Macfarlane (see above, Chapter 6, p. 113), they none the less probably exhibited considerable variation on the collectivistic-individualistic continuum, as witnessed by regional variations in inheritance customs and differential participation of their members, as individuals, in the labour market. It is equally likely that they varied also in terms of the nature and extent of their dependence on the market and in the degree to which production was oriented to profit maximisation.

It would be a mistake to suppose, therefore, that there was a single family type which, in England at any rate, was transformed by proto-industrialisation. None the less, Medick's claim that protoindustrialisation created a family form which was genuinely transitional between the family as a propertyowning unit of production, consumption and reproduction, and the family as a unit of labour supply but which nevertheless combined the same functions as the property-owning family, may be accepted. As such, it marks a more important stage in the emergence of the proletarian family than Laslett's servant-employing household, and may be regarded as a direct ancestor of the proletarian family as such.

The difference between the continental situation described by Medick and that pertaining in Britain is made evident by reference to Levine's study (Levine, 1977) of four contrasting England communities, using family reconstitution methods. Levine chose for study two communities characterised by rural manufacture/protoindustry and two which remained agrarian. In one protoindustrial community, Shepshed, in Leicestershire, protoindustrial manufacture displaced craft industry in the eighteenth century. In the second, Colyton, in Devon, previously the subject of a reconstitution study by Wrigley (1968, 1969), protoindustrialisation occurred in the late sixteenth and early seventeenth centuries, but the settlement became deindustrialised during the late seventeenth century. In Colyton, however, proto-industrial activity was an ancillary source of income to 'husbandmen, cottagers and labourers'. In both agrarian communities economic activity consisted of production of corn for the market, in one case (Tevling, in Essex) througout the period of study, but in the other (Battesford, in Leicestershire) corn production gave way to pastoral and dairy agriculture.

In spite of the fact that his model of protoindustrialisation is in many respects similar to Medick's, Levine (1977, pp. 9–15) places much more stress than does Medick on the proletarianisation (or 'protoproletarianisation') of rural workers, and less on the nexus between family organisation and protoindustrial methods of production in explaining the preindustrial rise in fertility. Basically Levine's thesis is that once propertyownership ceases to be a condition of production, the necessity for late marriage and restricted family size is removed, and that the chance of gaining income through labour alone will mean that the opportunity for early marriage will be seized. Increased family size will result, in the next generation, in an increase both in supply of labour and in the proportion of proletarianised labour, thus forcing down its price and creating the necessity of increasing the family's supply of labour in order to attain subsistence in the manner described by Medick. In contrast to Medick, Levin argues that the impulse to mechanise, to shift to factory production, arose from the discrepancy between production costs when rural industry was ancillary to the economy of the 'ganze Haus' as in parts of Germany, and when (as in England) rural manufacture constituted the sole or main source of family income. Undercutting by rural industry in regions with peasant households, necessitated the adoption in England of machine methods, which low labour costs would have otherwise inhibited (ibid., pp. 33–4), creating a permanent state of 'industrial involution' (Geertz, 1963).

Levine's study does, however, substantiate the proposition that family form was crucially determined at this period, by the location of the family in the system of relations of production. His data would seem to support the view that changes in family form in the last half of the eighteenth century in England are to be understood as the result of a continuous process of proletarianisation. Proletarianisation involved the disappearance of the necessity for late marriage and family limitation associated with both craft and smallholding family enterprises (as we should now term them), while opportunities of employment for adult children made early marriage possible. In the protoindustrial sector early marriage and high fertility early in the marriage constituted an optimum short-term strategy for individuals because of the logic of the domestic system of production and provided an opportunity for early marriage to the children of labourers and smallholders. Expansion of the protoindustrial sector did not *require* the pre-existence of the collectivistic family type described by Medick, and it seems likely that collective elements in English protoindustrial families were created by the conditions of protoindustrial production rather than being survivals from an earlier family form.

INDUSTRIALISATION AND THE FAMILY IN ENGLAND

It follows from the foregoing discussion that industrial workers were recruited from a range of different family types. In some areas where commercial family farming and capitalist farming had not developed, workers would have been recruited from smallholding families. They would also have been recruited from the families of agricultural labourers and from those of protoindustrial workers. How did the family forms of industrial workers differ from those of their predecessors and their twentieth-century counterparts?

If the consciousness of sociologists contains any common preconceptions on this issue, they are likely to derive from Smelser's (1959) study of the Lancashire cotton industry. Now largely ignored because of its unfashionable Parsonian functionalist theoretical apparatus, and recently subject to trenchant historical and methodological criticism by Anderson (1976), Smelser's study was of considerable importance when published because it questioned the truth of an historical myth, which sees 'industrialisation' as a process occurring in the last two decades of the eighteenth and the first half of the nineteenth century which destroyed the extended family/domestic mode of production and replaced it by the nuclear family, which functioned as a unit of consumption only and a supplier of workers (as individuals) to the labour market of a capitalist-industrial society.

Smelser argued that the first stage of factory production utilised the family, since male workers recruited their assistants from close kin. Hence, the family continued to exist as a co-operative productive unit within the factory itself, and was only destroyed by technological changes during the latter part of the period. The reader should understand that this is not the only conclusion of Smelser's work, nor even that element in it which is most important. It is our central concern here.

Clearly, Smelser is assuming that the family form preceding industrialisation was collectivistic at least as far as production was concerned. It follows from the discussion in this chapter so far that this conclusion is unwarranted. It is not, therefore, surprising that Anderson is able to argue that 'if there was a trend away from family employment ... it cannot have been very great, because such employment was at no time particularly widespread' (ibid., p. 325). Anderson also points out that

> few handloom weavers [whose families would have been of what we have termed the protoindustrial type] entered factory employment. It seems, by contrast, likely that ex-agricultural labourers and farm servants (and particularly their children) were significant among the recruits. (ibid., p. 326)

None the less Anderson concurs with Smelser that 'the family continued to perform important economic functions in the early cotton towns' (ibid., 1976, p. 321; Anderson, 1971, pp. 117–20) but doubts the validity of Smelser's argument that they ceased to be of importance after 1830, and that that period witnessed the differentiation of family and work structures, and produced a corresponding differentiation within the family itself (Smelser, 1959, p. 265). The nub of Anderson's argument is that though technological and legal changes undoubtedly took place in the 1820s and 1830s which meant that a principal operative was no longer able to produce, in the factory, by relying solely on close kin for assistance, this does not mean that the practice of recruiting kin to provide some of that assistance ceased. Since some of those being recruited to industry were farm servants or agricultural labourers, the shift to a factory employment may have resulted (in Smelser's terms) in the '*de*-differentiation' of the family.

It is of the first importance that we distinguish between the significance of the transition to factory production as a transition in the mode of production, and the associated transition between family forms. There can be no question that factory production presupposed an entirely different organisation of production from that involved in family farming, augmented by farm servants, and protoindustrial production. Although many industrial enterprises were family concerns (cf., for example, Joyce, 1980, chs 1 and 4) and kinship was widely used as a mechanism of recruitment (Anderson, 1971, pp. 118-20), the family itself was not the unit of production, and the fundamental social relation upon which the factory as a social collectivity was built was that of a contract between capital and labour whose terms were to a large part determined by market conditions. The displacement of the family by the factory as the unit of production does not, however, entail that families did not constitute propertyholding groups whose members jointly provided the capital and management of enterprises using the factory system of production; nor does it entail that family groups did not function as work groups within the organisation of the factory. The extent to which family groups continued to function within the new mode of production is an empirical question to which there can never be a simple answer as this varied enormously between industries and regions. What is clear, however, is that the family continued to be of importance throughout the nineteenth century, and that the transition to factory production did not create, in a short period of time, a proletariat composed of (male) individuals competing in a free market for employment, which would enable them to support the dependent members of their nuclear families. Parsons's nuclear family in so far as it constitutes a model of any empirical situation is a pure type of family associated with that pure type beloved of classical economists, 'a perfect (labour) market'. The function of a pure type is to delineate a state of affairs, to which reality may approximate, but which it never reaches.

In an attempt to become clearer as to what actually happened in the century-long transition from a preindustrial to a mature industrial economy, we shall consider the findings of three recent studies, Anderson (1971), Foster (1974) and Joyce (1980).

Anderson's study refers to Preston in Lancashire in the 1840s and 1850s. Lancashire was chosen because 'all through the Industrial Revolution Lancashire typified or led industrial Britain', the majority of the population were employed in factory-based industry for some period of their lives, and the area experienced 'all the characteristic social problems of early industrialisation'. 'In Lancashire ... if anywhere the disruptive effects of industrialisation on kinship relationships should have been found in large measure' (Anderson, 1971, p. 18). Yet Anderson is able to document, impressively, the extent to which, in many occupations in Preston, principal workers recruited their own children as assistants. He notes, however, that only a minority of assistants were at any given time recruited by kin;

he also points to several features which distinguish production in family work groups within a factory from production in craft or protoindustrial family types. In contradistinction to the children of family farming and craft families, children were (to adapt Laslett) life-cycle assistants. They were so employed only when young and later became either principal workers themselves or left for other occupations. This circumstance parallels closely the situation of children in the protoindustrial family. Unlike those children, however, the children of factory operatives could always get employment as assistants to persons other than their parents, and were not dependent (as were 'protoindustrial' children) on their family membership for employment (ibid., ch. 9, *passim*).

Anderson emphasises, however, that the available evidence points to the importance of family membership in obtaining regular occupation, and suggests that this was more important among the higher social strata of the working population. Parental influence with employers was, therefore, an important factor in determining the individual's life chances: the father, although no longer economically independent, still controlled sufficient resources effectively to influence the behaviour of his children. As against this Anderson points out that the availability of relatively high wages to teenagers meant it was to the *short-term* advantage of some teenagers to leave home at that stage. Some of these did, and those that did not were able to use their ability to do so to negotiate favourable terms on which they remained in the parental household.

The picture Anderson paints is one in which the values and sentiments associated with family systems in those areas where the family had traditionally been the unit of economic production had broken down under the impact of industrialisation and been replaced by what he terms 'short run calculative individualism'. This shift to calculative, individualistic values is also likely to have occurred (we have already seen) in the protoindustrial family in which the young adult typically left the parental household as soon as it was to his/her economic advantage to do so, even if penury for the parents was the result. The problem which Anderson attempts to solve is as follows: why was it, given the collapse of traditional norms governing family and kinship relations, that these relationships were assiduously maintained in Preston throughout the course of the life cycle, and maintained even when no net gain was likely immediately to accrue to one of the parties involved and in the absence of strong community controls over individual behaviour? For Anderson wishes to claim that family and kinship relations, far from being destroyed by industrialisation, provided a vital mechanism of adjustment to it.

While it is not possible to give an adequate summary of Anderson's findings here, the continued importance of families and kin relationships is evidenced by the high proportion of households of household heads containing extranuclear kin (23 per cent: ibid., p. 44), the geographical clustering of kin (ibid., pp. 55–62 *passim*), the low incidence of employment of very young children and indirect evidence as to the predominance of strong effective bonds between parent and child within the nuclear family (ibid., ch. 6). Anderson claims that the continued importance of kinship outside the nuclear family derives from the fact that they provided the only means of support in what he calls 'critical life situations':

> sickness, death, and unemployment, the problems of old age and those resulting from a housing shortage, the difficulties of finding good employment and the special problems of working mothers and of immigrants needing advice and shelter in a strange community. (ibid., p. 171)

Anderson's explanation depends on a theoretical framework which he elaborates at some length and with considerable sophistication. Very simply, however, he sees family life in traditional rural areas as characterised by *normatively* governed relationships involving an exchange of services over a relatively *long term*. Long-term reciprocation of services is possible only when uncertainty about the other party's ability and willingness to reciprocate is low. Uncertainty will be low if it is impossible for individuals to escape the social sanctions against counternorm behaviour, and if individuals are likely to have resources which will enable them to fulfil their obligations. These conditions are fulfilled in a small rural settlement with stable populations when the individual is economically dependent on family membership and the family is a propertyholding unit. In an urban industrial situation characterised by mobility of population and family independent sources of income, and when the majority of the population are propertyless and live little above the borders of subsistence, the certainty that any individual will be able to reciprocate aid is low and the absence of strong social sanctions means that there is little guarantee that he/she will. On the other hand Anderson quotes evidence to suggest that a *generalised* obligation to assist kin was still felt, and suggests that this reduced the uncertainty concerning whether reciprocation would be forthcoming. The high incidence of critical life situations in the new towns meant that assistance was needed, but the high degree of uncertainty meant that it was only offered if it was likely to be repaid in the fairly short term. Hence, kinship relations ceased to be associated with a set of specific prescriptions concerning who owed what obligation to whom under specified conditions, and served instead to constitute a reservoir of relationships where certainty of reciprocation was sufficiently high to enable short-term exchanges of aid to be negotiated, *ad hoc*.

Anderson's theoretical approach deserves more extensive exposition and comment than can be given here. The significance of his work as far as our understanding of the family is concerned (apart from the valuable information which it contributes) is that it prevents us from assuming that behaviour which is ostensibly the same as between two different situations, is an index of sociologically similar phenomena. The importance of industrialisation is not that it destroyed the family, or the kinship system, or decreased the number of composite households, but that it transformed the *character* of the domestic group, and the character of people's relations with their kinsfolk. This transformation came about as a result of the change in the mode of production which meant that employment, not family membership, became a precondition of adult existence; as a result of geographical mobility and increase in settlement size which diminished the efficiency of traditional controls over individual behaviour; and, lastly, as a result of poverty and economic uncertainty which necessitated the adoption of a short-term calculative attitude, even towards kin, because it was quite simply a condition of survival.

Foster's work (1974) unlike Anderson's is not primarily concerned with the family, but with the emergence of the working class as a class both 'in' and 'for' itself through the industrialisation process in Lancashire. Foster's material refers chiefly to Oldham which differed from Preston (studied by Anderson) in that it did not experience the same growth of population, having had a sizeable preindustrial population of whom a majority belonged to weaving families of the protoindustrial type. During the 1830s weaving was industrialised and spinning developed until it employed a small majority of the labour force. The new industrial structure was subject to recurrent crises, in response to which it attempted to substitute child and female for skilled male labour (ibid., pp. 80–3). Foster shows that a very substantial proportion of the population were below, or little above, the subsistence level, even in a 'good' year (his figures refer to 1849) and that 'poverty was not so much the special experience of a particular group as a regular feature of the life of almost all working families at certain stages in their development, especially old age, or before young children could start earning' (ibid., p. 96). The results of this poverty were manifested in the high incidence of accomodation-sharing and young children and mothers in early stages of the family cycle going out to work.

Thus far, Foster's work confirms Anderson's empirical judgements as to the poverty of the population and the frequency of 'critical life situations' and their importance in shaping family behaviour. Anderson's investigations in Preston throw doubt, however, on whether accommodation sharing was associated with the existence of large numbers of dependent children. They show that in Preston sharing accommodation occurred in the earliest years of marriage and not in the later part of the reproductive period, largely, Anderson suggests, because the available housing would not have been large enough to accommodate a composite household of such a large size as it would then have reached. In other words, the very poverty which

Foster rightly emphasises would have placed severe limitations on the ability of families to aid one another. Aid was not (in Anderson's terms) only short term, but low cost, because high-cost aid was impossible. But the very poverty which made high-cost aid impractical meant that even low-cost aid was important, and it was well worth maintaining extended kin relationships to benefit from it.

Although Foster's work recognises the significance of the shift in the mode of production and corroborates the view of the protoindustrial and newly industrial family that has been put forward in this chapter, it almost entirely neglects the effect of family structure and family attitudes on what we should now term 'industrial relations'. This is surprising, since he explicitly recognises the importance of the puritan family (Schuecking, 1969) in legitimating the dominance of the emergent bourgeoisie over wage labour in the preindustrial period. When he attempts to explain how working-class agitation in the 1840s resulted not in the overthrow of the capitalist system, but in a period of 'liberalisation' which saw a stabilisation of employer–employee relations, he explicitly considers not only the concessions made by the bourgeoisie, but also 'old traditional forms of control as they survived into the mid century' (ibid., p. 214). He does not, however, consider the family.

This omission is rectified by Joyce (1980), whose book involves a critique of both Smelser (1959) and Foster (1974). The central matter at issue between the three authors is the explanation of the outburst of radical working-class agitation in the 1840s and its later transformation into the moderate reformism of what would now be termed 'traditional' English working-class political movements. The family is implicated in both Smelser's and Joyce's accounts. Smelser, a Parsonian functionalist, saw industrialisation as requiring a greater differentiation of the 'social system' of the family, and working-class protest as a response to these pressures which disappears once the system has adapted to new economic conditions. Foster, a Marxist, sees working-class radicalism as a response to the exploitation and working conditions associated with factory production, and understands its demise in terms of the success of the employers in dividing the working class and creating an aristocracy of labour responsible for enforcing industrial discipline, which identified with the employers.

Joyce attempts to synthesise the elements of truth in both these accounts. He accepts the growth of hierarchical differentiation in the textile industry and the creation of an occupationally less homogeneous labourforce. But he assumes, tacitly, the importance of the family group as a unit in any stratification system, and the importance of the local community as a setting exercising a profound influence on class relations. These assumptions make it difficult to accept Foster's thesis as it stands, because they direct our attention to the fact that the spinner 'was the head of a household diversified over the whole [status] range of cotton occupations ... it is a decidedly o[d]d situation when the plebeians are the rightful and recognised progeny of the aristocrats'. Moreover the whole range of occupations would be found within the same neighbourhood. In sociological terms the restriction on social intercourse across strata boundaries, which is a defining characteristic of a social stratum, would be absent and the consequent enmeshment of members of the working 'aristocracy' in relationships with those in other occupations would inhibit their peculiar identification with the interests of the employers *as against* those of the rest of the proletariat. Moreover, Joyce claims that while technical changes in Lancashire during the 1840s weakened family links within the factory, subsequent changes in the 1850s strengthened them again, so that work, household and neighbourhood were characterised by the same pattern of basically familial relations (ibid., p. 56) and that similar considerations apply to Lancashire weaving (ibid., p. 58). After a period of upheaval in the 1840s, the family was reconstituted within the textile factory, and family and work relationships constituted the basic structure of the neighbourhood. This development mirrored the paternalistic attitudes of the dynastic families of the employers and served to assimilate class divisions to patterns of familial relations which cloaked the economic dependence of the proletariat on the capitalist, just as in an earlier formation it had cloaked the economic dependence of family members on those who controlled family property.

This argument is startling and uncongenial to some historians and has attracted much criticism, but Joyce notes that 'given the evidence available it is a problematic one to sustain' (ibid., p. 80). It is best regarded as a hypothetical course of events which serves to explain the character of labour relations in Lancashire during the second half of the nineteenth century. The relative lack of class hostility is explained by the fact that in the 1840s the worker effectively lost control over the production process, thus rendering him totally dependent on the manufacturer. The next generation grew up in 'urban villages' whose population were totally dependent on the owner of the works which constituted their foci. Their response to this situation was to adopt an attitude of deference to their employer in return for security of employment and rising real wages and the fringe benefits increasingly provided by an employer class which had learnt the lesson of the troubled mid-century years, and was moving into alliance with the landed aristocracy to whom paternalistic attitudes were traditional. In Anderson's terms a calculative deference was initially exchanged for short-term benefits, but as the population of the 'villages' within the town stabilised and conditions of trade improved there was a shift to a normative and longer-term deferential orientation, which involved the social identification of the workers with their neighbourhood/factory and, therefore, of their interests with those of their employer as against those of other areas, enterprises and trades. Central to this shift in consciousness was the ability of the employers to represent capital–labour relations as of the same kind as father–family relations, and this ability depended crucially on the continued importance of family relationships in structuring both management and labour processes. The demise of this familial culture came at the turn of the century with the replacement of the family firm by the limited company and the decrease in the isolation of the population of urban villages brought about by cheap rail travel and the advent of the bicycle.

Compressing Joyce's argument even further what he claims is as follows: the first stage of industrialisation did create class hostility, poverty and social disorganisation manifested in revolutionary action. This however was not the revolution of a true proletariat, but the protest of craft workers at the loss of their independence. The second generation, mid-century, workers were indeed proletarians, but the social conditions of class formation and mass action were no longer present and the production processes involved in textiles were such as not to eradicate all traces of preindustrial patterns of work organisation. The result was a failure to develop a distinctive proletarian consciousness.

These considerations are of vital importance for the understanding of family forms after industrialisation. Once the transition to factory production has been made, we can no longer even make preliminary distinctions between family forms with reference to their productive activities. Instead we need to make distinctions in terms of the class situation and the mode of articulation of the family with other institutions and groups. In other words, neither household composition, type of kinship system, nor relation to the means of production are adequate criteria, separately or together, for distinguishing the diversity of family forms which exist within a society with a bilateral kinship system, a predominantly individualistic family type, and in which, being capitalist in its basic structure, the majority of the population live by selling their individual labour power. The problem of establishing more sophisticated categories for distinguishing family forms in such societies is the central problem facing the sociology of the family in capitalist-industrial societies. This does not mean, however, that we can attempt to establish pure types of family which carry no reference to their social setting. On the contrary, Anderson's and Foster's work suggests that such typologies can only be constructed by relating empirical data about family behaviour to the characteristics of the social setting in which it takes place, and this involves studying family life in the context of investigations of locality and neighbourhood relations, of work organisation and labour market situations, which vary not only between historical periods, but between settlements and regions. It is notable that Anderson, Foster and Joyce, though focusing specifically on a particular settlement, all include data on or inference to other settlements or regions (though it has not been possible to make this evident in the foregoing discussion).

It follows not merely that there is a necessarily close relationship between studies of the family and local (or 'community') studies, but an equally close relationship between the study of the family and that of social stratification. British work in this field has in the last fifteen years begun to distinguish between types of worker in terms of their labour-market situation, occupational history, relation to and type of community, and work and political orientation (see Lockwood, 1966; Goldthorpe, *et al.*, 1969; Bulmer, 1975). A better understanding of the diversity of family forms is partly dependent on the success of efforts to achieve a better understanding of differentiation within the working class, but this clearly includes differentiation between family forms which cannot but vitally affect 'attitudes and behaviour' as Goldthorpe and Lockwood clearly recognise.

Even if we were able to establish, however, a sophisticated set of categories which enabled us to delineate a range of family *forms*, this would not enable us to specify the content of those forms. If we fail to apprehend the character of the interpersonal relationships associated with a particular form, we shall be unable to establish another and vitally important link between family and society: the way in which formative experiences within the domestic group affect the subsequent attitudes and behaviour of its members in society at large. We need never to forget that the domestic group is the site of the crucial articulation of culture with personality, and that if different family forms are associated with different 'images of society', they are equally associated with different models of man. It is well worth remarking that the pre-given, taken-for-granted, unarticulated presuppositions which sociologists of phenomenological and ethnomethodological persuasions have, in recent years, claimed to underlie the surface regularities of social interaction captured by conventional social science, must include as an essential component assumptions about the nature of human-beings as such and in general which have their origin in our first and most intimate experience of 'others'. It is one of the many merits of Lawrence Stone's contribution to our understanding of the emergence of contemporary family life that he attempts to relate the manner in which the domestic group is articulated with other groups and institutions in society to the character of interpersonal relations found within it. He provides us, therefore, with a way of characterising the process of transformation of domestic life which differs from that adopted in this chapter, and which will form the subject of Chapter 8. It would be a mistake, however, to regard the two chapters as instantiating two incompatible historical methodologies, 'materialist' and 'idealist', or two rival social theories. It is absurd to attempt to understand the changing nature of a human group in terms solely of its place in the mode of production, or solely in terms of the structure of relations within it and between it and other groups, or solely in terms of the cultural meanings generated by and attached to it. It is only by grasping the interplay of these different aspects of its being, that full comprehension can be achieved.

Chapter 8

The Character of English Family Life before Industrialisation

In his major work *Family, Sex and Marriage in England, 1500–1800* Stone (1977) adopts a fairly systematic schema to delineate changes in the character of domestic life during the period under consideration. Stone's work is informed by structural-functional thinking in sociology – though he is highly critical of some of its aspects. As a result he tends to regard the sociological as one aspect of the family, an approach which differs from that employed here. His definition of the family – kinsfolk who live under the same roof (ibid., p. 21) – corresponds to our definition of the domestic group (see, above, p. 40), but this is of little significance here since most of his material concerns what, in our terms, are familial domestic groups.

The schema he adopts (ibid., p. 18) involves distinguishing six aspects of family life. The central aspects are the biological, the economic and the political. The 'biological' refers to the basic demographic patterns; the 'economic' to the family's role in both production and the transmission of property; and the 'political' to the distribution of power and authority within the family. These three may be regarded as dimensions of family form to which reference must be made if family types are to be distinguished, in a way which discloses the nature of the family as both a structure and a process. What we have termed the character of family life is encompassed by two further dimensions: the 'psychological' which refers to the character of affective relations between family members, and the 'sexual' which refers to the character of sexual beliefs and practices. The remaining aspect is 'the relation between the nuclear unit and other forms of social organisation, notably the kin, the community, the school, the church and the state'. It refers quite clearly to what we have termed the 'articulation' of the family, but does not include articulation at the economic level. When Stone comes to describe 'the modern family', however, he does not deploy all six dimensions, but characterises it in terms of 'four key features': 'intensified affective bonding of the nuclear core at the expense of neighbours and [less close] kin; a strong sense of individual autonomy and the right to personal freedom in the pursuit of happiness; a weakening of the association of sexual pleasure with sin and guilt; and a growing desire for physical privacy.' It is this description that justifies the claim that he is centrally concerned with the *character* of family life. His work is an attempt to show the relation between changes in form and changes in content, rather than to explain changes in form themselves. Like any good historian Stone tells us a story, and the story is of the emergence of that type of family life characterised by what he terms (reasonably enough in view of the foregoing characterisation) 'affective individualism'.

Stone's other dimensions necessarily play a vital role in defining the stages of this development, because to describe 'family life' as having these characteristics necessarily implies that relations within the domestic group differ markedly from those 'outside it'. Stone's story begins at a point in time – the sixteenth century – at which (he claims) the way the domestic sphere was articulated with other spheres was of such a kind that this differentiation was absent. He paints a picture of a situation where the chief social boundary is drawn not between the members and non-members of a domestic group, but around that category of related persons, living and dead, to whom the members of a given domestic group owed obligations:

> Lacking firm boundaries [the domestic group] was open to support, advice, investigation and interference from outside, from neighbours and from kin, and internal privacy was non-existent. The family, therefore, was an open-ended, low-keyed, unemotional, authoritarian institution which served certain essential political, economic, sexual, procreative and nurturant purposes. It was also very short-lived, being frequently dissolved by the death of the husband or wife or the death or early departure from the home of the children ... it was neither very durable nor emotionally or sexually very demanding. The closest analogy to a sixteenth century home is a bird's nest. (ibid., pp. 6–7)

Stone calls this family type the *open lineage family*: Its 'articulation' and demographic, economic and 'political' features define a form which has implications for the character of family life defined in terms of attitudes and feelings.

The decline in the strength of obligations to kin and to local community and their substitution by obligations to church and state resulted in ' "boundary awareness" becoming more exclusively confined to the nuclear family' and was accompanied by an increase in paternal authority. The open lineage became the *restricted patriarchal nuclear family*. This in turn gave way to a predominantly nuclear domestic group characterised by individual autonomy, strong affective bonds, child centredness, and family and individual privacy.

This type Stone terms the *closed domesticated nuclear family* and claims that it was well established in the middle and upper sectors of English society by 1750, and that the period since then has witnessed its diffusion throughout the whole society.

Like all models, this model (even if adequate) is clearly a gross simplification of an enormously complex reality. There is nothing simplistic about Stone's handling of it, however. He does not claim that what might appear to a sociologist to be stages of familial evolution constitute a unilinear model of development, nor that any one of them was broadly characteristic of English society at any given point in time. Indeed, he stresses that the timing of the emergence of each stage varied between strata and regions. To trace their emergence is an enormously complicated process, which is the task of his book. The stages are not, therefore, a substitute for the writing of the history of the family: they are a device to make writing that history possible.

The weakness of Stone's approach is that its data-base is written materials originating in an age when the majority of the population was illiterate. This means that Stone's history is chiefly a history of family life among the 'middle and upper sectors' of English society, rather than a family history of the whole society. Of course, Stone is aware of this problem, but seeks to overcome it by claiming that the process of change involved what he terms 'the stratified diffusion of new ideas and practices' (ibid., p. 10) and that the literate and articulate classes were the 'pace-makers of cultural change'. It would be absurd to deny the influence exerted by upper strata on the lower, or the importance of ideas in determining the specifics of social behaviour. However, one can only *assume* downward cultural diffusion if one denies the importance of class situation as a determinant of family type; but Stone insists on the importance of class situation. He reconciles these two apparently contradictory beliefs by regarding classes as the sites of *sub*cultures, which suggests that he regards family types as the product of 'culture' conditioned by material circumstances and not vice versa. In this respect Stone's work would appear to be tainted with an idealism which many contemporary sociologists would find suspect.

It is clearly impossible even to begin to summarise a descriptive history of the kind provided for us by Stone, the chief virtue of whose extensive and very readable work is that it creates in the reader a sense of the difference between our own age and that of previous epochs. Instead we shall consider two questions with regard to Stone's work: what sort of connection does he establish between family form and the character of family life (to use our terminology – not his), and how does he understand the transition from the family life of the 'open lineage family' of the sixteenth century to the 'closed domesticated nuclear family' which he claims originated in the eighteenth and spread more widely in the nineteenth century?

SOCIAL STRUCTURE, FAMILY FORM AND THE CHARACTER OF FAMILY LIFE IN THE SIXTEENTH CENTURY

Stone's thesis, and also his problem, is of great importance for our understanding of the emergence of the contemporary family. It is also profoundly shocking to sociologists who (whether they concur with it or dissent from it) were raised on the functionalist understanding of the 'family'. For Stone's thesis is, in essence, that in the sixteenth century *no* kinship *group* was of great structural importance to the society or of paramount emotional significance to the individual, because there were no clearly bounded kin groups. Even the people occupying those kinship positions constituting the elementary family did not, even in the nuclear phase, constitute a distinct bounded group with which the functions usually attributed to 'the nuclear family' were uniquely associated. This was not, however, because these functions were shared by a wider kinship group of which the nuclear family was part. It was because the predominant principles of both kinship and social organisation in general focused on the concepts of 'lineage' and 'kin'.

Stone's account is deficient in that he fails to point out that in a bilateral system there can be no bounded groups which constitute lineages or kindreds, and that he does not make it sufficiently clear that in his account of kinship (which Trumbach, 1978, has rightly described as perfunctory) 'lineage' and 'kin' are concepts which informed sixteenth-century life and are not anthropological or sociological concepts. For a consideration of the sixteenth-century concepts and their relation to 'family' and 'household', it is necessary to turn to Flandrin's illuminating discussion (1979, pp. 4–23). A more thorough analysis of English aristocratic kinship is to be found in Trumbach (1978), who accuses Stone of failing adequately to distinguish 'kindred' and 'patrilineage'. Both Stone and Trumbach none the less describe a society in which kinship is of central importance for the structuring of social relationships in the political and economic spheres. It operated as a means of transmission of both property and social honour, as a means of social differentiation and social identification and, hence, as a means of mobilisation of support in both political and economic life. Trumbach, however, regards 'friendship' rather than kinship as the predominant structural principle.

In consequence the significance of the domestic group was small compared with that of the recognised line of descent, while success in life depended vitally on the good offices of an individual's kin. Marriage was understood as being primarily of significance for the continuation of the line, the transmission of property and the extension through affinal kinship of that web of connections through which influence could be exerted. The significance of the nuclear family lay in its being the product of an alliance to further the political and economic interests of two kindreds, and as a means of ensuring the continuance of a 'line' of descent through which the integrity of property could be assured. It was just this significance which meant that neither the domestic group, nor the individuals which composed it, could attain that autonomy which we associate with the modern family. Family life was subject to continued interference on the part of kin, and this interference was possible because of the necessity of their influence and patronage throughout the whole life course.

In contrast to kin, the domestic group was of only transitory importance. At most social levels children were sent away from home at an early age to be servants and apprentices in the houses of others wherein much of their later socialisation and education took place. Childhood within the domestic group was short, therefore, and frequently marred by the death of one of the parents, or, for the parents, by loss of their children. Marriages were also frequently dissolved by the death of one of the spouses. In these circumstances identification was with line and kindred, rather than with the members of a domestic group.

Stone's problem, given his thesis as to the nature of the sixteenth-century family, is to explain how this family was transformed into the 'closed domesticated nuclear family' of the eighteenth and nineteenth centuries. His central difficulty is that his description is clearly that of upper-strata life. This he resolves by claiming that among the lower orders, while the family was not the means of continuance of a noble line, it certainly preserved family property, in all but the lowest, propertyless, strata. If plebeian families were not open to interference by powerful kin, they were certainly at the mercy of control by inquisitive neighbours, living as they did in small settlements and in houses which afforded little privacy. Demographically, plebeian families would have been as transient as noble families if not more so (see also Flandrin, 1979, pp. 34–49).

Stone describes the character of family life associated with the open lineage family as one in which there is little evidence of close bonding between parents and children and of affection between spouses. The basic orientation (to use Anderson's terminology) was calculative: 'no-one is to be trusted since anyone and everyone – wife, servants, children, friends, neighbours or patrons – are only kept loyal by self-interest, and may, therefore, at any moment turn out to be enemies' (Stone, 1977, p. 96). 'The majority of individuals found it difficult to establish close emotional ties with any other person' (ibid., p. 99). Within the family 'there was a general psychological atmosphere of distance, manipulation and deference' (ibid., p. 117).

The character of family life and, indeed, of interpersonal relationships generally in sixteenth-century society may be understood from Stone's account to result from the economic and political functions of kinship, whose importance meant that creating an environment within which affectionate relationships could develop was held to be of little relative importance; from the resultant hierarchical structure of relations among kin, based on property and influence; and lastly, from the public nature of family life in both the physical and structural senses. Intimacy and individual autonomy were alike impossible. In addition, Stone specifically notes four further factors: 'the lack of a unique mother figure in the first two years of life (due to the practice of wet nursing), the constant loss of close relatives ... through premature death, the physical imprisonment of the infant in tight swaddling clothes in early months and [methods of childrearing that involved] the deliberate breaking of the child's will' (Stone, 1977, p. 101). Demographic factors and childrearing practices operated to create a family from which emotion was absent and a social life which was cold, suspicious and violence-prone.

Stone's explanation of why the family form was as it was is chiefly structural: it was a family type 'entirely appropriate to the social and economic world of the sixteenth century in which property was the only security against total destitution, in which connections and patronage were the keys to success' (ibid., p. 118). It was also both an expression of a particular culture and a mechanism (not so much for transmitting the values of that culture) as, through the way it structured relationships and its methods of childrearing, for creating the personality types consonant with that culture. 'The family' was, therefore, an institution of vital importance 'to the society' in the sense that the structuration of the family process and of the relationships involved was functional for the maintenance of both the culture and structure of the society of which it was part. The fact that the domestic group was not a stable, distinct group, membership of which was of great significance to the members of that society, in no way gainsays this fact. If Stone's picture is correct, however, it makes it impossible for us to think (as we might even after reading Anderson) that a calculative orientation towards kin was uniquely the product of industrialisation. It is in no way to deny that industrialisation caused the shift in kinship attitudes that Anderson suggests, to recognise that such attitudes had pre-existed industrialisation, and that any move to a calculative and instrumental approach in kinship relations associated with industrialisation did not amount to the destruction of an ancient let alone a natural – pattern.

Is Stone's account a credible one? This will continue to be a matter of historical debate, and he differs as to the amount of affection which existed in families at this period with historians such as Demos (1970), E. Morgan (1966) and Hunt (1970). However, his portrait of the character of *social* life in the sixteenth and early seventeenth century is unlikely to be disputed, as is his characterisation of social relations in small rural communities (see, for example, Le Roy Ladurie, 1978). If he is right here, then this must affect one's reading of the evidence as to the character of family life, and lead one to favour an interpretation similar to Stone's.

Certainly, Stone's central thesis concerning the 'unimportance' and openness of domestic life is strongly supported by other writers. The French historian Ariès, in his study of childhood (Ariès, 1962), describes the transition with which Stone is concerned so aptly that selected quotations from Ariès's work might well have served as masthead quotations for Stone's chapters. Of the sixteenth century Ariès writes:

> The movement of collective life carried along in a single torrent all ages and classes, leaving nobody anytime for solitude and privacy. In these crowded, collective existences there was no room for a private sector. The family fulfilled a function: it ensured the transmission of life, property and names; but it did not penetrate very far into human sensibility. (ibid., p. 395)

Flandrin (1979) equally stresses the importance of lineal and kinship relationships and the absence of privacy among French peasant communities.

Whatever the demerits of Stone's work, it does establish the absence of durable closed domestic groups which were composed of members of elementary families and whose life was characterised by intense emotional relationships. It does provide us with a framework for understanding why the family form described persisted. If we may take this much for granted, we may now turn to consider how he accounts for the transition to the 'closed domesticated nuclear family'.

THE TRANSITION TO THE CLOSED DOMESTICATED NUCLEAR FAMILY

Patriarchy

Stone's first attempt at chronicling this transition is to be found in an article in Rosenberg's *The Family in History* (1975). The argument is refined and the account expanded in Stone (1977). Its basic structure is simple. The period 1500–1700 saw a decline in the importance of kinship and clientage, the emergence of the modern state and the invasion of the home by Protestant conceptions of morality and family conduct, enforced by communal intervention in domestic affairs in support of the new norms. The first changes meant that relationships with close kin – those with whom one was or had been co-resident – became of greater importance; the last involved an increasing stress on personal relations between individuals, particularly within marriage, while the centralisation of political authority was associated with the development of paternal domination within the domestic group.

Stone argues that it is legitimate to describe the sixteenth and seventeenth centuries as witnessing a transition from a society composed of lineages and kindreds, 'held together by vague claims of obedience to the most powerful kinship network of all, headed by the King', 'from an association of cousins in the kin into an association of subjects to the sovereign monarch' (ibid., p. 133). He, therefore, concurs with James (1974) that this transition involved a shift from a 'lineage' to a 'civil' society, which Stone describes in Parsonian terms as the shift from 'particularism' to 'universalism'. The decline of 'kinship and clientage' and the rise of state power are therefore not two separate movements, but different aspects of the same movement, in which social relationships at both the political and economic levels become universalistic and kin (particularistic) relationships necessarily become a restricted and subordinate principle of social organisation. 'As loyalty to kinship declines, it shifted not only inward towards the nuclear core, but also outward towards the state, whose policies and actions were to no small extent responsible for the decline of the kin' (Stone, 1977, p. 134).

The rise of state power necessitated the destruction of all those bases of power constituted by 'intermediary organisations' and groupings. Protestantism, Stone argues, by destroying loyalties to the city, the parish and the confraternity, sanctified and symbolised by Catholic ritual, and undermining the local power of the church as a worshipping community and its priest, both isolated the domestic group by destroying the local groups of which it had been part and simultaneously created a vacuum in that it destroyed the central institution for moral and religious instruction. The puritan solution was to devolve these functions to the family and, more particularly to the head of the household (ibid., p. 140). Whether Stone realises it or not, this is a version of the 'mass society' thesis which explains the rise of politically autocratic regimes in the twentieth century such as that of Nazi Germany by the destruction of institutions which intermediate between the individual and the state (Neumann, 1965; Selznick, 1960; Giner, 1976). In the seventeenth century 'the individual' was not ready to appear and means for the control of a mass of individuals were not available. Social control was to be exercised not directly by the state, but indirectly through the family, whose head was to take over the ideological functions of the priest. It is at this point in history that we first encounter the claim made by every functionalist sociological textbook that 'the family is the basis of society'. At the same time the Protestant conception of marriage as a divinely ordained state, superior, not inferior, to chastity, and the Protestant stress on the unique worth of the individual, combined to transform attitudes towards marriage, affection slowly coming to be seen as a necessity, in 'holy matrimony'.

What differentiates this emergent nuclear family from the modern type (as defined by Stone) are two things: the absence of individual autonomy and the presence of paternal domination. The subordination of subjects to their monarch was justified by claiming, in the words of James I, that 'Kings are compared to fathers in families: for a King is truly . . . the politic father of his people' (quoted by Stone, 1977, p. 152). The justification of paternal dominance in the household derived from the Protestant removal of other sources of authority and their replacement by 'the word of God'. The communal celebration of the Mass was replaced by family prayers and scripture readings by the head of the household. The greater literacy of men meant that they exercised control over the means of legitimation of authority as well as control over property. Household members were no longer able to modify paternal authority by appeal to outside sources of legitimation the church, nor to outsiders who, through their command of resources, could influence the household head. Moreover, legal changes gave the propertyholder greater power to dispose of his property and this inevitably increased his power over his heirs. They also gave the husband extensive control over his wife's property. In the words Stone chooses: 'by marriage husband and wife became one person in law and that person was the husband' (ibid., p. 195). At the same time as religious teaching was exalting matrimony and loving relations within it, it was also emphasising to a greater extent than ever before the subordination of women to their husbands and their more general inferiority to men.

That the period witnessed a decline in the importance of lineage and kin, the development of the state and religious transformation which affected the character of domestic life is not in dispute. What is much more problematic is how we are to understand the relation between these events, and how exactly we are to characterise the associated changes in the family. Stone entitles the section of his book (1977) dealing with the transition to the restricted patriarchal family, 'The reinforcement of patriarchy'. What he describes is, however, the emergence of something new rather than the reinforcement of something old.

This point can best be made by drawing on Trumbach's (1978) study. Trumbach claims that Stone fails adequately to distinguish between kindred and patrilineage, that is to say, between a system of cognatic kinship and patrilineal principles of transmission of property and descent. The latter were, he claims, grafted on to the former in the tenth century and declined in importance after 1500, and were never of importance among the peasantry. The rise and fall of what Trumbach terms 'patrilineal ideology' is however not the same as the rise and fall of patriarchalism, which is not a principle of the transmission of property, or of descent, but is a term referring to a system of government (Schochet, 1975). It cannot refer to the government of a closed domestic group before 1500, however, for, if Stone is right, the closed domestic group is a subsequent development. The period 1500–1650 saw the rise of patriarchalism as a means of political legitimation of state power, and since this means had been previously used, it may be said to be a 'reinforcement' of patriarchal ideology. In the family it reinforced *male dominance*, but it *instituted* patriarchy as the system of government of the newly emergent closed domestic group, and cannot be said on Stone's argument to have reinforced it.

Trumbach brings out well, as Stone does not, that patriarchy (as we have defined it) was not a reinforcement of a remnant patrilineal ideology, but a result of its decline. For the preservation of a patriline involved the preference for primogeniture, and the treatment of marriage as an alliance. The shift away from patrilineal ideology 'is apparent in [the aristocracy's] strengthening the right of younger children and in their treatment of marriage not as an alliance, but first as an act of incorporation and then of love' (Trumbach, 1978). This shift did not in itself alter the status of children *vis-à-vis* the parental generation or greatly affect the dependence of women on men, but it did render women more dependent on their husband and children more dependent on their fathers. The shift from patrilineal ideology and the decline of kinship and clientage simultaneously involved the institution of a patriarchal family, but as we have already noted the decline of kinship and clientage was only one aspect of a social transition which involved the rise of the state and its adoption of a patriarchal ideology at the national level. 'State', 'family' and 'patriarchy' are, therefore, different aspects of an emergent new social order, legitimated by reference to a new interpretation of a traditional religion. This makes difficult any causal explanation of the emergence of the new family form, which must be seen rather as one aspect of an immanent process. Protestant beliefs, the rise of the state and the emphasis on patriarchy are all aspects of the new order to which reference must be made if the transition is to be *understood*, rather than *explained*.

Stone himself feels that his explanations of the rise of patriarchy (which are more extensive than there has been space to record here see Stone, 1977, p. 216) are not fully satisfactory and postulates that patriarchy was a manifestation of a more generally authoritarian atmosphere which was a result of anxiety occasioned by the breakdown of the mediaeval worldview. This posits a psychological mechanism which links cultural stability and the content of the intellectual and moral climate, but it does not of course explain either the collapse of the mediaeval world, nor the features of its successor. In so far as Stone does attempt a more general explanation it hinges on the concept of 'social order' (understood in the legal and political sense) at the societal level and on the concept of 'security' at the individual and psychological level. In the absence of a strong, stable legal-political order, individuals seek security and protection through a network of alliances. With the creation of a stable legal-political order, the need for such networks declines. There is, therefore, an oscillation between the importance of personal networks and the stability of social order in the legal and political sense.

The 'restricted patriarchal family' is, therefore, a product simultaneously of the emergence of the state on the one hand, and of cultural confusion on the other, of the slow (if uneven) growth of political order and security and an increase in cultural insecurity. The family emerges as an authoritarian institution charged with the establishment and maintenance of the new cultural values, necessary to the stability of the emergent legal and political order. The scene is thus set for Stone to explain further stages in the transition.

Before concluding our account of Stone's narrative, it is necessary to make four points. First, the image of the emergent society, family and family–society relation that Stone presents is a functionalist one in that it concentrates on the notion of social order, sees that order as dependent on a cultural consensus guaranteeing the legitimacy of state power and accords to the family the important task ensuring that consensus.

Secondly, by insisting that this pattern is newly emergent in the seventeenth century, Stone makes it clear that this image is not an image of any society, but of 'modern' society whose foundations were laid at this period. That is to say, he historically relativises the functionalist worldview. Thirdly, he fails to provide any general approach to the study of social life which could provide the basis for the explanation of the transition he chronicles.

Lastly, what the student of the family must learn from Stone is that, however important were the changes in family form and character associated with industrialisation, the *beginning* of the emergence of the modern family is to be located not in the period of industrialisation, but where any historian could expect it to be located, in the period immediately after 1500. This is so whether one's emphasis is on cultural and political changes, as in Stone's (1977) account, or whether one emphasises instead the spread of capitalist agriculture and the function of the state in an emergent world economy (Wallerstein, 1974).

Individualism and Affection

The further development of the family during the late seventeenth and early eighteenth century did not involve greater equality between the sexes. It did however involve, according to Stone, a decline in the importance of patriarchy as a system of domestic government in as much as there was a trend 'to greater freedom for children and a more equal partnership between the spouses' (Stone, 1977, p. 221), an increase in the degree of affection and the emergence of childhood as we now understand it as a relatively privileged period of life with its own institutions which differentiated children from the adult world. A more detailed discussion of the historical emergence of childhood is to be found in Ariès (1962). Both social life in general and family life in particular were characterised by an increase not only in affection, but also in what Stone terms 'individualism'. By this he means 'two rather distinct things: a growing introspection and interest in the individual personality and, secondly, a demand for personal autonomy and a corresponding respect for the individual's right to privacy, to self-expression and to the free exercise of his (or her) will within limits set by the need for social cohesion' (Stone, 1977, pp. 223–4). (The reader should be warned that there are many other senses of the term; see Lukes, 1973.) Puritanism had laid the foundation of individualism by stressing the conscience of the individual above the authority of the church, and the importance of personal morality and private devotion as opposed to ritual conformity and public worship. But if the individual person was the 'atom' of the puritan world, there also lay the root of sin and wickedness which had to be controlled if not extirpated. The reaction to puritanism after the Restoration in 1660 was essentially a hedonistic reaction to the asceticism of puritanism; it involved a freeing of personal conduct from the crippling restraints placed upon it by the harsh precepts of puritan morality and a rejection of the claims of religion to prescribe the details of personal conduct. Individualism was left unshaken, however.

This reaction was accompanied by profound changes in political thought. The view of 'society' as a collection of individuals who freely give up some of their natural rights to make social life possible grew in influence. This and the 'revolution' of 1688 in which the divinely ordained father of his people was forced to flee the country and another prince was *invited* to replace him eroded the patriarchal legitimation of authority until it was possible for David Hume to remark, in 1741, that 'to talk of the King as God's Vice regent on earth, would but excite laughter in everyone' (quoted in Stone, 1977, p. 231).

The collapse of patriarchal legitimation for political authority was followed by its collapse in respect of paternal authority. Marriage came to be seen less as a state than as a contract freely entered into for the mutual benefit of the contracting parties, a view of the matter prejudicial both to the absolute authority of the husband and the rights of parents to arrange the marriages of their children. Changes in the law and practice of settlement at marriage gave the wife more control over property and restricted the power of the father to disinherit his children. The decline in religious enthusiasm meant that family prayers were less widely used, and the father ceased to perform any religious function. Within limits the pursuit of individual happiness in domestic relations was recognised as a legitimate goal, even if it frequently clashed with notions of filial and wifely duty, and the interests of family property and social honour.

At the same time a number of bizarre innovations occurred in everyday life. In the domestic architecture of the rich, small rooms linked by corridors and allowing considerable privacy began to replace the sequences of intercommunicating chambers and antechambers which were previously normal. Separate servants' quarters began to be built, and apprentices slowly ceased to be members of their masters' households. These changes were accompanied by equally extraordinary practices, such as washing – in extreme cases all over – the use of handkerchiefs and of personal plates and cutlery at meals. Everyday life among 'the quality' saw the growth of a new sensibility towards the body, which necessitated that copulation and elimination became private activities, and even the public activity of eating became individualised.

Stone is right to draw our attention to these changes, to make us recognise that what we commonly take for granted is not universal, but an historical product, and that the process of that production is inextricably bound up with the historical production of 'the modern family'. It is reasonable enough to term these changes 'individualism'. It is less reasonable to define individualism *as* these changes. It is not surprising, therefore, that forty-four pages after his definition (quoted above), we find Stone talking as if individualism meant 'the abandonment of the principle of human interchangeability and the rise of the concept that each person is unique' (ibid., p. 268). This is a much more sociological definition, and thus defined, its rise may be understood as the result of the development of much higher levels of the division of labour. Stone locates the origin of individualistic sentiments in the rising bourgeoisie, from whence they spread to the squirearchy and lower nobility, but he speaks as if this new spirit of the age was one to which the economic condition of the bourgeoisie especially predisposed them. This is no explanation of why the spirit of the age underwent this transition.

None the less Stone's discussion is both sophisticated and insightful. This is particularly so with regard to the stress he places on the existence in the eighteenth century of a *plurality* of types of marital and parent–child relations, all of which are understood as a response to the changes in the culture that he describes, but are differentiated by the different functions performed by families in different strata, particularly their economic function.

Marriage is analysed with regard to mate selection, authority relations, the character of personal relations and sexual exclusivity. Using these dimensions Stone establishes four types of marriage, whose incidence he claims varied between social strata. At the highest level the dominant pattern of marriage is anachronistic and is a modified form of that found in the 'lineage' type of family. Marriages are contracted with a view to the interests of patriline and kindred; the woman brings property to the marriage and retains considerable power over it; husband–wife relations are not authoritarian; and there is little affect and little sexual exclusivity. Among the lesser 'quality' and the bourgeoisie choice of mate was determined within the limits of class endogamy by personal choice; marital roles were segregated and the wife had some part in decisionmaking; affect was high and sexual gratification was concentrated within the marriage. Among the petit bourgeoisie and the aristocracy of labour the potential economic contribution of the spouses was a prime factor in selection; husband–wife relations tended to be authoritarian; there was a high level of affect and of sexual exclusiveness. The family life of the 'propertyless poor' was in marked contrast: freedom of mate selection; male domination and brutality to children and wife; little affect or sexual exclusivity.

Six associated modes of childrearing are also distinguished. The aristocracy were 'negligent', entrusting their offspring to the care of servants and tutors. The poor were either 'brutal and exploitative' or 'brutal and careful', depending on whether the economic position of the family was such that the children were assets ('careful') or liabilities ('exploitative'). In between was the child-centred family of the bourgeoisie and squirearchy, high on affectivity and permissiveness. However, the old repressive methods sometimes lived on even in the child-centred family, just as puritanism persisted. The puritan methods, associated with the petit bourgeoisie, substituted for physical punishment 'the overwhelming pressures of prayer, moralising, and threats of damnation' as a means of control.

The continuance of the puritan influence provided the cultural base for the development of the Victorian family at which Stone glances briefly. This he characterises in terms of a swing back in the direction of the restricted lineage family: increased regulation of personal behaviour; strengthening of paternal authority and a decline in the status of women; and a return to prudery and repression in sexual matters. This swing is then seen as being reversed in the twentieth century and the stress on affective individualism developed even further.

ATTEMPTS AT EXPLANATION

Stone is anxious to point out that the types he defines are pure types, and the process he deploys these types to describe was one whose outcome at the empirical level was 'not so much the replacement of one (empirical) type by another as ... a growing diversity of family types, a wider pool of cultural alternatives' (Stone, 1977, p. 659). From these alternatives, different strata selected different elements so that (in our terminology) families having the same form might differ markedly in the character of their life. This greater diversity was made possible not by the family's 'losing functions', but ceasing to be the central social institution through which societal functions were exercised. During the eighteenth century it did not cease to perform economic, political and religious functions, but it did cease to be essential to economic, political and religious life; it ceased to carry the same structural weight.

Stone, however, takes the view that 'what needs explaining is not a change of structure ... but of sentiment', the 'shift in the whole cultural system'. He then rejects several possible explanations. *Modernisation theory*, understood in Nisbet's (1967) sense, is rejected on the perfectly proper ground that historical schemes which posit a unilinear development are either analytic devices and not explanatory, or (if descriptive) simply erroneous, since they fail to do justice to the differences within cultures or epochs and cannot accommodate reversals and swings of the kind which any empirical history must disclose. He regards Toennies's (1955) *Gemeinschaft–Gesellschaft* distinction as valid as an *analytic* distinction but treats it *historically* in a Durkheimian (1964) manner. Societies always contain elements of both characteristics and are to be distinguished in terms of their proportion and distribution, and the birth of the modern world cannot be understood as a move from one to the other. Specifically, as social relations have become more impersonal and anonymous, so familial relations have become more intimate and affectual.

Stone insists that the change in sentiment he describes cannot be explained in de Tocqueville's manner – 'freedom is then infused into the domestic circle by political habits and by religious opinions' (de Tocqueville, 1968, quoted in Stone, 1977, p. 666). He insists on the importance of the growth of a large, independent and self-confident middle class having close social ties with the landed classes – presumably to provide the fertile soil in which affectivity, individuality and privacy could thrive and from which these cultural values could be disseminated – but if so, then his explanation depends in part on a structural change which itself needs to be explained.

Stone reserves his main attack however for those who, in his view, have sought to explain change in the family in terms of 'industrial capitalism', and among these he includes both Parsons and Smelser and Marx and Engels. His criticism of both functionalism and Marxism reveals, in the view of the present writer, his failure to understand the essence of both positions. The passages cited from Parsons cannot bear the reading he places on them, and he erroneously supposes that a Marxian approach involves relating Stone's 'modern family' to *industrial* capitalism, rather than to the more general and temporarily extended transition to capitalist relations of production.

Leaving this aside his case against industrialisation as a cause of the modern family is that (1) it did not originate in the 'new' class characteristic of capitalist social formations (the proletariat); (2) its appearance predated industrialisation; (3) there is mounting evidence that the factory did not break up the family unit (see above, Chapter 7, p. 125 ff.); and (4) both historical and contemporary sociological evidence suggests that 'the modern family' is not uniquely adapted to social conditions in contemporary advanced industrial economies.

DISCUSSION

And there Professor Stone leaves us: infinitely better informed, with our sensibilities widened, but without providing an explanation of why, as opposed to how, the *'sentiments'* or *mentalités* which characterise family life changed so markedly. In answer to the second question that we posed above (p. 138) concerning Stone's work – how does he understand the transition between family types? – it must be said that Stone understands it, primarily, idealistically: in terms of a reflection in family life of a more general transformation of the collective consciousness, which is itself not explained. Structural factors determine the site of origin and pattern of diffusion of new *mentalités*, and are not understood as their source. To the first question posed above – how does he understand the relation of family form and the character of family life? – the answer is that he does not attempt to comprehend his material in this way. That is to say, he does not attempt to define a set of family forms in terms of their authority and demographic structures, economic activities and modes of articulation and then relate these forms to the personality, attitudes, beliefs and practices following from them. Of the four dimensions which we have described as dimensions of family form, authority structure is used by Stone to describe the character of family life and the other three are seen as *distinct* factors affecting the character of that life. His pure types of family involve some but not all of his six dimensions, and the more recent is the type, the greater the emphasis placed on 'character' (in his terms 'psychological', 'sexual' and 'political' authority aspects) rather than 'form'.

There can be little doubt that he is right to stress the importance of the demographic dimension in accounting for changes in 'character'. It is unfortunate that in his discussion of the economic dimension he has, given his sources, to concentrate on changes in the law of property, and that the function of the family as a productive unit in the lower strata is lost to view. However, his whole account depends crucially on the third dimension, which we have termed 'articulation' and which he describes as 'the relation between the nuclear unit and other forms of social organisation, notably the kin, community, the school, the Church and the State'. The emergence of 'the modern family' is predicated in Stone's account on what might be termed a transformation of the 'mode of articulation' of the kinship positions constituting the elementary family in its nuclear phase, with positions in other spheres of social life, which resulted in the nuclear family becoming a bounded group, distinct from 'public' life, within the privacy of which, a domestic life characterised by affectivity, individuality and *personal* privacy could develop. Stone remarks at one point that in the 'big, impersonal, bureaucratic, meritocratic, competitive, contractual, individualistic ... *Gesellschaft* world of today, the nuclear family has developed and strengthened its emotional cohesion as a last *Gemeinschaft* refuge' (Stone, 1977, p. 660). This implies that the structural differentiation of the nuclear family makes possible an adaptive psychological response to the stresses imposed by the character of social relations outside it. This constitutes an 'explanation sketch' which suggests a way of beginning to try and understand why changes in articulation were followed by changes in the affective character of family life.

The strength of Stone's work, from the point of view of this book is that, by paying so much attention to the 'character' of family life, he is able to distinguish a whole range of family types which immediately pre-existed industrialisation and, hence, delivers us from such simplicities as the belief that industrialisation destroyed 'the extended family', or that, since 'the family' was already 'nuclear', industrialisation had no effect at all.

The magnitude of the theme 'family and industrial society' should by now be apparent. To understand the transitions in the form and character of the family life which accompanied the great social transition of the late eighteenth and early nineteenth centuries requires a specification of the nature of that social transition, which in turn requires a specification of the form and character of the social formations which preceded and succeeded it. This, however, is the problematic of classical theoretical sociology. A discussion of Stone's work makes it clear that an historical understanding of the emergence of the modern family is dependent not only on a painstaking and scholarly examination of evidence, but also on the construction of a theoretical framework for its interpretation, and that this framework must involve the abstraction of the strategic structural features of preceding and succeeding social forms. It is also necessary to struggle with the central and perennial problem of the relation between structural form and the content of social consciousness at the levels of both family and society.

Stone makes it clear that the transformation of both the form of the family and the character of its life is an essential element in that transition, because of the role of the domestic group in constituting the character of the individuals of which a society is composed. We have already seen that family transformation is an aspect of the transformation of the mode of production and that Stone's sources do not enable him to deal with production as opposed to property. What Stone inexcusably ignores is the complex *interaction* between sentiment and demographic factors. Mortality undoubtedly affected sentiment, but the reverse is also true. Not only are attitudes to children and childrearing practices likely to affect infant mortality, but attitudes to sexuality clearly are an important factor affecting births. The character of family life affects both the demographic form of the family and the demographic structure of the society which is, in turn, a vital factor in determining its social structure and a condition of its transformation. If it is impossible to study the family except as an element of a total structure or formation, it is equally impossible to study the transformation of social totalities without an investigation of the changing nature of the family. This is less because the family is a central social institution through which institutions governing other social spheres are articulated, than because the family plays a central role in articulating the past and the future. However little structural weight it bears at a given moment, the family always constitutes a crucial linking mechanism in the process of social change.

Chapter 9

Distinguishing Family Types in Capitalist-Industrial Society

We have referred above to the inadequacies of 'great divide' theories of history, but have so far concentrated on the inadequacies of their characterisation of 'the past', that is, of preindustrial social life. They are equally inadequate as resources for understanding the family in 'the present', that is, within social formations characterised by the capitalist mode of production and industrial means of production. For in such societies families may not be distinguished, as we have done in Chapter 7, by reference to their participation in different modes of production. The vast majority of families in such societies are 'proletarian' families in the sense that their members subsist by selling their labour power, or are dependent upon someone who does sell his/her labour power. Equally they are all 'bourgeois' families in the sense of being 'closed domesticated nuclear families'. Hence, there is a tendency to speak of '*the* family in capitalist society' or '*the* family in industrial society' as if there was no differentiation of family type either synchronically or diachronically.

The growing amount of recent work on the family, and the position of women, sexuality and childhood in the nineteenth century, reveals what one would expect: very considerable diversity. As Vincent (1979) has pointed out, 'with a subject so large and relatively unexplored as the Victorian family, it is still much too early for any sort of satisfactory synthesis to emerge'. Consequently it has not yet yielded the categories which would enable a sociological history of family life after industrialisation to be written. Yet it is difficult to see how, in default of such a history, the diversity of family life in contemporary society can be fully understood, since many present family forms are survivals and modifications of earlier forms. Certainly, there are also innovative forms, but these cannot be recognised as innovative, as 'new', nor can their newness be specified, without some determinate conception of what constitutes the 'old'.

This chapter will not attempt, therefore, to carry forward Stone's narrative of the evolution of the family to the present day. Rather, it will attempt to suggest one way in which family types may be conceptualised. Before doing so, however, it is necessary to consider how in principle any attempts of this kind should proceed.

To say that historical work has not yet yielded the categories for systematic analysis of family variation is not to say that it is not beginning to furnish us with the materials for their construction. Indeed, whether we look at French structuralist-historical writing, or traditional British and American studies of the family, or to Stone's work itself, there can be detected an insistent emphasis on what we have termed the mode of articulation of the family. This is obscured by the fact that 'articulation' takes an indirect object, and what 'the family' is articulated *with* will depend on how a writer 'thinks' social life. Parsons, for example, though his functionalist approach is antipathetic to a 'structuralist' understanding of the family, and does not deal with family variation within industrial societies, is clearly concerned with the articulation of familial and *economic* institutions. Stone is concerned with the articulation of relationships within the domestic group with kin relationships, just as Young and Willmott (1957) and Rosser and Harris (1965) were. Bott's (1957) study may also be said to be concerned with the articulation of the family. It is, however, concerned with a further relation. It considers not merely the relations between family members and others in their social milieux, but also the relation between the structure of relationships constituting the family and the structure of the set of relationships in which family members were embedded. Bott's work was an attempt to explain variations in the internal structure of families by reference to the types of network with which that structure was articulated.

In contrast to Bott, Stone, influenced by psychohistorians such as de Mause (1976) and Hunt (1970), is concerned with the internal structure of the family in a different sense – with the 'psychological interior' of the family, to use Handel's (1968) phrase. The question must now be asked: if it is not possible to distinguish adequately family types in contemporary society without reference to their 'character', can differences in character be distinguished without deploying what are essentially psychological categories? Such a question will doubtless cause many conventional sociologists to shudder, either because the term 'psychological' is thought to refer to internal states rather than to overt behaviour or because they have been brought up as good Durkheimians to identify the psychological as the opposite of the social. The present writer regards both these views as mistaken. It might be thought possible to avoid 'psychologising' the interior of the family by speaking of changes in sentiments. Indeed, the writers whom we have considered and who have emphasised the changing character of family life are often bracketed together as sharing a common concern with sentiments. This is the case, for example, in Anderson's (1980) lucid and succinct discussion. The notion of sentiments is avoided here for two reasons. It covers too wide a range of phenomena, and does not differentiate elements produced within the family and cultural elements which inform family activities but are synchronically independent of them. Secondly, it is associated, as Anderson points out, with an expressionistic and idealistic approach to the explanation of change in the character of family life. For these reasons, we prefer to face squarely the issue of the place of psychological categories in the description and understanding of change in family character. What is meant by 'psychological' is best indicated by an indirect approach.

If one eschews approaches to the study of family life which regard the family as a natural grouping which is culturally elaborated in different ways in different cultures, an essentially functionalist view, or sees 'the nuclear family' as the natural result of men's attempt to satisfy their needs once freed from the thraldom of custom and superstition (the Enlightenment or 'modernisation' view), then one faces the task of defining one's object of study in a way which does not make similar presuppositions. The most obvious way to do this is to focus on universal human activities, such as biological reproduction and the co-operative performance of domestic tasks, and to regard these activities as the *site* of a *range* of historically and culturally specific constructions. However, this strategy has certain parodoxical consequences. If we accept one of the tenets of psychology, that early life experiences are of unique importance in the constitution of human-beings as social persons, domestic groups within which biological reproduction takes place constitute a social location where, in Poster's (1978) words, 'psychic structure is most decisively prominent'. This is paradoxical in the sense that, as Poster rightly argues, the predominance of the natal group in determining the psychic structure of human individuals reaches its apogee in the 'bourgeois' type of family and is infinitely less significant in other earlier family forms. To define the object of study of students of the family in such a way as to make the determination of the psychic structure a key definitional element would appear to be yet another instance of reading back into history the characteristics of the modern family.

Poster's proposal is, however, only paradoxical and not contradictory. The determination of psychic structure by early life experiences first becomes *recognisable* when those experiences are concentrated within a small closed group. However, that determination may be assumed to be universal, and the corresponding question which further defines the locus of interest of family studies concerns the consequences of different types of arrangements of reproductive and domestic tasks for the formation of psychic structure.

The type of psychic structure generated by an individual's early experiences within his or her natal group will depend crucially on its *emotional* structure. Poster, who rejects Freudian claims to have discovered a universal emotional structure in which all human-beings are necessarily involved and accuses Freud of lacking any coherent social theory of the family, sees this emotional structure as intimately tied to the differentiation of the natal group in terms of age and sex. Age and sex are therefore universal categories, but the patterns of emotional relations subsisting between these categories are culturally and historically specific. Hence, Poster proposes that we define the object of study of students of the family as the 'place where psychic structure is internalised and becomes a mechanism for instituting the hierarchies of age and sex' (1978, p. 144).

This, however, presumes both reproduction and the performance of household tasks, since Poster in a good functionalist manner (in one sense of the term) goes on to claim that Freud's theory of psychosexual development (oral, anal, genital) provides foundational elements for the analysis of emotional structure. In our terms: reproduction involves rearing, and rearing involves nurturance (oral), waste disposal (anal) and (according to Poster) the development of strategies 'to cope with the child's exploration of its genitals . . . In so doing, families present to the child a pattern of love and authority which helps form the child's psyche' (ibid., p. 150).

In contrast to Freud, Poster insists that childrearing practices must be regarded as interactional processes and not understood simply as subject–object (parent–child) relations. Parsons, of course, insisted that socialisation is an interactional process. In contrast to Parsons, Poster claims that it is inadequate to define the parent–child relation simply in terms of its functions of cultural transmission and the production of personality types consonant with the requirements of the social system and embodying elements of the cultural system. Psychic structure is a product of interaction within a specific emotional economy. The term 'personality' is not used, presumably to avoid its interpretation as a cluster of dispositions on the one hand, or as a set of internalised value-orientations on the other. 'Psychic structure' would appear to have the connotation 'emotional structure'. Families (groups within which children are reared) are also to be understood as emotional structures. The child does not necessarily internalise these psychosocial structures, but acquires distinctive patterns of emotional response through participating in them.

Poster's work is extremely stimulating and highly suggestive, but somewhat programmatic. Indeed, it has been necessary to elaborate it slightly even to write the above account. It includes one or two oddities: why, for example, are waste disposal and genital exploration universal 'problems' that have to be 'coped with' in all cultural and historical circumstances? Its chief difficulty is that it does not begin to consider the problem of how to classify 'emotions', which presumably constitute the differentiated elements of any psychical or psychosocial emotional structure. The only categories Poster generates are 'love' and 'authority' but, while in no way denying the centrality of these two concepts in providing an initial orientation to the 'interior' of the family, they do not constitute an adequate typology of emotion; 'authority' is not the name of an emotion.

Any attempt at specifying emotional structure must run up against a fundamental difficulty which is as follows. Emotions, like other experiences, whether internal or external, are only constituted as intelligible through the categories of a given culture. If there are emotional universals, they are not accessible, and what is accessible is part of the very culture which defines the notion 'family' and the social relations which constitute its social structure and determine its emotional structure. In this sense we cannot escape projecting back concepts arising out of our own family form into the past or on to other cultures.

In spite of these difficulties, any orientation to the family which regards it as the locus of the constitution of personality, but does not regard personality as the result of internalisation of culture, has considerable advantages from the sociological standpoint, and does not (as might be thought) imply either an individualistic or atomistic social theory, or the psychologisation of culture.

Culture is usually regarded as being initially acquired through interaction within the family. In sociology the model of such acquisition is usually either the symbolic interactionist model elaborated by G. H. Mead (1934) or the neo-Freudian model developed by Parsons (1956). Both are normative in intent: they attempt to explain how new entrants to an ongoing culture acquire it: how the state of 'having been successfully socialised' is achieved. They 'link' personality and culture only by identifying them: in Mead's case as different moments of the same process, and in Parsons's as different expressions of the same structure. They, therefore, generate residual categories of 'deviant' personality types or 'socialisation failure' to be accounted for by factors, or in terms of categories, external to the model. What is required instead is a model of a process through which genuinely independent categories of culture or personality are linked and which is adequate to explain a range of different outcomes, and a specification of personality which includes cognitive and emotional as well as evaluative elements. Here we shall concentrate on the emotional aspects.

If 'personality' is defined in terms of individual emotional structure, and 'culture' as a totality of categories, values and expectations, then the family may be seen as the site of the process which simultaneously generates the former while transmitting the latter. The new entrant to the culture both learns to feel certain emotions and to associate them with cultural meanings. As a result cultural items come to have an emotional meaning, and emotional experiences become culturally significant. However, exactly what emotion becomes associated with what cultural items will vary from individual to individual. Individuals may be differentiated in terms of their emotional structure specified in terms of the type and intensity of emotion attached to cultural items, but that differentiation is only possible by virtue of this common possession of the same culture.

The cultural items to which emotion will be attached will, however, be both constitutive of the family group itself and of other spheres of interaction within the society. Pre-eminent among them will be cultural meanings and prescriptions connected with age–sex categories, since these dimensions are the basic axes of differentiation of the biological group. The family is the prime *locus* for the development of individual responses to what Poster calls 'authority', but which is better termed 'superordinate-subordinate relations'. Aggression, deference, or obedience to superordinates are the behavioural correlates of emotional responses to the experience of domination and control. The family is simultaneously the site of the development of emotional responses connected with gender definitions. However, since hierarchical and gender differentiations are general throughout all societies, the emotional responses acquired in the family will constitute a determinant of behaviour in all social spheres. Age and sex as principles of differentiation necessarily result in hierarchical relations between the generations and gender differentiation within them. It is by no means clear, however, that gender relations must also be hierarchically ordered, though they usually are. What is clear is that it is mistaken to suppose that 'age' is to 'sex' as 'hierarchy' is to 'gender' as 'authority' is to 'love'. Rather, material-object properties are the basis of cultural distinctions which are invested with emotion. That is to say, meanings are invested with emotions, and because these meanings are general and not particular, they can be generalised to spheres other than that in which they originate.

It is not being suggested, however, that human action is intelligible solely in terms of emotional response. Rather, individual action is to be understood in terms of that response, as well as in rational and cultural terms. It is not being suggested that the understanding of social life is possible simply on the basis of an understanding of individual action. It is being suggested that even at the level of collective events some attention must be paid to the emotional significance of situations to agents, as well as to purposive elements and structural constraints, and that the family is of central importance in determining the nature of that emotional significance.

The advantage of this orientation from the sociological standpoint is that it constitutes the family as the locus of a process, which (however closely that locus is determined by other social processes) is autonomous in its operation. This provides an avenue of escape from a functionalist approach which sees the family as determined by other elements in a social system and, in turn, determining the character of the individuals whose collective life exhibits that system. It also provides a way of escape from expressivist and functionalist tendencies in Marxism which see the family as an expression of the essence of capitalist social formations, or as functionally necessary means of maintaining such formations. David Morgan (1979) has pointed out the parallelism between Gouldner's (1970) notion of functional autonomy and the Althusserian (1971) notion of relative autonomy, both of which have originated to avoid the inadequacy of theoretical formulations which see 'parts' as being totally determined by wholes. However, both theoretical traditions claim autonomy for 'the family'. That is not what is being suggested here. Reproduction and domestic activities define a 'site' on which different types of group (whose members engage in those activities) are formed. The forms of such groups (families) are relatively closely determined by other social processes which do not universally occur within them. These forms, in turn, vitally affect but do not in any simple way determine the character and outcome of the process of personality constitution which does characteristically occur within them – which *process* may be said to enjoy relative autonomy *vis-à-vis* other fundamental social processes.

For this reason, it is desirable to avoid defining the family in terms of its reproductive function (in industrial society/for capital), while recognising that it is precisely its connection with reproduction that gives the family its strategic importance as a social institution. However, because of that importance, a central problematic for the sociological study of the family must be the relation between the psychodynamic processes occurring within the social group within which children are reared and other major social processes. This relation must be understood as being itself a process which involves the determination of family form by other processes, and the determination of those processes, over time, by the supply of new members of the population with a specific range of types of emotional structure.

In a different language, and in Johnson's (1979) words, 'families are sites where ideologies are produced in the form of subjectivities'. But this production is not to be seen as necessarily functional for capital. 'Capitalism is far from being a self-policing system ... those processes (i.e. the reproduction of labour) necessarily require continual management' (ibid., p. 237). Johnson is writing about working-class culture, and claiming that while the forms of consciousness and subjectivities of the working class are generated by the labour process, this generation involves processes which are relatively autonomous, and from the standpoint of capital, indeterminate in their outcome.

The approach proposed here, except for its use of the term 'emotion', resonates with a number of contemporary approaches to aspects of family life. In particular, Laing's work (see Laing 1971) is premissed on the assumption that individuals interiorise family structure which they then map on to social situations other than those in which those structures originate, including of course their own families of procreation. Moreover, Laing writes:

the dynamics and structure found in those groups called families in our society may not be evident in those groups called families in other places and times. The relevance of the dynamics and structure of the family to the formation of personality is unlikely to be constant in different societies or even in our own.

This understanding is, however, developed to aid the comprehension of·the process of definition of *individuals* as mentally 'ill', and to explain *individual* behaviour, and this aim naturally leads him in a different direction from that taken here. This is also true of the psychotherapeutic approach to the family (see, for example, Walrond-Skinner, 1979). For while the approaches constituting this orientation share in common a view of the family as a system of relations spanning more than two generations (Lieberman, 1981), they are divided by their therapeutic aims and the theoretical apparatus they employ. As a result there has been no possibility of the emergence of any consensus on family typologies, and were there to be such it would be determined by the orientation's diagnostic-therapeutic aims. Such a typology would necessarily be different from that devised for sociological purposes. The distinctive focus of psychological and psychotherapeutic approaches is upon the psychodynamic processes occurring within childrearing groups themselves, rather than upon the *relation* between those processes and other social processes. A sociological typology must in contrast be concerned with discriminating between families in terms both of their mode of articulation in the social structural sense, and the personality types they typically produce – these types being defined in terms of the emotional meanings with which they typically invest cultural objects.

THE SENNETT APPROACH

One of the most stimulating contributions to our understanding of how the coming of modern (that is, urban-industrial-capitalist) society affected family life has been made by Richard Sennett. Sennett investigates both past and present: the emergence of the modern distinction between 'public' and 'private' domains in *The Fall of Public Man* (1974), the character of family life in nineteenth-century urban America in *Families against the City* (1970a) and in a reflection on city life and personal identity in the tradition of Simmel and Wirth: *The Uses of Disorder* (1970b). Lastly, Sennett and Jonathan Cobb, in *The Hidden Injuries of Class* (1972), a work not overtly about the family at all, provide a stimulating and provocative study of hierarchical relationships in American society which centres on the relationship between family and work.

The picture of eighteenth-century society which Sennett paints in *The Fall of Public Man* is that of a social universe composed of two spheres, the public and the private. The latter is rooted in the natural, the former is the sphere of civilisation – the realm of culture. The private is composed of a multitude of enclosed spaces; the public, an open space which reunites what the private sphere has divided. The private was however not yet identified with the individual, the particular. It was a realm within which people realised their natural, human being, just as the public was a sphere in which they realised their social and cultural being. In neither sphere was there room for the expression of individuality in the sense of psychic difference, of 'personality'. Private, family relations were thought to express natural affections and emotions common to all men; public relations expressed artificial cultural differences between social categories and groups. The private sphere was becoming centred around dependent children, yet concern was not yet with their developing personalities, nor with their function in perpetuating something of their parents as individuals. Rather, the centrality of children derived from the view that their dependency gave them the natural right to the care and protection of their natural parents. Public life was not seen yet as dangerous or threatening as opposed to the security of the private. Rather, public and private represented two different types of social order and security.

Sennett sees these two types of order and the stable complementary relation between them being eroded in the nineteenth century. This erosion resulted from two processes, each affecting both spheres. The first source is obvious: the rise of industrial capitalism. Sennett sees this as resulting in the localisation of the city – the development of separate class-homogeneous localities (the bourgeoisie alone retaining access to the truly public sphere) and intense uncertainty in economic life. At the same time, however, the public sphere came to be identified more and more with the market for commodities. These commodities, produced and exchanged for their use according to the dominant nineteenth-century ideology, came to function as social signs, not (like the clothes of the eighteenth century) of who one was in a stable social order, but of one's success in the disorderly economy of the nineteenth. At the same time they functioned as signs of identity. If this was the case, however, identity must have come to mean something not associated with either the public or private spheres which had defined the previous social universe.

The second process that Sennett refers to is the development of a new way of understanding and experiencing human existence in which human actions are not understood as the expression of a transcendent natural or social order, but as the embodiment of individual difference. These differences depend for their existence on their being perceived, by the agent or by others, for whom they are constitutive signs of the agent's inner self. Put another way, Sennett is saying that people no longer knew who they were in terms of a stable social order. Not being thus defined, they located identity in a hidden inner self. Not knowing who they were, they sought to define their selves and those of others by scrutinising external signs, much as the Calvinist – according to Weber – scrutinised his working activity for signs of divine favour. The nature of the individual came to be thought automatically expressed in his/her appearance and action. Hence, one's inner self could be inadvertently *betrayed*. To betray oneself in public became a deep-rooted fear, and hence the public sphere came to be no longer an arena of the spontaneous expression of social difference, but a threatening arena which could only be safely entered when individuality of appearance was masked by conventional uniform, and behaviour strictly regulated by conventional form. Yet social differences continued to be of vital importance and these were signified by the minutiae of dress – minute signs which could be read only by social equals.

This second process is nothing less than the birth of personality in the modern sense which involves the identification of the inner self and the outward sign. Personality could only be *safely* revealed in the private sphere, which should logically have become the sphere of individual spontaneity as opposed to the public sphere of conventional forms, a stable refuge from the world outside, isolated from its cares and uncertainties. Sennett points out, however, that while there is some truth in this picture, it cannot be the whole truth, if the foregoing analysis is correct. The problem of identity could not have ceased to be a problem the moment the threshold of the family dwelling was crossed. Indeed, as far as children were concerned they needed to be prepared to enter the threatening public sphere. In which case they needed 'strong' personalities capable of not betraying themselves in public. This was achieved in the Victorian family in two ways. First, by the importation into the family of fixed forms of behaviour. Spontaneity on the part of parents and children was inhibited. The parents were required to display stable presentations of self, that the children might learn stability in their own self-presentations. The family now not only functioned as a means of protection for the dependent as in the eighteenth century; it assumed in Ariès's (1962) words 'a moral and spiritual function: it moulded bodies and souls'. The family became a sphere characterised by stability and predictability of interaction in contrast to the uncertainty of the public world. Secondly, this was made possible by the nuclear family form, which simplifies the structure of the domestic group, restricting interaction of children to the first ascending generation only. With this development the private sphere of the family became the opposite of the public, rather than complementary to it. At the same time it was elevated as the seat of moral virtue of truly human (that is, personal) relationships as opposed to the impersonal world of threatening and unplaceable strangers.

Sennett is attempting to delineate a profound transformation which is simultaneously emotional and cultural. In a sense he is describing the *birth* of what has been termed the psychological interior of the family. For before the family became closed, before in Ariès's words, 'it raised the wall of private life between family and society', it had no *interior*; before it developed the function of personality formation, it was not the one social sphere 'in which psychic structure is most decisively prominent' (Poster, 1978); and before it was both closed and simplified to its elementary form, whatever its importance, it could not have been the predominant 'mechanism for institutionalising the hierarchies of age and sex'. Yet the later development of the family is not to be understood in these terms alone; the character of the modern family was decisively influenced by the decline of the public sphere itself.

In *The Fall* Sennett concludes by chronicling what he sees as the 'end of public culture', which involved what might be termed the wholesale psychologisation of life. Sennett with every warrant defines 'civility' as

> the activity which protects people from each other and yet allows them to enjoy each other's company. Wearing a mask is the essence of sociability ... Civility has as its aim the shielding of others from being burdened with oneself. (Sennett, 1974, p. 264)

A mask does not simply function to hide the wearer; it also proclaims who he/she is. It makes possible public expression of feeling and emotion precisely because this does not imply the total abandonment of all reserve. It functions to give psychic content a social form and, thus, to enable the social actors to distance themselves from their own feelings rather than identify with them. On these terms those public activities which sociologists term 'instrumental' may be 'expressive', without destroying the possibility of stable interaction. However, as we have seen, the nineteenth century witnessed the decay of all forms of public expression and the meaning of acts and relationships became purely 'psychological' – significant only as emblems of self, of personality. The persona (mask) degenerates into the personality, yet nowhere in public can personality be expressed. Hence, the opposite of the 'public' becomes not the 'private', but the *intimate*; the intimate becomes the locus of one's true humanity, and that locus is family and locality.

According to one 'great divide' theory of history much beloved of sociologists, this atrophy of the public sphere as an arena of authentic human expression is the last stage in the transition from *Gemeinschaft* to *Gesellschaft*, from Community to Society, family and locality constituting the last remnants of true Community. Sennett is quite clear, however, that if the modern family became a community as a result of the nineteenth-century changes he describes, it became a 'community' of a very modern kind. Community as the opposite of the public sphere has come to mean intimacy, the realm of expression of individual differences of personality and feeling in which psychological closeness is made to substitute for a true unity of being and feeling. But, Sennett claims, 'the closer people come, the less sociable, the more painful, the more fratricidal their relations'. Hence, he concludes his book with a short discussion of the 'tyrannies of intimacy'.

It is important to recognise that Sennett is neither attacking nor defending the family, nor is he making an empirical generalisation about all families in modern society. He is attempting, rather, to delineate through historical analysis the nature of our cultural predicament. Denied community in the public sphere, we seek intimacy in the family which makes demands upon the family which it cannot meet. As a result we feel the family to be suffocating and seek to escape into the public world only to find it impersonal and sterile. The *origins* of the degeneration of public life which eventually produced the identification of intimacy and privacy are to be found, he claims, in the nineteenth-century city. Obviously, it occurred at different times in different places and in different sectors of society.

Sennett's other historical work concerns one of those locations, late nineteenth-century Chicago. It constitutes the origin of one of the themes of Sennett's work which focuses on the notion that the 'isolated nuclear family' was not, in Parsons's words, a means of 'adaptation and integration', but 'a tool people used to resist the economic and demographic changes rather than a means of participating in them' (Sennett, 1974, p. 178), hence the title of the Chicago study: *Families against the City*. Sennett now feels that he overestimated the extent to which it was possible to escape into the family, for reasons we have discussed above. But this revision does not affect the other part of his thesis: that the escape (or attempted escape) into the family was counterproductive. As he puts it, the Chicago study 'tries to show how an intense and warm family life under certain conditions destroyed bonds between father and son, destroyed as well the strength the members of the family possessed to deal with the urban world around them' (Sennett, 1970, p. 5).

Sennett's study is of a particular area of Chicago called Union Park, a once-upper-class area which had, by the 1880s, become 'middle class' – in English terms its residents were drawn chiefly from strata we term lower-middle, middle-middle and 'respectable' working class. Sennett's first claim, based on literary evidence, is that this class shift was accompanied by a decline in interfamily sociability, and a simplification and impersonalisation of social life. As a result the family group was the only locus of face-to-face relationships: 'the family became *the* medium for interpersonal expression.' At the same time he claims that husbands had little authority in the home in which they spent so much time: fathers had become 'no longer leaders but rather supporters of directing mothers'. This, while plausible, must on the basis of the evidence he cites however remain little more than speculation.

What he does establish beyond doubt is the predominance of the nuclear family household, a low level of economic activity of wives, that children typically went straight from their elementary family of origin to form their own nuclear family, and that this transition was normatively unstructured. His *interpretation* is that the whole system was associated with fear and anxiety. He is able to *show* that the occupational strata occupied by Union Park inhabitants were substantially recruited from lower strata, and that their sons frequently were in lower occupations than their fathers. In other words, status could not be maintained at the point at which it really matters, at the border of the respectable 'middle' class, and that the rewards of upward mobility could not be passed on by fathers to children. Marriage was delayed, therefore, until the son had proved his success in maintaining the occupational status of the family, and it was judgements about when it was *safe* (in occupational terms) to start a family that determined the departure of adult children from their natal home to establish a family of their own.

In an examination of intragenerational occupational mobility Sennett claims that members of small nuclear families had lower upward mobility rates over the period 1876–90 than did members of large nuclear families or composite households. The same conclusions held when geographical mobility was considered. Sennett interprets these results in the following way. The adults in nuclear families in Union Park were attempting to escape the uncertainty and confusion of urban life. They were concerned to obtain a secure job, and a house in a residential area to exclude the turbulent world outside. As a consequence their children grew up in a protected environment, isolated from the dynamic world in which they would have to live. Three factors prevented fathers from educating their children for entry into that world. First, the fathers regarded 'home' as the opposite of that world and sought to exclude it. Secondly, they were the only wage-earners in their families and, hence, no occasion for conversation about work ever arose. Thirdly, even if it had, the nuclear family father's work strategy was to secure the sort of job in which he was protected from competition and not required to show enterprise and in which he did not seek promotion. Hence, he would not be able to prepare his children to act effectively in a fluid and changing occupational milieu.

In contrast composite households frequently contained several persons engaged in paid work whose conversation would have brought the world of work into the home. In addition, composite household fathers were more upwardly mobile and would have both greater experience of and more positive attitudes towards the external society.

As a result the behaviour of the children of the two family types differed, composite household children being more inclined to change residence in search of work, more successful in moving upwards and emotionally more secure. Nuclear family children in contrast clung on to their parents until a secure job offered itself and made it possible for them to establish a family of their own on the same lines as their parents'.

Sennett wishes to claim that in its pure form the nuclear family is dysfunctional in industrial society, and that its extension is functional for the education and mobility of children. The closed nuclear family is a response to industrial society, but a pathological and maladaptive one. This analysis, while having the virtue of suggesting that major social change can generate a maladaptive response, does not consider that response from the standpoint of the social system. Indeed, the creation of a stratum whose members had the psychological character Sennett describes may have been highly functional for capitalism at a certain stage in its development.

Moreover, Sennett ignores the influence of kin outside the nuclear family's household. He needs to show that they were sufficiently distant to have no part in the upbringing of children if his claims about the dysfunctionality of the nuclear family are to be supported. Methodologically the work is unsatisfactory in that he provides no evidence about the psychological interior of such families and his claims on this account are no more than plausible conjectures.

There is little doubt that this study of Sennett's is badly flawed and merits the criticism which it has attracted. It is, however, a very important book, for two reasons. First, it questions the simple notion of fit between family form and societies with industrial systems of production. Secondly, it attempts to relate psychological interior, family form and mode of articulation in an interesting and original way, which emphasises the relative autonomy of both form and the process of personality formation occurring within it.

Underlying both the Chicago study and the *Uses of Disorder* is one of Sennett's central hypotheses. It is, at its simplest, that the growing complexity and uncertainty of social existence in the city resulted in a flight from the cosmopolitanism, richness and diversity traditionally associated with urban as opposed to rural life, and a search for a *simplification* of social experience born out of a desire for *order and stability*. This simplification is to be found in the nineteenth century in the creation of class homogeneous neighbourhoods like Union Park, and in the twentieth in the flight to suburbia. It is to be found equally in the preference for the simplest family form: the closed domestic nuclear family, and Sennett claims that one simplification supports the other: intense family life is easier to achieve in suburbia than in the city.

Intensity in family relationships and a planned built environment which segregates social groups are both, for Sennett, the result of an adolescent fear of disorder and they mutually reinforce one another. The individual identifies with his/her social attributes and seeks in interaction confirmation of that identity, and feels threatened when it is not forthcoming. This requires retreat into a socially homogeneous neighbourhood. As a result individuals do not achieve full personal autonomy, as they would have to were they unable to substitute social for personal identity. Family life is, therefore, characterised by the intense desire to eliminate differences between family members through minimising age and generational distinctions and seeking psychological closeness. Disorder in the family cannot be permitted, hence conflicts between members cannot be expressed. Children growing up in intense families of this kind fail to develop psychological autonomy and repeat the pattern of neighbourhood segregation and intense family life. Sennett pleads for a recognition of the uses of diversity and disorder in personal maturation and castigates the fear of disorder in much the same way as Fromm (1942) has castigated the fear of freedom.

This thesis is plausible as a psychosocial hypothesis but utterly lacking in cogency as a sociohistorical explanation. Sennett is simply postulating a 'fit' between suburbanisation and family nucleation, just as Parsons did between family and industrial society. However, to understand a relation is not to explain its occurrence. Sennett believes that there was once a time when (in Ariès's words) 'The movement of collective life carried along in a single torrent all ages and classes' (Ariès, 1962, p. 411). Exactly when is not clear, but it would appear to be in the nineteenth-century American city. The escape from the torrent began in neighbourhoods like Union Park in the 1880s and concluded with the suburbanisation of much of urban America after the Second World War. If Sennett is right, why did people start trying to escape? Why was the torrent of city life suddenly so intolerable? Is this a peculiarly urban American experience?

Sennett gives no answer to these questions, but if we wish to attempt to construct them, we must turn to his third work to be considered here, *The Hidden Injuries of Class* (Sennett and Cobb, 1972). This work based on participant observation and a series of depth-interviews in Boston in 1970 begins to approach, if in an oblique manner, the issue of stratification as a determinant of family experience which has a significant, if ghostly, presence in Sennett's other works. 'Class' here refers not to a theoretical abstraction, but to the social experience which a class society generates among those who occupy lower positions in the class hierarchy. What Sennett writes is a mixture of ethnography and descriptive psychology and does not deploy basic sociological concepts. It is impossible to summarise it briefly and remain true to Sennett's own interpretation. What follows is, therefore, a reconceptualisation in sociological terms of that interpretation. It is no substitute for reading an insightful and stimulating book.

The hidden injury of 'class' is, for Sennett, status deprivation in the strict sense of that term; that is to say, the absence of any recognised place, position, or standing in society at large. This exclusion derives partly from absence of autonomy at work, and partly from exclusion from the realm of middle-class (in the English sense) educated culture. For those experiencing their class position in this way, the home is their only area of autonomy; the socially homogeneous neighbourhood, their only refuge from psychologically painful cross-strata interaction.

Sennett wishes to claim that 'class' (that is, social hierarchy) produces hidden (that is, psychic) injury because social conflicts rooted in the unequal distribution of resources are internalised and occur within the worker. It is of the first importance to understand that Sennett is not psychologising 'class'. On the contrary, he wishes to claim that one of the mechanisms through which a class society in America is maintained and reproduced is through the displacement of conflicts between social groups by psychological conflicts within individuals. *He* is not psychologising class, but claiming that, in *American society*, class is psychologised. Nor is he psychologising culture. Rather, he wishes to claim that it is because a particular ideology (that is, mystification) of class relations is a dominant component of American culture that class conflicts are displaced by psychological ones.

Sennett's thesis would seem to run as follows. The inhabitants of American industrial cities derive from two sources: foreign immigration, and rural-urban migration. The first initially formed ethnic enclaves constituting little societies within which they retained a social status. The second carried an ideology of independence of social bonds as a criterion of identity and worth appropriate to an individualistic frontier society. This ideology could not be maintained in the urban industrial context in the face of the experience of social dependence on employers and the labour market. In consequence this ideology changed into one which emphasised individual success in competition with others as the criterion of self-worth, thus creating an elite who had achieved what Sennett calls 'the badges of ability', and a mass who hadn't, whose members as individuals felt a sense of personal failure. The catch in this ideology is that it identifies social inequality with feelings of self-worth and forces people to aquiesce to the former as the price of retaining the hope of achieving the latter. At the emotional level the mass are angry at the system of social inequality which degrades them; but they are ambivalent about their right to be angry, because they *feel* (that is, they have learnt to feel) that this subordinate position must be their own fault. As Eisenstadt noted (1956), peer-group formation is the basic way of accommodating status deprivation. As educational sociologists have demonstrated, the development of a counterculture is a way in which the mass can retain some dignity in the face of their adjudged failure in terms of the impersonal 'objective' standards of the elite. As a result workers not only feel angry and simultaneously ambivalent about that anger, they also experience a conflict of loyalties as between two opposed types of respect. To seek respect by social mobility is to betray one's peers; to retain peer respect is to forgo hierarchical respect in the society as a whole. This applies equally to geographical mobility and the family: to move is to reject one's peers; to refuse to move is to appear dependent in a society which values independence and mobility. This dilemma is particularly acute among parents from 'ethnic' neighbourhoods in the city, but the conflict between status in a group with a traditional culture, and the desire for respect accorded to those wearing the badges of ability in a competitive one, is only a special case of the conflict which all American workers experience, between lateral solidarity and vertical mobility. Sennett suggests that an important mechanism leading to the disintegration of traditional extended families of immigrant groups is that hierarchical (age) relations between adults in the family acquire an emotional significance learnt in the world of work. One of his informants commented that if you have to say 'yes sir, no sir' to your boss all day, you don't want to come home in the evening and 'yes sir' and 'no sir' your father. The once-acceptable hierarchy of age statuses in the family becomes unacceptable when it assimilated into the unacceptable, status-denying hierarchy based on the badges of achievement.

The opposition between lateral solidarity and vertical mobility, or between aspirations towards mobility and the failure to achieve it, can be overcome if there is a special identification on the part of a worker between himself and his children. In Sennett's terms the worker 'sacrifices' himself through long hours of work to provide a home for his family which is better than his natal home (thus earning self-respect in consumption which he has failed to obtain in production) and educational opportunities for his children which he never enjoyed. *He* may not be worthy of respect, but they will be, and he will be the one that made it possible. However, he never asks his wife or children whether they *want* him to make this sacrifice; rather, he uses the moral superiority which his sacrificial giving provides him to insist that they conduct themselves in the way he wishes. The effect of this stratagem is to shift the chief conflicts arising out of his class position on to his children and his wife. He avoids, but forces his children to face, the opposition between peer solidarity and upward mobility, while his wife is denied the freedom to negotiate a personally acceptable balance between the segments of her marital role. Both are forced to follow the path of the husband and sacrifice freedom as a means to self-respect. 'The tragedy of loving as sacrifice', says Sennett, 'is that those who are pushed to feel grateful cannot.

Sacrifice appears to the children as a way parents have of manipulating them, rather than really loving them'. Workers who sacrifice freedom for vicarious respect feel threatened not by the system of inequality which forces them to make that sacrifice, but by those who by their actions call into question the value of that sacrifice: rebellious students, welfare 'chisellers' and ethnic groups whose members still belong to an enclave within which they can obtain a respect not tied to the badges of ability respected by the society as a whole. The desperate search for respect which is the outcome of the hidden injuries of class issues in conflict and hostility not between classes, but within the disadvantaged strata themselves; between spouses and children and those who choose different paths of escape from common dilemmas.

In his last book, then, Sennett clearly locates the mechanism which produces the closed, intense nuclear family. It is a self-defeating search for self-respect, born out of status deprivation in a culture which makes each person feel individually responsible for what happens to them, and identifies self with the badges of achievement. Such a response can presumably be found in all class societies where the particular cultural conditions which he specifies prevail. Sennett is defining a type of family by specifying its psychological interior, but relating the incidence of such interiors to the family's class position and culture. He is certainly defining a process occurring within domestic groups which has a definite structure and produces individuals with a distinct type of emotional structure specified by relating emotion (anger, anxiety) to specific sociocultural items. Without prejudice to the correctness and applicability of this analysis, it represents one of the first attempts to define a family type in the way it has been suggested is necessary if the diversity of family types in industrial society is to be charted and understood.

It is not being suggested that Sennett's type is adequate either as a description of the psychological interior of families under capitalism or as an embodiment of the principles for constructing family types. In particular far more attention needs to be paid to the cultural and emotional significance of the two basic relations within the nuclear group: between spouses, and between parents and children. We shall return to the former relation in Chapter 10 but conclude the present chapter by considering parent–child relations more closely.

THE SIGNIFICANCE OF CHILDREN

Parent–child relations are in one sense a curiously neglected area of sociology and history. There is a vast literature on childrearing methods and practices on the one hand, and on the other an extended debate on the extended family which centres on relations between parents and adult children. The *sentiments* school of family history gives a prominent place to parental sentiments towards children.

There is a growing number of historical studies of childhood. However, these studies always proceed from a standpoint which takes for granted the inevitability of children. In Macintyre's words: 'sociologists have taken normal reproduction and the problems attached to it, for granted as part of the natural order' (1976, p. 151). In contrast she points out that we cannot 'assume *a priori* that people have babies because they are married, or marry in order to have babies; nor that people have babies because they have had sex, or that they have had sex in order to produce babies' (ibid., p. 102). It is easier not to make these assumptions at a time when the birth rate is declining and the number of childless couples increasing. However, in such a situation there is still a tendency to regard the absence of children as problematic and to seek to understand it as deviance from a natural pattern, rather than to regard the dominant pattern itself as problematic and explain departure from it in terms of the same mechanisms that produce it (see Veevers, 1980).

As a result the question 'why do people have children?' remains largely unanswered beyond the platitudes that intercourse has a tendency to result in conception, and that where the culture assumes that marriage and a family (that is, children) are normal events in the life course, the social pressures to marry and have children are intense. From a sociological point of view, however, the cultural meaning with which children are invested is highly variable as between sectors and strata of a given population and between populations; and the emotional meaning may be equally variable at the levels of both categories and individuals.

Where a family has both a title and a property to transmit through a system of primogeniture, the birth of the first male child will be conceptualised as the birth of an *heir*. In a traditional culture the birth of a new generation is a way of defeating time, of preserving a traditional mode of life handed down from the past. In both cases the social significance of the child predominates over its significance to the individual. In contrast the significance of a child to the (male) workers described in Sennett's (1972) study, is that it constitutes a continuation of its father and, hence, perpetuates his hope of moving up the hierarchy and achieving social respect. Equally a child may signify the personal immortality of the parent. An elementary taxonomy of the significance of children could be obtained by permutating the distinction between past and present, and between the collectivity and the individual. The polar meanings are continuing a past collective existence into the present, and continuing a present individual existence into the future. While it would be a mistake to suppose either polar type to be typical of any given historical period, the period since the eighteenth century in Europe and North America has certainly been associated with an increased emphasis on the future as opposed to the past, and the increased individualisation of social life. Clearly, Sennett's workers belong to the 'modern' rather than to the 'tradi-

tional' type. Such distinctions do not explain historic.
point of making them is to understand the differer.
attached to children in any society at a given point in

Children may be regarded also as the means whereby
the status of *parent*. The significance of this status vari
the genders, however. Paternity may symbolise publicl
identity of the father and maternity that of the mother. 1
mistake to suppose that this is necessarily of more significance for the
woman than for the man, since the importance attached to paternity
as a sign of virility in some cultures is immense. It does not follow that
the significance of parenthood is not different as between the sexes.
The most obvious difference is that maternity universally involves
gestation, parturition and lactation as well as conception, and in most
cultures, rearing as well. In consequence 'being a good mother' not
only involves more profound physical experiences and consumes a
great deal more time and effort than mere paternity (that is,
generation and economic support); it also has a social-moral element
absent from paternity. Hence, though culturally defined failure in
maternity may be felt no more severely than failure in paternity, the
damage it causes to the woman's gender identity will be far more
extensive than failure in paternity is to a man's.

If the culture defines maternity as natural to women, that is, an
expression of their natural being, to abstain from maternity will
appear not only unnatural, but also a sign of failure at the level of
interpersonal relationships. Hence, for a woman to have children may
be a cultural sign of her normality as *person*.

These considerations do not by themselves suggest a typology of the
cultural significance of parenthood, largely because the significance
we have specified is so general. What varies is, rather, the cultural
expectations which define what good (natural) parenting involves, and
this depends on the significance accorded to childhood. Once
childhood has come to be understood as a period of moral formation
of the individual; once it has come to be commonsensically accepted
that early intrafamilial experiences have a decisive effect on adult
character; when it comes to be believed that normal development
depends upon parental love, then the significance of parental care is
enormously extended.

In a society where people lack clearly defined statuses and roles, and
identity has to be negotiated and the respect and acceptance of others
achieved, for both men and women children acquire a significance as a
means to the creation of identity and the achievement of respect. A
typification of parent–child relations based on their significance as
determinants of parents' identities should, therefore, begin with a
typification of the meanings attached to childhood and maturation.
The key question is whether the social emotional development of the
child is thought to occur naturally, provided the parents care for it
physically and provide it with the security of belonging to a relatively

group, or whether it is thought to depend on a mixture of technical and moral qualities in the parent.

These cultural elements constitutive of family relationships will clearly have a considerable effect on its emotional structure. Where the emphasis is on the individual as opposed to the collectivity; on the future rather than on the present; where children are means to the secure identity of the parents and affection the means to the successful achievement of that end, parents' feelings towards children are likely to be extremely powerful and fraught with anxiety. The realisation of the parents' aims requires strict control over the child, but to attempt to achieve this by means of generating a disciplined submission to forms of behaviour will be regarded as impermissible, as it is repugnant to the cultural values of individualism. Hence, the parent must resort to emotional control, which is quite consistent with the cultural emphasis on love as a means to the production of normal adults, but self-defeating in that the children recognise its instrumental character and, as Sennett has pointed out, regard parental efforts for the children's welfare as merely a ploy in a power-game to control them.

The basic family 'situation' then becomes one in which the personal integrity of the parents can only be achieved by the sacrifice of the autonomy of the children, who are forced to reject their parents in order to escape emotional suffocation or remain forever emotionally dependent upon them. This contradiction may be regarded as the central contradiction of the process of individual reproduction in societies with cultures that stress self-determination and self-realisation as the touchstone of moral conduct, as opposed to cultures which emphasise external conformity to conventional forms. Social reproduction does not merely involve individual reproduction, however. It also involves the reproduction of social groups and categories, and in class societies the most important individual identity which is reproduced through children is a class identity. This involves two elements: the transmission to the children of the resources necessary to maintain the parents' position in the reward hierarchy and the property (if any) on which their position in the productive process depends; and the transmission of a 'class' culture, the ideology and that type of subjectivity associated with the class position of the parents. This is problematic and difficult unless the parent can segregate the child from the influences of other class cultures. The need for the parent to control the child further emphasises the importance of emotional control. Hence, it is not surprising that in a class society children have symbolised their rejection of parental domination by rejecting the cultural signs of class membership which have become so highly emotionally charged in the course of their upbringing. Such rejections have a profound emotional and personal as well as cultural or political significance. They are, however, characteristic of relatively privileged strata, where the parents have some social advantage to pass on to their children. Families in negatively privileged strata, in contrast, can pass on nothing but relative social disadvantage. For higher strata parents, children symbolise their positive class identity, which can be threatened by cultural and social contamination by lower strata. Lower-strata parents are faced with a spoiled identity (to use Goffman's phrase). Hence, non-mobile children will signify a continuation of a negative identity, but mobile children will, in one very real sense, cease to constitute a continuation of their parents' identity at all. If the status deprivation involved in the existence of class is accommodated by the development of a working-class counterculture, then the significance of children will approximate to that for parents from relatively privileged strata.

There is, however, another way of approaching the problem of the significance of children. So far, we have considered their significance in the 'bourgeois' family, that is to say, in a small, closed, domesticated nuclear family, and the way in which (in such a family) a particular type of culture generates a specific emotional structure. It is equally legitimate to regard the contemporary Western family as a proletarian family in as much as neither the family nor its members own or control the means of production. If we generalise the notion of the absence of productive function, it is possible to claim that capitalist societies are characterised by the absence of socially structured and sanctioned opportunities for self-expression through creative activities. Sennett has described public life as having degenerated into a set of empty forms which are only animated by the personalisation of public issues. From a Marxian standpoint, this is the inevitable result of the determination of public issues by economic forces, thus depriving all but the owners or controllers of capital of the power even to influence events. At the same time the capitalist mode of production necessarily entails that the majority of the population work under the direction and control of others, while the reliance on industrial means of production combined with bureaucratic control means that much work provides little or no creative outlet. Hence, the only social spheres where people can be creative are the domestic and the ideological. We can exercise our creative powers by interpreting the world differently (as long as we don't try to change it). We can make heavens and future utopias in our heads. The only thing we can create in reality is children.

The bourgeois family as characterised by Ariès and Stone is 'child-centred', and this child-centredness, though associated with the rising bourgeoisie, appears to predate the industrialisation process. However, it is not the child-centredness of the family that is at issue here. What is being suggested is not that the family in capitalist-industrial societies became child-centred, but that, with proletarianisation, the family becomes the only creative sphere left to the parents and consequently children came to take on an entirely new significance. They signify not the continuation of their parents' identities, but their parents' capacity for production. Production, however, involves control. If we try to understand the significance of children from the standpoint of the Marxian approach, therefore, we arrive at much the same position as before: an opposition between the self-realisation of the parents and the autonomy of the children.

The emotional correlates of this type of significance are once again an intense involvement of the parents with their children, and a fear of their loss, which is inevitable if the children are to become autonomous. Though this involvement may be transferred to younger children, the period of 'child production' is strictly limited. There are two ways in which these limitations can be overcome, given the present sexual division of labour. For the man, a form of serial monogamy may allow him to extend his productive period indefinitely. For the woman, a close association with her daughter(s) may permit her substantially to extend her involvement in the child-production process.

If the culture defines female gender in terms of childbearing and rearing, and social life is so structured as to militate against female participation in social spheres outside the family, then it will be women who are forced to identify their productive capacities most strongly with child production and who are most likely to attempt to retain some involvement in the process of child production through participation in rearing their daughters' children. This puts a different perspective on the importance of the mother–daughter tie, which might now be explained in the following manner. The cultural identification of female personhood with the reproductive function and rearing activities and the exclusion of women from other areas of social activity, results in the concentration of women's creative capabilities in the maternal role. To prevent the extinction of all creative outlet with the maturation of the children, the mother attempts to inculcate dependence rather than autonomy in the daughter, thus creating a need on the daughter's part for her mother's support when the daughter starts having her own children, thus ensuring a continuing child-production role for the mother. This strategy is possible because the absence of autonomy in the daughter can be masked, and the supply of the needs which she herself has created can be represented by the mother as a continuation of her maternal role of loving mother to her daughter. This is possible, in turn, because maternal help at crisis points in the developmental cycle of the daughter's household supplies a genuine need on the part of the daughter. The threat to autonomy posed by the mother is experienced not by the daughter, but by the daughter's husband, who sees the mother as supplanting his parental role and usurping his creative child-producing function.

Such behaviour on the part of mothers ought to be more frequent the fewer creative opportunities exist outside child production. It is reasonable to suppose the existence of such opportunities to be related to the stratification structure and, hence, for the incidence of intense mother–daughter relations and daughter's husband–daughter's mother conflict to be most frequent in working-class strata, which appears on the available evidence to be the case. Thus, the significance of that popularly well attested but academically largely ignored phenomenon, husband–mother rivalry in the working class, has to be understood in terms of the disabilities placed on women and the significance of children in capitalist societies.

This chapter began by suggesting that the contribution of historians to the study of the family had not enabled us to distinguish family types within capitalist-industrial societies, since the predominant type was nuclear, 'bourgeois' and 'proletarian'. It was argued that such a classification must proceed by distinguishing types of family interiors in terms of the psychosocial processes going on within them. These processes were seen to be determined by what was termed the 'emotional structure' of the family and resulted in the production of persons having a determinate character, understood as a typical emotional structure. Emotional structure was to be specified in terms of the emotional responses to cultural items.

Sennett's work, it is claimed, is an instance of this approach, and constitutes an attempt to specify the character of distinctively modern families. Sennett clearly sees such families as being the sites of distinctive psychosocial processes which result from the emotional structure of such families which is, in turn, determined by their mode of articulation. This involves not only the pattern of relations with others outside the family, but also their place in the system of stratification and the significance accorded to family relations and activities by the culture of the society in which they are set.

The last section of this chapter examined in more detail the significance of children in modern families. This involved an attempt to typify the cultural meaning of children in general, the meaning of children to parents via the cultural meaning attached to childhood, the variant meanings as between strata attaching to children when seen as the means of individual and social reproduction, and concluded with a sketch of a Marxian approach to the significance of children in societies where families are the only remaining sphere of autonomous productive-creative activity.

We have not, however, considered how family types may be distinguished in terms of types of marriage, nor have we investigated the possibility of constructing a Marxian approach to the family in capitalist societies. It is these issues that we shall explore in Chapter 10. For if our understanding of the family in industrial society has been immeasurably broadened and deepened by the work of historians, it has also been extended by sociologists working in the Marxist tradition. It is to their contribution that we now turn.

Section II:

Marxist Perspectives

The Household and Family under Capitalism

If Parsons has a very clear theory of the modern family but an inadequate theory of the nature of industrial society, the opposite is true of those who work in the Marxist tradition. Marxism provides us with an elaborate theory of capitalist society, but tells us very little about the family. This is partly because, as Gerstein has pointed out, Marx's analysis was focused entirely on capital, not on wage labour (1973, p. 108). It is also partly because Marx's work is still informed by that eighteenth-century understanding of 'private and public' in which the private was the sphere of natural affection and feeling. Marx was chiefly concerned to show that the basis of *public* life was economic rather than political, and that the anatomy of the new society was to be understood in terms of the opposition of capital and labour, and the conflict of interest between bourgeoisie and proletariat. This inevitably had the consequence that, the bourgeoisie apart, the family had no public/economic role. (See the discussion in Zaretsky, 1976, pp. 62–3; a useful discussion of Marx and Engels's attitudes to the family is Draper, 1970.)

Subsequently Marxists have stressed the opposition between family and economy and the functionality of the family for capitalism: it is a prime means of transmission of bourgeois ideology; its particularism militates against the class universalism of the proletariat; it dampens discontent in the economic sphere by providing workers with a psychological outlet denied them in the labour process. These functionalist platitudes in Marxist terminology do not amount to a theory of the family in capitalist society, and it is only recently that debate at the theoretical level has developed. This debate has very largely been inspired by the growth of the women's movement, and of Marxist-feminist approaches to the understanding of sexual divisions in society.

The problematics of feminism also have a familiar functionalist ring: Is 'women's oppression' or 'patriarchy' (that is, the control of both production and reproduction by males) universal and what is its role in capitalist society? (Compare: is the nuclear family universal and if so what is its role in industrial society?) These problematics provide the framework within which the debate is couched. There is also another and purely non-academic opposition involved between those who want to enlist women's support for proletarian struggles, and those who want to enlist proletarian support for women's struggles. There is also an opposition between those who claim primacy for the mode of production and those who claim primacy for patriarchy in the explanation of women's oppression. The main academic fallout from these debates is an analysis of the domestic group as an economic unit and of its relation to the process of production. We shall however postpone further discussion of this debate and turn, first, to even more fundamental matters. Leaving aside the question of the role of the family and the oppression of women under capitalism, the question which needs to be considered is: what would an historical-materialist analysis of the family look like?

The central tenet of historical materialism is that humans are material beings as well as conscious, idealising ones, and that, therefore, the most fundamental of all the relations in which they are placed is their relation to the natural world. This relation is not one of passive determination by nature, but an active one, that of *production*. Humankind actively produce the means of the reproduction of their material life, and they do so in association with one another. Hence, the most fundamental *social* relations are those concerned with material production. If this understanding were to be elaborated into a purely static structural analysis, which might be called structural (as opposed to historical) materialism, the resultant mode of analysis would be very close to that of structural functionalism. All other types of social relation would be seen as fitting one another through the necessity of their being consonant with the relations involved in material production. (Structural-functionalist analysis assumes, just as much as Marxist analyses, that 'the material' determinates in the last instance.)

The distinction between 'structural materialism' and historical materialism is twofold. In the first place, in historical materialism, the humankind–nature relation is not only one of production, it is also historically specific. This is so because, throughout its history, humankind is seen as constantly developing its capacity to produce, and in so doing transforming its relation to nature and its relations of production. Hence, historical materialism constitutes, as an object for study, not a static structure but a dynamic process. In consequence, though historical materialism is concerned with structure, these structures are seen as moments of a larger historical process.

Secondly, the structures that exist at any historical moment are understood as generating their own specific processes. This means that analyses can examine structure, process and the outcomes of process specified in terms of their effects on the maintenance of the structure. It is possible, then, to generate a set of statements specifying the relation between structure, process and outcome which describe contradictions as well as congruence between structural elements at the theoretical level without those statements themselves being contradictory and, therefore, unintelligible. It follows that we are not committed, when adopting an *historical*-materialist approach, to showing that capitalist social formations necessarily require a certain family form which serves to maintain the capitalist system of production. What is required is that we show the way in which the development of the capitalist mode of production affected *pre-existent* family forms, and investigate the outcome of such transformations in terms of their tendency to maintain or undermine the stability of the formation concerned. Indeed, it could be argued that an historical-materialist approach, because it emphasises the notions of contradiction and determination by historical conditions, provides more scope for empirical research than functionalism. Why, then, has the family been neglected by historical materialists?

The family is the site of the reproduction of human-beings. Economic production and human reproduction are the two activities without which any society cannot persist, and both activities are, each in its own way, equally fundamental. However, while in economic production the means of production are highly variable and have varied enormously, the means of biological reproduction appear, in contrast, as relatively fixed. The transformation of family life would appear to be always the resultant of the transformation of economic life, not because of any universal power of the latter to determine the former, but because of the absence of any dynamic process within the sphere of biological reproduction which could transform the *relations* of reproduction. The intrusion of technology into the sphere of reproduction is, of course, altering this situation and the possibilities inherent in artificial insemination and test-tube conceptions are immense. These new technological advances have not, however, actually been utilised on any scale. In consequence, with the sole exception of contraceptive techniques, technology has not revolutionised the means of biological reproduction. Variation in family form is in consequence seen to be a resultant of variation between formations in the mode of production and, within formations, of variation between reproductive groups in their relation to the productive process.

An alternative to focusing exclusively on reproduction is to focus on the reproductive *group*, and to consider the *material basis* of family relations. What is the 'real foundation' on which any family, understood as a form of social life, is based? There are obviously two sets of relations involved: those between children and parents, and between the spouses. Let us, first, consider parents and children.

The real foundation of the parent–child relation is the dependence of the infant on the mother for nurturance. The total dependence of the human infant is universal; so is the biological capability of the mother to provide nurturance. Let us assume she does. Then it is in relation to the mother that the infant first develops the capacity to make self–other distinctions, and that first social relation is simultaneously one of gratification and frustration. The satisfaction of the child's material needs is directly dependent upon the co-operation of an uncontrollable other. The other has a monopoly of the means of the reproduction of the child's material life. In consequence of this dependence the child necessarily experiences satisfaction, deprivation, anger and anxiety as those means are regularly or irregularly supplied or withheld, and these feelings will be associated uniquely with the person who rears it.

There will be only one other relation of equal intensity in the child's later life, the relationship with its sexual partner as an adult. Here again the other will have, in a monogamous relationship, a monopoly of the means of gratification of need, but in this case Ego will also have a monopoly of the gratification of the other's need. Both relations are dependent relations, but in the childhood relation dependence is asymmetrical, while in the adult relation dependence is symmetrical. The transition between the two is, in theory, between hierarchical dependence and functional interdependence; or in terms of nineteenth-century social thought, between differentiation by rank and differentiation by function.

The condition of the adult relationship constituting a truly sym-metrical relationship at the emotional level, will be the prior emancipation of the dependence of both parties on others, and their ability to act autonomously, that is, to utilise in interaction not only their need of the other, but also the other's need of them.

The emotional life of the individual may be seen, therefore, as rooted in relationships involving the monopoly of material resources by others, out of which monopoly arises the necessity of the co-operation and consent of others as a condition of individual action. However, the family (like history) must be seen as a process and a family structure (like a mode of production) will be characterised by its own distinctive processes. At the emotional level the family process may be seen to have two phases. The first phase involves learning by the infant to accept limitation on its desires and activities by others. The second involves learning on the part of the adult members to accept limitation on their desires and activities as the family's children move towards independence and autonomy. Clearly, elements of both phases are present throughout the cycle. The phases are distinguished by the relative weight placed on each.

There is nothing particularly new or original in this, but it is none the less of considerable importance. Such an approach regards the family as essentially the site of struggle and conflict between parents and children rooted in the material nature of its members, as opposed to the locus of the free play of 'natural affection'. It does not regard this conflict as pathological, any more than class conflict in capitalist social formations is seen by historical materialism as pathological.

Conflict is inevitable in and appropriate to both structures. Moreover, just as class conflict is a necessary moment in the process of humanity's realisation of its being, so is familial conflict a necessary moment in the full realisation of the emotional potentialities of both parents (qua parents) and children. It is this conflict which generates the emotional structure of the children and modifies that of the parents. Even more fundamentally it is this conflict which generates *emotion* as opposed to merely diffuse states of physiological arousal. It is a material process which generates both love and hatred, altruism and egoism, security and anxiety. The family is not based on natural affection; it is the natural locus of the generation of the whole range of human feeling.

Now, it may properly be objected at this point that the discussion thus far has assumed a particular family form, as indeed it has. In which case, what is universal about the process which has been sketched? What would appear to be universal is the opposition between rearers and reared, and what has been said about 'the family' which is universal in its application derives from its being a childrearing group. Any childrearing group will be characterised by the developmental process rooted in the conflict we have described and will generate the emotional structure of the individuals raised within it. This has the implication that an historical-materialist approach would ask of each society not only: what is its mode of production, but also: what is its mode of reproduction? Reproduction, like production, may be regarded as a universal, but as always embodied in a culturally and historically specific form. In industrial societies in comparison with other cultures, and epochs, the reproductive group is quite remarkably restricted in form. It may be said, therefore, that the *reproductive group* (rather than the kinship group) has shrunk to its nuclear core.

The concentration of child care within the nuclear family has been a constant theme in social comment on the family throughout the 1970s, beginning with Leach's attack in *A Runaway World* (1967) and continuing through the whole range of publications inspired by the women's movement, while in *The Two Worlds of Childhood* (1970) Bronfenbrenner has emphasised the isolation of both the family and the educational system. The significance of the restricted form of reproductive group in industrial societies is that the emotions generated by the childrearing process are concentrated among very few individuals. As a result the emotions it generates are not only intense, but the emotional domination of the junior by the senior generation is more total. Where the child is deprived by interaction with a member of the parental generation, there is only one other member of that generation with whom it can interact by way of compensation; that member may not be available, and where he or she is, the compensation will necessarily be significant in terms of the marital relation between the two parents. Bott's study of *Family and*

Social Network (1957) argued that relationships between spouses were more intensive when deprived of other sources of assistance external to the marital relation. The same is true of both parents and children in the absence of alternative external resources.

This has extraordinarily important consequences. In the first place, it means that the inevitable conflicts between rearer and reared may become conceptualised as generational conflicts, in the absence of any other solidary relations between children and the generation senior to them. In the second place, the *universally* necessary conflicts between rearers and reared will be intensified by the restricted nature of the group and compounded by other conflicts arising from its peculiar structure. Freudian psychoanalytic theory may be seen as concerned with just such a situation. Because it follows from the approach adopted here that conflict is essential to the rearing process, it does not follow that all conflicts characteristic of a particular mode of reproduction are necessarily universal; nor because conflict is a necessary precondition of the development of mature adults, that all conflicts within rearing groups necessarily have this effect. Indeed, what Sennett terms the *simplification* of family structure (see Chapter 9, p. 167) may constitute a complication of the rearing process which has precisely the opposite effect, that is, to militate against the production of autonomous adults.

An attempt to specify the real basis of family life is both of fundamental importance and, by itself, unable to take our analysis very far, since to say that it is a *basis* is to claim that it is the foundation of culturally and historically specific constructions which constitute the proper object of study. The specification of a mode of reproduction must involve a specification of the mode of production, of the relation of the two modes and the variation in this relation as between classes.

The analysis of the specific constructions erected on this base will involve a specification of the dominant ideology and its effect on the consciousness people have of the mode of reproduction in which they participate. Such an analysis will also require a specification of the mode of articulation of the group within which childrearing takes place. This will involve establishing both its place in the productive process and its relations with other groups and spheres of institutionalised activity.

The mode of articulation of childrearing groups will determine their form and structure and this, in turn, will affect the universal reproductive processes going on within them. In particular it will determine the means available to the parents to ensure their domination over the children, and enforce their control, other than the asymmetrical distribution of resources inherent in the rearer-reared relationship itself.

The capitalist mode of production involves, by definition, the concentration of capital and the existence of a class of people who can only produce by selling their labour power to those who own or control capital. Of itself such a specification says nothing about the mode of reproduction within capitalist social formations. It does not logically necessitate that the reproductive group be open or closed, large or small, or that it must have a particular sexual division of labour. Nor does it necessitate that members of such groups sell their labour power individually or collectively: only that they sell it. The family form which emerged from industrialisation is to be understood, rather, as the result of the interaction of the development of a capitalist mode of production with pre-existent family forms. The capitalist mode of production entails that the family cannot be the basic unit of economic production. The adoption of industrial means of production, involving standardised and repetitive work and bureaucratic control has militated against the employment of families as groups rather than as individuals. The family form was already restricted in size and composition prior to the transition to the capitalist mode of production and the adoption of industrial means of production. The question that requires answering is: why were women and children steadily excluded from the labour process during the nineteenth century, thus completing the 'closure' of the family and ensuring the spread of the bourgeois family type among the proletariat? Was this *necessitated* by the *capitalist* mode of production or is it an historically specific form of *patriarchal domination*, or some admixture of the two?

THE DOMESTIC LABOUR DEBATE

The response to these questions from those working in the tradition of historical materialism has been to emphasise that the domestic group under capitalism is not only the site of biological reproduction and of the production of subjectivities and ideologies, but the site of the reproduction of labour power, both daily and generationally. This is a vital move to make, since it strips away the cloak of ideological self-consciousness of the family as the opposite of the economic sphere. If there did not exist a 'non-economic' institution (the family) which reared the next generation of workers and provided services to workers on a daily basis thus enabling them to labour, then workers would necessarily have to buy in such services. In non-Marxist terms these costs would be added to the living costs of the worker and thus raise the wage floor, the level below which employers could not reduce wages. Hence, the existence of domestic labour lowers the minimum cost of labour to the advantage of capital.

This argument is basically extremely simple. It has two disadvantages. First, it is an essentially functionalist argument. If correct, it shows that the institution of domestic labour within the wider division of labour was functional for capital. But it does not explain why that happened or why it was that domestic labour was universally performed by women. Secondly, it poses certain difficulties for Marxist theory.

According to the assumptions of Marxist economics, the value of a commodity is determined by the labour time necessary for its production. Domestic labour contributes to the production of labour power and, hence, would seem to contribute to its value. But how much does it contribute to that value? Since domestic labour power is not sold and is not therefore a commodity, we cannot compare it directly with the labour power to whose production it contributes. There are two ways out of this difficulty. One, adopted by Seccombe (1974), is to regard the value of domestic labour as equivalent to its production costs. The alternative is to suppose that the value which domestic labour contributes to the value of labour power is given by the hours of domestic labour involved as compared with the hours of wage labour required to purchase the consumption goods necessary for the reproduction of the wage labourer's labour power (Harrison, 1973). This, however, could only be consistent with the view that domestic labour lowers wage costs if it is accepted that labour power can, as a result, be exchanged below its value.

These issues depend for their resolution on that of wider problems in Marxist theory and on our understanding of the relation between what goes on in the household and what goes on in the factory. What sort of labour is domestic labour? Is it necessary, useful, or productive, or all three? Is it part of the capitalist mode of production, a vestige of an earlier mode, or is it what has been termed a 'client' mode? The answers to these questions not only bear on the answers to questions about the value of domestic labour; they also raise fundamental questions about the exact meaning and application of the different categories of labour and the usage of the term 'mode of production' itself.

A further set of issues is also involved, and these concern the productivity of domestic labour as opposed to wage labour generally and wage labour producing consumption goods, since the ratios of these rates of productivity will determine the willingness of domestic labourers to abandon domestic for wage labour and the preference of capital for extracting surplus value from erstwhile domestic labourers, as opposed to accepting wage labour which is subsidised by domestic work.

Because there are so many issues, because they interlock and because their significance is not confined to the substantive question of the relation between domestic labour and the capitalist mode of production – but involves questions of interpretation of the Marxian corpus itself – the debate has been extraordinarily complex. It has been further complicated by the 'addition' of the distinctive feminist problematic, which concerns the identification of domestic labour with women, an identification which predates the development of the capitalist mode. Moreover, some writers have had primarily theoretical aims, while others have used theoretical categories to analyse concrete historical developments. This has led to a confusion between on the one hand the historical explanation of contingent features of hierarchical gender relations and/or capitalist social formations, and on the other the attempt to show that certain features of either phenomenon are necessary in the sense of being theoretically derivable.

A further difficulty attaches to presenting this debate here, since the purpose of this chapter is not to elucidate the finer points of Marxist theory, nor to account for the existence of patriarchal domination, but to explore the yield of the debate in terms of its clarification of the relation between character of family life and capitalist social formations. What follows does not, therefore, constitute an adequate account of the debate from the standpoint of the protagonists, but is rather the result of an abstraction from the debate for the purposes of the present chapter. It is written on the premiss that a goodly proportion of readers of books on the family will be moderately ignorant of even the rudiments of Marxist economics.

Domestic Labour and Value

One of the few consensuses that seem to have emerged from the debate is that domestic labour does not produce *labour power*. What it produces are *use-values* which are consumed within the household. It transforms commodities purchased out of wages received by the household into consumable form and provides services to other household members. The effect of the consumption it makes possible is the reproduction of labour power both daily and generationally, and the reproduction of the household to which the wage labourer belongs. The family, therefore, is located between two markets: the market for labour which it supplies, and the market for consumer goods ('wage goods') which it consumes. Hence, domestic labour mediates these two markets and brings them into relation. However, whereas household members sell labour power to capital, engage in social labour and consume wage goods produced by social labour, labour within the household is private labour. As Seccombe puts it: '[domestic labour] contributes directly to the creation of the commodity labour power while having no *direct* relation with capital. It is this special *duality* which defines the character of domestic labour under capitalism' (1974, p. 9; first emphasis added). It is exactly the duality that creates problems for further analysis.

Seccombe attempts to determine the value contributed to labour power by domestic labour by means of an analogy with personal service workers the value of whose products is, according to Marx, determined by the production costs involved in maintaining or producing them (ibid., p. 10). Seccombe is almost certainly wrong. The problem to be faced is what proportion does domestic labour (a non-commoditised labour) contribute to the value of the commodity 'labour power'. This problematic is not analogous to that of domestic service, which is: what determines the value of the commoditised labour power of domestic servants. Domestic labour is not sold, and domestic services do not necessarily contribute to the production of a commodity.

Seccombe uses the analogy with personal service because he wants to insist that domestic labour is not 'productive' labour. Unlike wage labour, it does not create value. The value it contributes to that of labour power must, therefore, be equivalent to its costs. The assertion that domestic labour is not productive, not value-creating, *when combined with the insistence that the value it contributes equals its costs*, leads to bizarre conclusions.

In a second article responding to critics of his first, Seccombe claims that the value of domestic labour is independent of the length of time worked: 'average domestic labour time will be that labour time necessary to convert the average wage into the average proletarian household at the average price of wage goods' (1975, p. 89). It follows that, if average wages fall, there is 'a hidden intensification of (domestic) labour'. However, irrespective of how hard domestic labourers work, the value they produce is always equal to the cost of their subsistence.

Now, clearly domestic labour is a silly occupation to be in if there is no relation between value and effort, and sensible domestic labourers should abandon their occupation and become wage labourers. Yet domestic labour persists. This is an absurd conclusion.

Let us turn, therefore, to Harrison's (1973) attempt to compute the value of domestic labour. Harrison assumes in an example that the productivity of domestic and wage labour is equal, that the wage labourer receives a wage equivalent to the value produced in five hours' wage labour time, that the domestic labourer works for ten hours and that the use-values produced by the domestic labourer plus the consumption goods purchased by the wage are together sufficient to reproduce the labour power of both labourers. The 'disposable income' of the household is, therefore, equal to the value produced in fifteen hours' labour. He then assumes that this 'income' is consumed equally by the two labourers, that is, each consumes seven and a half hours. The value of the wage labourer's labour power is, therefore, seven and a half hours but the wage is only equivalent to five hours. It follows that the wage labourer is exchanging his labour below its value, and that the employer is paying only for the *consumption goods* necessary for the reproduction of labour power but not for the equally necessary domestic labour. The domestic labourer is receiving two and a half hours-worth of value produced in the capitalist sector, but supplying to the wage labourer five hours-worth of domestic labour. This reduces the size of the necessary wage which capital has to pay the wage labourer by the difference (two and a half hours), and once this reduction has taken place, that value has been transferred from the household to the capitalist sector.

If we define surplus domestic labour (not value) as the difference in labour time between that time necessary for the daily reproduction of the domestic labourer and the time actually worked, then we may say that the domestic labourer (in the example) does five hours' surplus *domestic* labour. The domestic labourer exchanges two and a half hours of this for consumption equal to half the household's wage. The net surplus labour of the domestic worker is therefore $(5 - 2\frac{1}{2} =)$ $2\frac{1}{2}$ hours, which is transferred via the wage labourer to capital. The profits of capital are, therefore, equal to the value of the surplus labour (surplus value) extracted from the wage labourer plus the value of the surplus labour extracted from the domestic labourer.

This constitutes a modification of Marxian theory. Labour remains the source of value and surplus *labour* the source of profit. However, profit is no longer seen as being determined solely by surplus *value* (the value of surplus labour extracted by capital from wage labour); it is determined also by the value of *surplus domestic labour*. It follows that labour exchanges below the true cost of its reproduction (value).

It is, however, only possible to add the duration of the two types of labour (domestic and wage) on the assumption of equal productivity. Once this unrealistic assumption is relaxed, it becomes apparent that the extent to which capital benefits from domestic labour depends on this ratio. If the productivity of wage labour is twice that of domestic labour, then the market value of domestic labour must be reduced by half. In consequence the wage labourer's reproduction will consume not $(2\frac{1}{2} + 5 =)$ $7\frac{1}{2}$ hours, but $(2\frac{1}{2} + 5/2 =)$ 5 hours-worth of marketable labour, and wage labour will exchange *at its value*. If domestic labour productivity is only a quarter of that of wage labour, then the value of the wage labourer's consumption will fall to $3\frac{3}{4}$ hours and labour will exchange *above its value*.

This seems to imply that it is not correct to suppose that wages (the price of labour) will fluctuate about the value of labour. They will rather fluctuate about the value of the bundle of consumable *commodities* whose consumption is necessary for the reproduction of the wage labourer and the wage labourer's household (wage goods). However, the mechanisms determining the long-run level of wages cannot take account of the variation of domestic labour imputs and their productivity. This implies that the constitutive concepts of *Marxist theory* do enable us to grasp the relation between domestic labour and capitalist production, but the *mechanisms of capitalist production* take no account of it and, hence, there are no propositions within Marx's theory of the capitalist mode of production (CMP) which refer to it. It is possible to construct a Marxian analysis of wage labour which incorporates domestic labour, but Marx omits it from his analysis of *Capital*, because, from the standpoint of capital, it may be regarded as one of the historical conditions determining the level of subsistence. As Lebowitz, in a penetrating comment on Harrison's paper has put it (Lebowitz, 1976): 'the rate of surplus value ... from the perspective of capital ... is the appropriate measure and is the relevant link to the rate of profit – because it is only concerned with what the capitalist must pay for.' He suggests that the rate of exploitation (E') be defined as the ratio of surplus to necessary labour. It will then follow that E' is only equivalent to the rate of surplus value where the *only* necessary labour performed is wage labour. Wage labour is a form of social labour. The category 'non-wage labour' may be termed 'private labour'. *Necessary* private labour is universal and capital certainly depends on it for its existence. But so would any mode of social production. With regard to private labour in its domestic form, Harrison demonstrates that what the relative benefits of domestic labour are to capital and labour will depend on specific circumstances.

If we now consider the matter from the viewpoint of the household, it follows from both Seccombe's and Harrison's analyses that its standard of living will depend not on wage labour alone, but also on the quantity and productivity of the domestic labour to be found within it. Hence, the only way in which that standard of living can be maintained in the face of falling real wage income or increased in the face of constant real wage income is by increasing the input of domestic labour. In so far as domestic labour inputs are variable and independent of the cost of their reproduction, the existence of the domestic form of private labour is functional for *households* in evening out variation in wage income and, hence, may contribute to the political stability of the social formation to which they belong.

We may conclude this section of the argument, therefore, by stating that domestic labour may be regarded as producing value, but the value it produces does not appear in the form of a price for a commodity and does not become abstract labour, since domestic labour is not a commodity. Domestic labour is functional for (that is, tends to maintain) social formations with capitalist modes of production, but it does not necessarily increase the rate of profit on capital. Domestic labour is an integral part of capitalist *social formations*, but it is not part of the capitalist mode of production as such, but an historical and moral condition of that mode of production.

Is domestic labour part of a 'client' mode of production? Harrison claims that it is, and Lebowitz that it is not. Harrison wishes to suggest that domestic labour stands to wage labour as forced labour in the colonial periphery stands to wage labour in metropolitan capitalist countries, where the surplus labour extracted from the periphery is used to pay higher wages to wage labour than would otherwise be possible, thus creating a politically compliant aristocracy of labour. This analogy of Harrison's is interesting and suggestive, but it does not depend upon the periphery having a different mode of production, as Harrison recognises. Harrison also recognises that the housework mode of production cannot reproduce itself: it is dependent on wage inputs from the capitalist mode of production. What it produces does not of itself provide all the necessary inputs for the next production period. But if this is correct, such a way of producing cannot be a mode of production in the Marxian sense, since it could not provide the foundation or basis of a distinct type of social formation.

Harrison insists that housework is a mode of production for excellent reasons, however, since he insists on the centrality of 'relations of production' to the notion of 'mode of production'. The social relations associated with housework are quite different from those of the CMP (he claims) and close to those associated with petty commodity production. Harrison's approach shows itself to be flawed, however, when he attempts to specify those relations. According to him, the houseworker does not work under authority, and is not separated from the means of production. These attributes are not, however, derivable from any *theoretical* specification of the nature of housework. If one is predisposed to question their truth, one must proceed by means of social inquiry and not theoretical argument.

Housework does not specify a mode of production because it is impossible to derive from that concept the relations which empirically characterise its performance. Rather, it is the case that the relations associated with that activity define housework as we understand it. *Empirically* domestic production is an activity which is symbiotic with capitalist production, outside the capitalist mode of production, and therefore a 'client' of it. *Theoretically*, however, it is merely a contingent historical condition of the operation of the CMP.

If we analyse the CMP from the standpoint of wage labour instead of capital, we are suddenly made aware of the vital importance of private labour (to use Lebowitz's term), of which housework is a specific form. While private labour is a necessary condition of social labour, there is nothing necessary about the forms it takes.

There is a profound sense in which Harrison's attempt to get at the essence of housework is as unsatisfactory as Seccombe's. If we pursue his analogy with colonialism, we are forced to ask: how (in the case of housework) is surplus labour extracted from the domestic labourer/houseworker? On this point Harrison has nothing to say whatever. For by conceptualising houseworkers as workers within a different mode of production, the *relation* between houseworkers and wageworkers is left untheorised. It is also left obscure precisely because it is not a market relation based on the exchange of commodities. The central question which is mysteriously left unasked (in all these accounts) is: what is the nature of the wage labourer–domestic labourer relation? An answer is clearly implied, however. If surplus labour is extracted from houseworkers by the wage labourers whose households they inhabit, the relation must be one of domination. The question must then be asked: what is the material basis of such domination in capitalist social formations? This question cannot be posed if it is claimed that housework constitutes a distinct mode of production.

Do Domestic Labourers Constitute a Reserve Army of Labour?

There would appear to be universal agreement that domestic workers do constitute a 'reserve army' *within* the household and that their function is to maintain the standard of household consumption in the face of varying real wages. This point has already been discussed. Of concern here is whether they constitute a reserve army in the classical sense. That is, does the institution of domestic labour serve to ensure the maintenance of a reserve of unwaged labourers who can be prevailed upon to sell their labour in times of high demand by capital for labour, and have their employment withdrawn without political and economic cost to capital when demand for labour is low?

There would appear to be some agreement that this is the case. Increasing participation of domestic workers in wage labour is understood by Seccombe to be the result of (1) increased productivity in domestic production; (2) increased productivity in the wage–goods sector *relative* to the domestic sector. The first gives houseworkers the time to engage in wage labour, and the second makes it advantageous for them to do so because the value of the goods bought with the wage is greater than the value which houseworkers can produce by their own labour in housework. Variation in economic activity rates of domestic workers is not to be understood in terms of the demand side of the labour market alone. The demand of capital for labour will only secure a supply if the conditions of domestic production make it possible and worthwhile for domestic workers to trade housework for wage labour. It follows that the answer to the question: 'is domestic labour functional for capital by providing a reserve army?' must be 'it depends'. It depends on domestic production itself which, though dependent on the CMP, is not part of it.

A similar conclusion is reached by Harrison. He asks whether the movement of a domestic labourer into wage labour is of benefit to capital, and concludes after analysis involving labour–time calculations that it depends on the effect of the shift upon the value of labour power. He claims that capital gains from the employment of domestic labourers if the value of labour power remains constant and the hours worked in the domestic sector are reduced by an amount less than the hours worked in the capitalist sector. Once again, capital does not *necessarily* benefit. Whether it does or not depends on what Harrison terms 'the composition of the means of subsistence', that is, the proportions of the value of subsistence contributed by housework and wage labour respectively.

Seccombe, therefore, attempts to explain what determines whether domestic labour comes on the labour market and Harrison what determines whether capital benefits. What Harrison never tells us is what determines 'the composition of the means of subsistence'. All the Marxist contributors to the debate assume that there are two sorts of labourer, domestic and wage, and that though domestic labourers sometime engage in wage labour, wage labourers never engage in domestic labour. It would appear that the analyses offered contain an assumption which is not made explicit, which is not derivable from the theoretical categories they employ.

This consideration takes us to the heart of the matter. Marxian theory constitutes as its object the capitalist mode of production and presupposes that an understanding of a mode of production is a pre-requisite of understanding the complex of social relations, ideologies and practices which have formed around that mode of production in any specific historical case. Marxian theory is not, in other words, a theory of capitalist *social formations* however indispensable it may be to their analysis. To put the matter another way: Marxian social thought furnishes us with a theory of the capitalist mode of production; it does not supply a sociology of capitalism. From a Marxian standpoint a social formation is a mode of production together with its historical conditions. These conditions may be intelligible from the standpoint of the theory, but they are not derivable from it. Rather, it is the case that the *operation* of a mode of production is derivable (in principle) from the statements of the theory and statements about contingent conditions.

In consequence, while we are able to apprehend household activities as involving the daily and generational reproduction of labour power, we cannot explain those activities in terms of their effects on the operation of social production in the CMP. This is to slip into a teleological and functionalist mode of explanation which involves trying to explain the *explanans* in terms of the *explanandum*. The same considerations apply to the analogies of the movement of house-workers into waged work. When this movement (and its reverse) occurs, it warrants our describing houseworkers as constituting a part of the reserve army of labour. However, so to describe the pheno-menon does not explain it; it merely reconceptualises an event in such a way as to make it intelligible as a condition of the operation of a theoretically defined system. This is not to deny that historically social production in the CMP has affected domestic work and the participa-tion of domestic labour in the labour market. Such effects can be investigated and described. To explain them, what is required is a theory of the household which enables us to theorise aspects of the operation of production in the CMP as conditions.

This basic methodological point is the substance of Anthias's (1980) excellent critique of an extremely valuable contribution by Beechey (1977), in which she accuses Beechey of making assumptions about the family in order to draw theoretical conclusions about the participation of women in wage labour. Anthias claims that conclusions, derived from the Marxist theory of the CMP, about *women* qua women are impossible because 'women' is not a term within the theory of the CMP. Anthias quotes with approval Hartman's (1979) remark that 'Marxist economic categories, like capital itself, are "sex blind"'. The truth of this observation has been shown in this chapter by writing the discussion of domestic labour without any reference to gender. Such reference is entirely unnecessary in order to discuss the relation between domestic and capitalist production, when that discussion assumes as a condition of the operation of production in the CMP that domestic production exists, and that there are two types of worker (wage and domestic). But it has thrown no light at all on the question of why there are two types of worker, and why the domestic worker is female. Nor could it possibly do so. It only throws light on the condition of women if we assume that domestic workers are female, as most contributors do. But from the feminist standpoint, and that of a family sociologist, that is precisely what is to be explained.

Beechey (1977) argues that the employment of *women* is advantageous to capital for two chief reasons. First, it lowers the value of labour generally and hence increases the rate of surplus value. This is so because the capitalist was already paying for the subsistence of married women through the wages of their husbands. If wives work more labour is performed per household, but subsistence costs remain the same hence the difference between value created in the labour process by household members and the cost of their subsistence (reproduction) is greater. Secondly, and alternatively, if we assume that the subsistence of the wife is already paid for through the husband's wage, then it is only necessary to pay the wife a wage which covers the extra costs of her going out to work. Hence, *the capitalist who employs a wife* can pay her less than the value of her labour power. By the same token, however, her labour can easily be disposed of when no longer required. Not only is the married woman not dependent on her wage for her subsistence, neither (in the absence of that wage) does she become a charge on the state, 'which refuses to recognise married women as individuals in their own right (e.g. denying them social security benefits if married or cohabiting)' (ibid., p. 57). She constitutes for capital, therefore, a 'preferred source of the industrial reserve army'.

Beechey then attempts to connect the category 'married women' with the categories of the theory of the CMP by pointing out that to retain married women in the home makes it possible for male labour power to be exchanged below its value which is advantageous for capital, but is inconsistent with the exploitation of women as a source of cheap and easily disposable wage labour. Except for the 'easily disposable' aspect, this adds nothing to the Seccombe–Harrison–Lebowitz discussion and involves a confusion. The maintenance of the family and of women's place within it is a precondition of women being a preferred source of the reserve army of labour. This is only a contradiction synchronically. It can be temporally mediated by the flow of housewives in and out of employment. The employment of women in wage labour *may*, but does not *necessarily*, conflict with the definition of the married woman as primarily a mother and house-wife. In this regard it is particularly important to recognise, as contri-butors to the domestic labour debate rarely have, the variation in domestic activity over the family cycle. Employment of married women after the children have left home need not militate against the performance of the roles of mother or housewife.

More important is the attempt which Beechey (1977) makes to relate female employment to the class struggle and, hence, to begin to answer the question posed above: why were women (and children) steadily excluded from the labour process during the nineteenth century? Her argument basically is that capital favoured the employ-ment of women and children in unskilled jobs in industry because skilled male operatives attempted to resist the process of deskilling involved in the introduction of machinery. In consequence the resistance of males to deskilling became a resistance to the employ-ment of women and children. As a result the ideological attempt to impose bourgeois family forms on the proletariat met with support from male workers seeking to preserve their jobs. To extend Beechey's argument: resistance to deskilling led to the introduction of women; this threatened male jobs; the threat of the loss of male jobs led to the acceptance of deskilling as the price of continued employment and female employment became acceptable to male workers only when it was in unskilled occupations and during periods of high labour demand. They could be employed so long as they didn't threaten regular skilled jobs. This led to the concentration of women in unskilled and unstable employment, to their becoming a reserve army of labour.

There is almost certainly some truth in Beechey's hypothesis. However, as an historical explanation sketch of the concentration of women in the secondary sector of the labour market, it only works if one begins with an initial situation in which men are in skilled employment and women out of employment and without skills. But that is precisely what needs to be explained. If we define our initial situation as that of the protoindustrial family producing through a domestic form of production, then there is no reason to suppose that either spouse is more or less skilled in the technology used, while with regard to new industrial technologies both spouses would have been equally unskilled. What requires explanation is the movement from this initial situation to the one chosen by Beechey. The transition from one to the other cannot be explained simply in terms of the establish-ment of the CMP and the adoption of industrial means of production, since initially capital preferred the employment of women and children. Beechey clearly believes this preference was due to the fact that they were partially supported by men working in the domestic economy. But in that case the same advantages would be obtained by employing men partially supported by women working in the domestic economy. Once again, the explanation proferred pre-supposes an historical condition.

Beechey has, however, also discussed this topic in an admirable article which was written earlier than her 1977 contribution (Beechey, 1978) and which is ignored by Anthias. There she makes it perfectly clear that she does presuppose the sexual division of labour and the subordination of women within a patriarchal family form as his-torical conditions of the operation of the CMP and that her project is not to attempt to derive them from an analysis of the CMP. Indeed, she criticises Barron and Norris (Barron and Norris, 1976) for attempting to locate their explanation of the concentration of women in the secondary sector of the labour market 'solely within the internal dynamics of the labour market' (Beechey, 1978, p. 180). What is required, Beechey goes on to claim, is 'a theory which links the organi-sation of the labour process to the sexual division of labour' (ibid., p. 180). At the same time, however, she insists 'that both Marx and Engels constitute the form of the labour process and also the form of the family as matters for historical investigation' (ibid., p. 184). She then attempts to show how 'Marx's analysis of the labour process . . . and his theory of the industrial reserve army can be used to *analyse* female wage labour in the CMP' (emphasis added), but concludes 'that the sexual division of labour and the family . . . must be assumed if the specificity of the position of female wage labour in the CMP is to be understood'. The main thrust of her argument is to 'emphasise the necessity of integrating an analysis of the sexual division of labour . . . into an analysis of the capitalist labour process'. She then proceeds to sketch how this might be done.

The development of the factory system of production, she claims, brought into being a new form of family whose functions were the reproduction of labour power and consumption. Generational re-production includes biological reproduction, sexual regulation and socialisation; daily reproduction involves domestic labour. The family is also the agency of the reproduction of class and gender relations, that is, the transmission of property and the inculcation of patriarchal ideology (Kuhn, 1978) on both a daily and a generational basis. As a unit of consumption it is essential to the process of commodity circulation.

This is a functional (as opposed to a functionalist) description of the family deploying categories derivable from the Marxist theory of the CMP rather than categories of functionalist theories of 'society'. This description permits us to understand the family as a condition of the CMP, but it does not enable us to understand the CMP, nor particular forms of the labour process and/or labour market structuration as conditions of the family. Such a description does, of course, specify the material basis of the family in capitalist social formations. But it is not the case (as Beechey claims) that the sexual division of labour is thereby ascribed a material basis.

Beechey's position has been discussed at some length because her contributions have certain qualities which are likely to make them 'seminal'. The confusions which surround them can be simply resolved if we assume that not only is Beechey not trying to explain the sexual division of labour *in terms of its functionality for the CMP*, she is not trying to provide a *theoretical explanation* of anything. Her demand for theory is simply a demand for a systematic set of analytic categories which can be used in the empirical study of different aspects of women's subordination. There is nothing wrong with this objective. However, if we wish to attempt to explain the forms of social life which have grown up upon the material basis which she specifies, then the type of explanation which we seek must be historical in character.

CONCLUSION

It would be a gross mistake to characterise the domestic labour debate as a debate between Marxists and feminists. What is at issue is the limits of two types of explanation: that provided by an economic theory, and that provided by historical analysis. Explanation of concrete phenomena requires both the utilisation of theoretical abstraction and empirical analysis. The complexities of the concrete cannot be derived from theory alone. Hence, feminists have been absolutely right to deny the possibility of explaining the oppression of women on the basis of the theory of the CMP. Not that there is anything special about their explanandum. Such attempts involve a methodological mistake. Marxist contributions have, it may be argued, made another mistake. Marxism is not to be identified with its scientific theory. Because most Marxists now reject the view that Marxism is a science of history, it does not follow that it must be either scientific or historical; or that as a science, it cannot be historical. If it is to be a guide to praxis, Marxist theory must be applied to historically and culturally concrete situations. In its application theory provides the categories for empirical analysis; it does not function to explain the phenomena studied in their entirety and without remainder. The historical analysis of the changing position of women is as important a corrective to analysis based solely on Marxist economic theory as it is to sociological analyses based solely on functionalist theory, and for much the same reason.

The upshot of all this is that while Marxist theory can provide us with categories essential to the analysis of the empirical relation subsisting between the family and the fundamental structure of capitalist social formations (the CMP); while historical materialism allows us to specify the material basis of any reproductive group, it does not furnish us with the necessary elements for the construction of a theory of the family, or of women's subordination. The sterile attempt to derive the contemporary family from the CMP tells us less about the content of family forms in capitalist social formations than non-Marxist works like Sennett's *Hidden Injuries of Class*. As a result of the domestic-labour debate we understand rather better the relation of the family to the labour process, but are little enlightened as to the way in which capitalism determines the form or content of family life.

There are two ways in which, from an historical-materialist standpoint, the understanding of the family can be further developed. The first is by increasing our historical knowledge of the process whereby the industrialisation process, and the transition to capitalism as the dominant mode of production, interacted with a variety of pre-existent family forms to produce the exclusion of women and children from wage labour and the predominance of the closed, domesticated nuclear family. The second is by focusing on the interaction between that process and transition, and the pre-existent sexual division of labour.

Pursuit of the second option leads quickly to the realisation that we don't know nearly enough about the variety of preindustrial forms of the sexual division of labour among the majority of the population, particularly the division of labour within the family. Pursuit of the first option leads equally swiftly to the conclusion that our understanding of the transformation of the family requires an examination of the changes in marital relationships – whose understanding depends, in part, on the changing activities of men and women outside the family and the resultant transformation of gender conceptions and definitions general throughout the society. Both options need, therefore, to be pursued simultaneously.

In order to understand the content of family forms in terms of changes in the articulation of those forms with other social spheres, the 'articulation' of different categories (husbands, wives and children) must be considered separately. Yet while the exclusion of women from the public sphere does not cause, but logically entails, their confinement in the domestic sphere, this confinement has consequences for the behaviour of males in the domestic sphere which, in turn, affects their behaviour in the public sphere. We are dealing, in other words, with a complex, interactional, developmental process. Understanding this process requires, as the domestic-labour debate has emphasised, that we consider the family not merely as a childrearing group, but also as a household. In opposition to the assumptions of that debate, however, the entity whose persistence we need to focus on is not the productive system, but the household. If we cease to be mesmerised by the CMP, and are willing to abandon theorisation at a high level of abstraction and focus instead upon human responses to the state of affairs created by the arrival of the

CMP, it is even possible to render intelligible the connection between women's subordination and the capitalist mode of production.

The exclusion of the woman from the labour process (where it occurred) constituted a state of affairs which, combined with long hours and near-subsistence wages, necessitated the adoption of a highly segregated pattern of marital behaviour as a household survival strategy. The (male) worker's life was structured by the demands made upon him by his employer: the household's survival depended on his fulfilling those demands. This, in turn, necessitated a domestic organisation designed to fulfil his needs. Just as the activity of the worker reflected the needs of capital, so the activity of the (female) houseworker reflected the needs of the (male) wage labourer. Each pair involves a relation between a determining and determined member, and that relation is by definition hierarchical. The combination of the loss of autonomy by the worker (the transition to the CMP) with the exclusion of women from the labour process resulted in the necessary subordination of the woman within the household. In other words, the domestic subordination of women must be understood *not in terms of its functionality for capital, but for the woman's household*. This subordination is then reinforced by the women's consequent economic dependence on the wage of the husband, transfer of part of which to her appears in the form of payment for services rendered.

The transformation involved in the shift from an economy in which the household is a unit of production to one in which the household is linked to the productive process only through the wage labour of the male, is the transformation of the household from a group whose basis is co-operative activity, to one whose basis is an exchange based on inequality, mediated by monetary payment. Unequal exchange mediated by monetary payment is exactly the basis of production under capitalism. The social relations characteristic of the capitalist mode of production are thus reproduced within social institutions not part of that mode of production but which, being linked to it, are thereby 'determined' or in modern parlance 'conditioned' by it. This is the sense in which the family under capitalism, though excluded from the CMP is a 'capitalist' family form.

The original material basis of the inferior status of women within the family lies, therefore, in the *de facto* exclusion of women from the labour process and the incorporation of men into that process as wage labourers. Their subordinate status is then reinforced by proletarian culture which arises on this basis and reflects that subordination. However, that culture is not a simple reflection of the experience of proletarian family life, but is conditioned synchronically by the ideological hegemony of the bourgeoisie, which is itself historically conditioned by pre-existent cultural definitions of gender.

The subordination of women within the family under capitalism is the result, then, of the subordination of labour to capital under certain conditions which made the former subordination a necessary condition of household survival. It was accepted at the material level because of its necessity, and at the ideal level because it was congruent with the dominant ideology. It may be argued that improvements in the productivity of domestic labour, combined with the higher wages and shorter hours of wage labour (as compared with the nineteenth century) have rendered that subordination unnecessary. In so far as that is the case it is maintained only by the power of gender and family ideology on the one hand, and the encapsulation of most women in the secondary section of the labour market on the other.

Women remain primarily domestic labourers/houseworkers and perform surplus domestic labour because, at the material level, they are better able to ensure subsistence in this fashion than if they were to rely on wage labour in the secondary sector. However, it is precisely because they can ensure their subsistence through performance of the domestic role that they are relegated to the secondary sector of the labour market. It is no longer their exclusion from the market, but their inferior position in it, that is the basis of their dependence on their husband's wage. Although wives' subservience to husbands is no longer required to ensure survival, its persistence is to be understood in terms of the wives' and husbands' unequal access to material resources outside the household. As a result the subordination of women no longer appears as natural necessity, but as something imposed upon women by men: employers and husbands. This has important consequences for marriage.

In the domestic mode of production both spouses equally participated in the productive process. During industrialisation both partners co-operated to ensure the household's survival. In contemporary circumstances where a majority of households are very significantly above subsistence level, the spouses are scarcely *required* to co-operate at all. The extent of co-operation has moved from the realm of necessity to that of freedom. It is precisely this freedom which makes apparent the greater power of the husband to determine marital decisions, a power which can now be seen as rooted in economic circumstances, not natural necessity. The ideology which has served to legitimate female subordination in marriage is then weakened or destroyed, while the basis of that subordination remains unshaken, thus enormously increasing the difficulty of sustaining a successful marital relationship. Attempts to avoid the difficulty by avoiding the type of relationship – in forming consensual unions – miss the point. Marriage in itself is merely a form whose content is specified by its historical conditions. Marriage in itself is not the basis of women's subordination, which is rooted in the differing relations of the parties to the productive process.

Section III:

The Family in Contemporary Britain

Chapter 11

Official Statistics and the Decline of the Family

The value of the sociological approach to contemporary social life is twofold. First, it provides new perspectives on the familiar; secondly, it provides information as to the manner in which social life is being transformed. There is a tendency to identify the first with the theoretical and the second with the empirical. This is a mistake. Empirical knowledge about the past can provide entirely new perspectives on the present, while what information we obtain about the present and the way in which it is categorised and presented depends inevitably upon the perspective employed and often on the prejudices of the investigator. Moreover 'perspectives' need not be theoretical. Indeed, one of the most influential books on the British family (Fletcher, 1973) orders his material in terms of a problematic which concerns 'the decline of the family' and argues robustly against the view that there has been a 'decline'. It is in no way to denigrate Fletcher's book to note that his chosen problematic is not in any sense a theoretical one, and that his work however much informed by sociological understanding and knowledge, is essentially a contribution to the popular debate on the decline of the family which he describes.

This chapter will briefly consider aspects of change in the family in contemporary Britain. It is assumed that family life is, like other areas of social life, in the process of continuous change. The purpose of the chapter is to examine the nature and direction of this change, but not to evaluate it. It is assumed that any manner of ordering social life presents difficulties and problems to those who have to live it, while at the same time avoiding difficulties and problems that might otherwise arise were it not so ordered. There is no objective way of evaluating the bundle of problems and difficulties created and avoided by any given institution operating under specific social and historical conditions. The task of academic study is not to interpret information in the light of a particular set of moral beliefs espoused by the academic, but to provide a better understanding of the situation to which the information refers so that the moral judgements of society members may be better informed. Before proceeding with this task, however, it may be as well to attempt to characterise briefly the dominant evaluative interpretations of familial change.

Current argumentation and discussion about the predicament of the family and its future involves two rhetorics: the rhetoric of responsibility, and the rhetoric of freedom. The opposition of these in their contemporary form dates from the period of the Enlightenment, and is encapsulated in Edmund Burke's remark that men should think more of their duties than their rights. The notion that the family is in decline centres essentially on the view that family members are neglecting their duties, are acting irresponsibly *vis-à-vis* other family members. To the 'decline' school, this is self-evident:

> The rising divorce rate demonstrates that spouses are putting personal satisfaction before marital and parental duty. The rising incidence of juvenile crime attests to a decline in parental authority and control, and a failure to give children a proper sense of social responsibility. The growing numbers of isolated and elderly people, the rising costs of housing provision and institutional care for the aged is eloquent witness of the neglect by adult children of their duties towards their parents. This is but one example of the growing lack of respect of the young for their elders which is manifested throughout the society in a refusal to accept legitimate authority, whether of the police (riots, crime, civil disobedience), employers (industrial conflict), of the State (local authorities and Trades Unions who reject the authority of Parliament) and, of course, of the Church. A stable, ordered society in which conflict is reduced to the minimum is only possible if it is rooted in stable and ordered families where children are brought up to be respectful, obedient and responsible citizens. That we do not live in such a society is taken as ample evidence of the decline of the family.

The rhetoric of freedom agrees with the rhetoric of responsibility that, in Edmund Leach's words, 'the family ... is the source of all our discontents'. Consider the following entertaining if somewhat extreme example of the *genre*:

> The family is oppression, the family is despotism, the exclusive rule of privileged groups, the broken harmony of the passions; the family is monopoly, the family is depravity, the family is God the oppressor, this greedy villain crucifying his son for love ... the family is misery, the family is the broken health of humanity; the family is a miasma, an epidemic; the family is evil incarnate and the state based upon it a poisoned organism; its destruction is near. (Kov in Riasonovsky, 1953)

The freedom or enlightenment school regards the family as a relic of an oppressive and collectivistic past, where humankind were enslaved by custom, tradition and religion, and the individual subordinated to the group. History is the story of people's progressive emancipation from control by collectivities: church, state and kin group. The last has shrunk to its nuclear core, so that the only forms of unfreedom and oppression that remain in this sphere are the subordination of children to parents and wives to husbands. Because the family 'is oppression, is despotism', the achievement of freedom necessarily requires it dissolution. Hence, in contrast to the duties emphasised by the rhetoric of responsibility, the rhetoric of freedom emphasises the rights of children, of wives and of spouses to realise their individual potentialities unrestrained by the authority of superordinate persons or that of an authoritative set of prescriptions which restrict those rights. Either the family must disappear altogether or it must be reconstituted as an association of free and equal individuals – instead of being based as at present on domination and subordination.

Neither of the types of rhetoric sketched crudely here is often found in its pure form, but they do constitute opposing tendencies in contemporary thought and Western culture, which are united in the importance they ascribe to the family and the way they define the issues: duties vs rights; responsibility vs freedom; collectivity vs the individual; and authority vs equality. They are united also in regarding the family (as this book has done) as denoting a social group and not merely a plurality of related persons.

There is, however, something very odd about the opposition. For what reasonable person can be 'against' freedom or 'against' responsibility? Moreover, in moral terms, freedom must be seen as a precondition of responsibility, not its opposite. It is easy to deride either rhetoric in its extreme form, but the temptation to do so must be avoided if we are to recognise that each expresses an apprehension of the family which is distorted and mystifying only in its dogmatic and one-sided mode of abstraction from its object, and that each embodies therefore a practical truth. Indeed, the two rhetorics should not be regarded as static expressions of opposing views, but as moments in a continuous dialogue which highlights different features of the institution which it concerns. The popular 'debate' about the family should not, however, be regarded as a resource for interpreting data, but rather as part of the topic of investigation.

The character of family life will necessarily differ as between different family groups, according to whether their members deploy the terms of one rhetoric or another in describing their situation. The debate is, therefore, constitutive of and not merely a gloss on the contemporary family. It is also a sign which points to the nature of the contemporary family, because it is a product of the very changes that have resulted in its coming into being. The concern with responsibility points towards an increase in personal choice and freedom in family matters, while the demand for freedom suggests that this increase has been partial and uneven, the freedoms gained increasing the salience of the unfreedoms that remain.

The sections of this chapter and Chapter 12 could quite properly constitute the chapters of a book. It will not be possible, therefore, to deal exhaustively with these topics. The purpose of the chapter is rather to highlight the crucial issues raised in each area. In some areas the relevant literature is potentially vast, in others it is sparse in the extreme. In all cases, however, it points to the occurrence of profound and important changes whose nature and direction are not yet clear. It is, then, like the other chapters in Part 2 of this book exploratory rather than definitive. It does seek, however, to identify topics and issues in the field of the sociology of the family which may be expected to be central during the next decade.

THE INCIDENCE OF MARRIAGE

In 1958 it was possible for Richard Titmuss (Titmuss, 1958) to note that *the proportion of the population who were married* had been increasing since 1911 and strikingly so since the mid-1930s, and that an increase of one-third over 1911–54 in the proportion of women aged 20–40 who were married, represented a truly remarkable rise. It is scarcely suprising, then, that this decline in the proportion of the population who are single has not continued at the same rate during the last thirty years. The *fall* itself has continued, however: single women who constituted a quarter of all women aged 15 and over in 1951, only constituted one-fifth in 1976 (*Demographic Review, 1977*, p. 12).

One of the chief causes of the dramatic fall in the proportion of single persons (and the increase in the proportion married) was the continuing decline in the age at which people married, which fell from 1915 to the early 1970s. Obviously, a falling age at marriage cannot continue indefinitely, and since the Second World War the rate of fall has slowed down. The median age at marriage of men fell from 25.8 in the quinquennium 1946–50 to 23.2 in 1965–70, and of women from 23.1 to 21.3 in the same period. During the later 1970s, however, the median age has *risen* slightly for both sexes: to 23.9 for men and 21.8 for women in 1980 (*Population Trends*, 1981). Another factor in the decline over the century in the proportions of single persons has been the changing sex ratio. In the past there has been a surplus of girls over boys in the marriageable ages arising from a higher incidence of infant mortality among males, and this surplus was of course inflated by the death of young men in the two world wars. The absence of any recent major war, and the reduction of mortality rates among male infants, had brought the sex ratio of people of marriageable age into balance by the mid-1960s. Since then, however, a surplus of males has emerged as a result of continued past reduction in the mortality of male infants, thus reducing the proportion of males who are able to marry within their own, broad, age range (Leete, 1979, p. 34).

The declining rate of fall in the *age* at first marriage, recent rises in it and changes in the sex ratio have affected the *rate of marriage*, which since the Second World War had been slowly rising. During the 1970s, however, the rate of marriage has declined sharply for both sexes, for men from 85.9 in 1970 to 63.3 in 1976, and for women from 98.6 to 76.8 in the same period. (The rates are the number of first marriages per 1,000 persons of the same sex – *Demographic Review, 1977*, table 4.2, p. 50.) Surely, so sharp a fall cannot be accounted for simply by the factors we have mentioned?

Changes in yearly rates, which attract media attention, are not indicators; that is to say, they do not vary consistently with determinate changes in family life. They are the product of a number of processes of which they are signs, and signs require interpretation. It is generally assumed that a high marriage rate shows the 'popularity of marriage' as an institution, and low marriage rates its decline. This is too simple an interpretation. Figure 11.1 compares the variation in first-marriage rates with the proportion married by ages 30 and 25 in the years 1964–76. The stability of the proportions curve is in marked contrast to the fluctuation in the rate curve. The fall in the marriage rate since 1972 would appear to be a result of a postponement of marriage rather than its abandonment. Interpretive caution is still required, however. The figure shows that the rising marriage rates in the 1960s do not indicate an increasing popularity of marriage, but merely reflect a fall in the age at marriage. It is still too early to say whether the converse is true of the 1970s, since those who 'should' have married then but didn't (hence the fall in the rate) had not

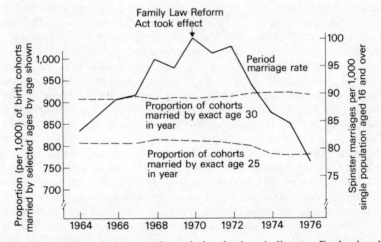

Figure 11.1 First marriage trends, period and cohort indicators, England and Wales, 1964–76 (see Leete, 1979).

attained the age of 30 by 1976. There is no evidence from figures like these that marriage is becoming less popular, but this does not mean to say that it is not.

FORMAL VS INFORMAL MARRIAGE

What would 'declining popularity of marriage' involve? In order to answer this question, important conceptual distinctions must be made. There have been marked changes in *the manner in which marriages are formalised* (or in Anglican jargon 'solemnised'). (People marry each other, they are not married by priests and ministers, clergy, or registrars; these officials merely bless, bless and register, or register an act of commitment by the parties marrying.) During the period 1964–76 the proportion of state-registered marriages increased from 22 to 34 per cent. A contributory factor to the decline in marriage rates may be a reluctance to formalise marriage at all. We may, therefore, be moving away from a situation in which the chief distinction is between those whose marriages are formalised by the state as opposed to the church, to one in which the predominant distinction is between those whose marriages are formalised and those whose marriages are not. A shift in this direction of deformalising marriage would not amount to its *deinstitutionalisation*, provided that the informal marriages embodied the same conception of marriage as that set forth publicly in marriage ceremonies. A gap would then open up between the proportion of the population married, and the proportion registered as married. This, while statistically extremely inconvenient, would not signal any fundamental change in family life. Such a development may be expected as the outcome of the progressive separation of private and public spheres, and the separation of law and morality which is its correlate.

How prevalent *informal marriage* is, it is impossible to say. It is, however, possible to estimate the incidence of *cohabitation*. Brown and Kiernan (1981) estimate that in 1979 3 per cent of all women and 5 per cent of the 20–24 age group were cohabiting. However, cohabitation is most frequent among divorced and separated persons, and in these groups should be seen as a response to their rather special situation, rather than as a new form of mating arrangement. They estimate the proportion of single women cohabiting at 8 per cent, but it is clear that a proportion of these are engaging in cohabitation as a preliminary to marriage rather than as a substitute for it. How large this proportion is, it is impossible to say in default of a longitudinal study, though as is noted below the Family Formation Survey (Dunnell, 1979) estimates premarital cohabitation at 10 per cent for the 1971–75 marriage cohort. The increased incidence of cohabitation is contributed to but by no means identical with the growth of informal marriage, and certainly involves mating arrangements which depart from traditional marriage.

CHANGES IN THE INSTITUTION OF MARRIAGE

Changes in the willingness to formalise marriage must be distinguished from changes in the institution of marriage, though empirically they may go together. For example, an unwillingness to formalise marriage may result from an unwillingness to enter into a lifelong, as opposed to long-term, commitment to another person. It has become popular to refer to a situation in which high rates of divorce are associated with high rates of remarriage as evidencing the popularity of 'serial monogamy'. This, however, involves the breaking (divorce) of a public contract of lifelong commitment (marriage). If the institution of marriage is changing from lifelong to serial monogamy and this is not reflected in social and legal forms, a declining rate of formalisation of marriage may result.

Neither of these changes would constitute a decline in the popularity of marriage, though the latter would constitute a decline in the popularity of *traditional* marriage, but both would lower the rate of formal marriage. Marriage involves however not merely a commitment to another person, but a sexual commitment. It also involves an acceptance of social responsibility for the rearing and maintenance of the children of the union. If it is the case that marriage is becoming the public ratification of previous (private) sexual unions, rather than public espousal being the precondition of such a union, then the need to marry in order to obtain the opportunity for sexual expression within the context of a stable relationship disappears. Moreover, if at the same time effective, cheap and simple contraceptive means are available, then the entry into a stable sexual relationship no longer requires a simultaneous acceptance of responsibility for its issue. The net result of these two factors (other things being equal) ought to be an increasing postponement of marriage by mates until such time as procreation was intended. Such a development would constitute a further erosion of *traditional* marriage, and raise the age at marriage, thus (in the short term) lowering marriage rates. It would not affect the proportions of the population who *eventually* married, but it would decrease the proportion of the population married *at any given time*. Such a development could well be defined as a 'decline in the popularity of marriage' and indicate a change in the character of the institution, but it would not necessarily constitute a weakening of that institution.

There is evidence to support the supposition that marriage increasingly follows rather than constitutes a precondition of a stable mating relationship. Dunnell (1979; summarised in *Demographic Review, 1977*, p. 57), in a study of family formation, collected data on the incidence of *premarital sexual intercourse* of women with their future spouses. The study provided evidence of a marked increase *in this form* of premarital sexual activity since the war. Only 34 per cent of women who married before 1951 at ages below 20 had had premarital intercourse with their future husbands, but of those marrying in the years 1971–6 at the same ages, the proportion was 82 per cent. Large rises were also recorded for those marrying at later ages. There is also evidence of the increased use of *modern contraceptive methods*. A sample survey of women having a legitimate birth in 1975 showed that nearly half had used the pill or an intrauterine device compared with fewer than one-quarter in a comparable survey in 1967–8 (Cartwright, 1978). Those who had never used any method of contraception constituted only 1 per cent.

It is reasonable to assume therefore that traditional marriage is being eroded, in as much as it is no longer a prerequisite of a stable mating relationship, and is frequently dispensed with as a prerequisite to such a relationship. The Family Formation Survey also found evidence of an increasing trend towards premarital *cohabitation*, 10 per cent of the women respondents married in the years 1971–5 having lived with their future husbands before marriage compared with 5 per cent of those married during the previous quinquennium. Marriage is ceasing to be a prerequisite of co-residence, as well as of a stable mating relationship (Dunnell, 1979). These data suggest that the rising age at marriage and falling marriage rates may be interpreted as indicating a major transformation in the nature of the institution of marriage.

THE DEINSTITUTIONALISATION OF MARRIAGE

The question that must now be asked is whether there is evidence that points not merely to change in the social definition and function of marriage, but to its decline. Clearly, if marriage is a prerequisite of neither mating, co-residence, nor childrearing, and does not regulate sexual access, it ceases to be in any sense the institution of marriage and simply becomes a type of relationship available to mates should they happen to choose it. That marriage has not yet lost its institutional status is clear, since the vast majority avail themselves of it, and it is still supported by legal sanctions. The question to be answered, however, is whether there is a *movement in the direction* of the deinstitutionalisation of marriage.

Two statistical measures are of importance here: the illegitimacy rate and the incidence of one-parent families. Both are ambiguous and misleading and need to be treated with caution. The *number of illegitimate births* reached a peak in the late 1960s and has declined steadily since then. The *illegitimacy rate* (the ratio of legitimate to illegitimate births) increased sharply throughout the 1960s, but during the 1970s the *rate of increase* of the illegitimacy rate has been somewhat less than during the 1960s. Since the *number* of illegitimate births has been declining, the rise in the rate in the 1970s is due to the faster decline in the number of legitimate births. The movement of the rate is not, therefore, an accurate reflection of the willingness of people to have children out of wedlock and their ability to avoid that consequence. The rise during the 1960s was associated with increased premarital sexual activity, and was consistent with an increased willingness to procreate outside marriage. The fall in numbers and the slowing of the speed of increase in the rate during the 1970s do not, however, support that interpretation. As Pearce and Farid (1977) point out, the British rate of 9 per cent (in 1976) is in striking contrast to Sweden where, in 1975, one-third of all births were illegitimate and reflected substantial proportions of couples cohabiting outside marriage. The evidence does not suggest that, at present, Britain is moving in that direction, though the rate in spite of a general increase in fertility had risen to 12 per cent by 1980 (*Population Trends*, 26, 1981).

It may, of course, be argued that the decline in the number of illegitimate births is a product of rising numbers of abortions after the liberalisation of the law on abortion in 1967. However, it is impossible to estimate what proportion of legal abortions would have taken place illegally had the 1967 Act not been passed. In any case, even if this argument were correct, it would not affect the issue discussed here. Whether people prevent extramarital births by sexual continence, contraception, or abortion, they seem to be getting better at it, with the result that fewer children than in the 1960s are being born out of wedlock. This does not suggest the widespread substitution of cohabitation for marriage as a *rearing* arrangement. This conclusion is not however inconsistent with the claim that procreating cohabiting couples are becoming more frequent, since the proportion of illegitimate births registered by both parents is increasing and reached 57 per cent in 1980. This entails that the illegitimacy rate is no longer a reliable indicator of the incidence of unwanted pregnancy, and that present levels of illegitimacy are only maintained by procreation within non-formalised unions.

It may be argued, however, that the increasing numbers of *one-parent 'families'* indicate a movement away from marriage as an institution. Leete (1978) has estimated that the number of one-parent families has increased in Britain from 570,000 to 750,000 in 1971–6, an increase of nearly a third. If it were the case that one-parent families were predominantly constituted by single persons with illegitimate children, this rise would be a definite sign that a growing minority of parents were procreating outside, at least, formal marriage. 'One-parent family' is, however, a misnomer. The statistics refer to a father or mother not living with their spouse, nor cohabiting, and having dependent children. This definition, used by the Finer Report (*Report of the Committee on One Parent Families,* 1974), was devised for administrative purposes, not sociological or demographic analysis. Strictly speaking, a 'one-parent family' is a *lone-parent household* with dependent children (LPH). Such households come into being through the breaking of marriage (or of cohabitation) by death or separation, as well as by extramarital procreation.

Leete (1978 table 4, p. 7) estimates that in 1976 17 per cent of female-headed LPHs had been created by death of a spouse and 64 per cent by divorce or separation from a spouse. Only 19 per cent were headed by single women. The number of LPHs created by divorce was the fastest-growing category in the years 1971–6, though the increase in the number of households headed by single women was considerable. The increase in this latter category is attributable to a declining propensity of fertile single women to marry or to have their child adopted, which is of course related to the increasing proportion who are cohabiting. The increase in one-parent families is primarily indicative of the increased instability of marriages rather than of an increasing propensity to procreate outside marriage. It may be concluded, therefore, that the shock-horror statistics so beloved of the popular press do not indicate the deinstitutionalisation of marriage, though they do suggest a decline in the traditional conception of marriage which had previously been institutionalised and, to a lesser extent, its deformalisation.

THE INCIDENCE OF DIVORCE

It may be objected at this point that the rise in the *divorce rates* since the last war, and particularly since the liberalisation of the divorce law in 1969, is evidence that marriage has ceased to be a lifelong commitment. This argument, if correct, would point in the direction of a further movement away from traditional marriage. Certainly, if you already *believe* that marriage is ceasing to be a lifelong commitment, then the rising divorce rates support that *belief*. If however you do not know what to believe, then the divorce statistics are of little help, since they are equally consistent with the belief that, while the social definition of marriage is unchanged, traditional marriages are increasingly unsuccessful. Both beliefs are likely to be partly true, but the proportion of marriages which end because of failure as opposed to a lack of commitment to a lifelong union is unknown and, probably, unknowable.

Divorce rates have in the past been low due to restricted legal grounds for divorce and the considerable costs of a legal action. Before the Second World War, the divorce rate never exceeded one per 1,000 married women. After the war, there was an enormous rise in the rate to nearly six per 1,000, which has been attributed to the disruptive effects of the war years on pre-existing marriages and the number of unions hastily contracted in that period. The rate then fell during the 1950s to twice its prewar level, but during the 1960s rose sharply, a rise due in part to more generous legal aid becoming available to divorce petitioners in 1960. In 1969 the Divorce Reform Act brought about profound changes in the law. These changes came into effect in January 1971, making divorce possible with the consent of both parties after a two-year waiting interval, and with the consent of only one party after a five-year delay. Since then the divorce rate has increased. It rose sharply for England and Wales from 5.7 in 1971 to 9.0 in 1972. It fell back to 8.2 in 1973 but since then has risen steadily to 9.8 in 1976 (Leete, 1979). The most recent figures for the UK show a continued rise to 1978, but a small fall in 1979 (*Social Trends*, 1981).

These rises have been popularly interpreted by the simple device of calculating the proportion formed by the number of divorces of the number of marriages contracted in a given year. This calculation is strictly meaningless, since the denominator varies with factors which have nothing to do with the propensity to divorce. More sophisticated estimates by demographers suggest that one in five marriages contracted during the 1970s will be broken by divorce within fifteen years (Leete, 1979). This would seem to be a very high failure rate. However, there is no means of knowing what the marital *breakdown* rate was before the legal changes of 1960 and 1969. Contemporary high rates of divorce do not necessarily indicate a higher incidence of breakdown, therefore, but are in some degree attributable to a greater formalisation of breakdown. However, since the legislative measures took effect and their initial impact has disappeared (since, that is, 1973), the rates have continued to rise. Whether the level of marital breakdown is exceptionally *high* compared with the past or not, the steady rise of the divorce rate certainly indicates a growing incidence of marital breakdown; that is, it is unlikely that it is due to a growth in the propensity to formalise marital breakdown alone.

Not only is marital breakdown increasing; divorce rates appear to be rising faster at earlier ages (Leete, 1979, table 32) and at shorter marriage durations (ibid., table 33 and figure 16). Moreover, the earlier the age at marriage, the earlier in the marriage the divorce occurs (ibid., figure 17). It is not true, therefore, that the present pattern of divorce can be understood as the result of the practice of 'serial monogamy' in the sense of a succession of relatively long-term stable unions, though this may be one element. In 1976 18 per cent of the divorces affected marriages of under five years' duration and almost half occurred in marriages which had lasted less than ten years. The falling length of duration at divorce would appear to imply that more and more nuclear families (families with dependent children) are disrupted by divorce. This seems to be confirmed by the increasing *number of children under 16 affected by divorces*, which rose from 71,000 in 1971 to 152,000 in 1976 (ibid., table 41). These figures are however misleading, for the same table demonstrates that the *proportion of divorcing couples with at least one child under 16* shows no clear trend during the early 1970s and was no higher in 1976 than in the first year of the decade. Since most couples 'wait' a year or two before having children, the shortening of marriage duration at divorce means that an increasing proportion of couples separate 'before' children are born, as well as 'transferring' some divorces from couples with children over 16 to children under 16. It is none the less true that the rise in the divorce rate *since 1960* must have increased the proportion of nuclear families affected given the trend to earlier and younger divorce.

There is, therefore, evidence of increasing marital instability. That is to say, *individual marriages* are increasingly fragile and that, therefore, nuclear families are increasingly fragile as the growth of one-parent households attests. This fragility of particular marriages is not to be confused with the weakening of the institution, though it may be understood as the result of changes in its nature. The continued institutionalisation of marriage is attested by the high rate of remarriage among divorced persons.

The fragility of marriage is strongly related to the age at marriage. Were 1976 age-specific rates to apply in the future the proportion of marriages contracted under the age of 20 which would end in divorce after fifteen years would be 33 per cent, while only 11 per cent of marriages contracted between 30–34 would so end (*Demographic Review, 1977*, p. 61, para. 4.29). Rising divorce rates are in part explicable in terms of past falls in the age at marriage, therefore. Given the low age at marriage, it is to be expected that 'young' divorces are the most swiftly followed by remarriage. Leete and Anthony (1979) in a pilot investigation of remarriage produce data which confirms this expectation. Some 60 per cent of those under 30 at divorce in their sample had remarried after four and half years compared with only one-third of the women and one-half of the men over 40. Overall, over half of the divorced persons sampled had remarried after four and a half years. These marked differences between ages in remarriage rates suggest differences in the character of the original marriage. The high rate of remarriage at younger ages suggests that the original marriage constituted a 'marital mistake', while the lower rates of remarriage at older ages suggest that the ending of the marriage may, in contrast, be thought of as a breakdown of a stable relationship, that is, a 'marital failure'.

A parallel distinction can also be made concerning the nature of the divorce. Marriages of short duration can be ended with less cost to the partners than marriages of longer duration in both economic and psychological terms. This is not to claim that divorce is not traumatic for the parties at shorter durations, but it is to claim that the patterns of interdependence will be less complex and less well established with the result that the period of disassociation will be shorter and its long-term effects less severe. For marriages of longer durations, the costs of divorce are very considerable, and these costs in themselves constitute a barrier to divorcing simply because of minor difficulties within the marriage. The rhetoric of irresponsibility is more appropriate to marriage than divorce, since the former *can* be entered into, in the words of the Prayer Book, 'lightly, wantonly and ill advisedly'. Thornes and Collard in a recent study of divorced persons comment:

When their serious marital problems started, the majority of couples did not quickly separate and marital difficulties, which frequently started very early in the marriage, tended to be tolerated for quite long periods. Nor did people quickly seek to legally end their marriages once cohabitation had ceased. (1979, p. 129)

Such a conclusion does not suggest that divorce is the result of a lack of commitment by the parties to each other, their children, or the institution; and Hart's (1976) study of divorced people supports the view that the social costs of divorce are considerable and must therefore act as a deterrent.

PROCREATION

The last demographic indicator which is sometimes thought to indicate a profound change in family life is the *number of births*. The appropriate measure is not of course the number of births, nor even the crude birth rate, but the general fertility rate, that is, births per 1,000 women aged 15–45. This fell from a high point of 91 in 1966 to a low of 58 in 1977. Since then there has been a small but distinct upturn to 64 in 1979. The total-period fertility rate (which is a calculation of the completed family size a woman would achieve were the age-specific fertility rates of a given year to apply throughout her fertile period) has also fallen sharply from a high of just under 3 in 1964 to well under 2 in 1977. This measure has also risen, however, during the years 1977–80 (*Population Trends*, 26, 1981).

A more detailed analysis of changes in age-specific legitimate fertility rates (*Demographic Review, 1977*) shows that during the 1960s when fertility rates were high, this was due to the high fertility of younger women, and that the fall in the 1970s, though affecting all age groups, has been greatest among older women. The variations in general fertility conceal a steady decline therefore in fertility at later ages, and reflect a growing concentration of births in the early part of the life course and therefore of the marriage. This decline in the fertility of older age groups has however been reversed since the birth rate began to rise again after 1977: the increase in the fertility of older age groups has, since that date, been greater among the young (*Population Trends*, 26, 1981). The increase in fertility was already by 1980 beginning to slow down, however. These two facts suggest that some part of the fall in fertility was due to the postponement of childbearing, rather than the decision to have fewer children; but it is too early to say whether this is a once-for-all phenomenon or the first signs of a move to later childbearing which will persist.

The other component of declining fertility is the reduction in the number of premarital conceptions and illegitimate births. The latter has already been discussed above. The premarital conception rate fell by almost half during 1964–76 (Leete, 1979) and this fall was most marked among marriages contracted at ages of 18 and over. Since it is unlikely that premarital sexual activity has declined, these falls are due to improved contraceptive techniques and to the greater availability of abortion, though in what proportions it is impossible to say. It would appear, therefore, that the decline in fertility has been due to a small degree to the decline in extramarital fertility, to a large extent to a wish and ability to avoid childbearing at later ages, as well as to a fall in fertility at the prime childbearing ages.

It isn't possible to infer from declining birth rates whether they reflect changes in the proportion of couples deciding not to have children or deciding merely to postpone childbearing. Dunnell's Family Formation Survey (1979) found no significant change between marriage cohorts in the preference of women for childlessness (the proportion being 1 per cent or less), and recent rises in fertility in later age groups suggest an element of postponement. Dunnell did record substantial changes in women's notions of socially desirable family size, which had fallen from 3.4 to 2.4 during 1967–76 (ibid., table 2.4). There is no evidence, therefore, which supports the view that people are increasingly unwilling to marry or to procreate within marriage, but there is evidence of a significant decline in the normative size of families. Increases in the number of third births as between 1978 and 1980 cast doubt, however, on the permanence of even this normative change.

The decline in the number of births experienced during 1966–77 cannot be used as evidence of either a rejection of marriage or a transformation of its nature. People still overwhelmingly expect to get married and to have children within marriage and are doing just that. The reasons for the recent decline in birth rates lie elsewhere, probably in economic circumstances and housing conditions, as well as in normative changes concerning family size. Why there should have been normative change downward, however, remains obscure.

CONCLUSION

It may be concluded, therefore, that the case that marriage and the family in Britain are at present in the process of 'deinstitutionalisation' is simply not proven. The demographic data do, however, strongly suggest a movement away from traditional conceptions of marriage and family life. In traditional societies interindividual relationships arise from one's membership of the group; the institutional is the precondition of the interpersonal. The evidence is consistent with the view that family life in Britain is increasingly moving away from that situation, to one in which the family is a merely residential group resulting from the establishment of a personal and private contract between individuals which is publicly registered and whose existence is dependent not upon their occupancy of an institutionalised status ('married'), but on the continuance of that interpersonal relationship.

Children are then significant in terms of the personalities of the parents; they are not significant in terms of the continuance of a group identity – national, cultural, or familial. The role of the state is seen not as preserving, buttressing, or defending the existence of institutionalised groups (families), but as regulating the private contracts of individuals and protecting the weaker parties to relationships resulting therefrom.

Though this does not amount to deinstitutionalisation, it does constitute a major shift of emphasis from institutions to the person, and the correct perception that this is taking place lies at the root of the rhetoric of responsibility. However, this substantive change is taking place in a culture which is still premissed on the reverse emphasis. Linguistic and other social practices, and legal and administrative arrangements, change only slowly and until they come fully into line with the new situation are felt to be oppressive and constraining. This disjunction lies at the root of the rhetoric of freedom. It does, however, have other roots. Marriage is, among other things, a contract. Marriage as an institution will be perceived as oppressive, whatever its form, as long as the resources of the contracting parties, external to the relationship, are unequal. It is to be expected that however great the formal equality between spouses, wives' sense of inequality in marriage will persist as long as they cannot, for whatever reason, participate on equal terms with men in the labour market.

The parent–child relationship is not, however, a contract, and children are their parents' inferiors in law, in access to external resources of all kinds and in terms of their internal resources. In a society whose structure consists of an ordered hierarchy of positions and where personal relationships depend on institutional membership and not vice versa, the subordination of the child within the family will not be perceived as an intolerable unfreedom. In a society operating on the opposite principles, however, parent–child relations appear as the last remnant of an oppressive social form. Yet to deregulate those relations, normatively or legally, is to deliver the child entirely into the hands of the naturally superior party; to regulate them is to give a natural inequality institutional support. If the exclusion of the child from the labour market be taken for granted, then the exclusion affecting children which parallels that of women, is the child's exclusion from other spheres of interaction outside the residential group, except the school where the child is also subordinated. Exclusion increases the dependence of the child upon his parents and renders the problem of parental-child relations even more acute.

THE CHANGING SHAPES OF THE FAMILY CYCLE

Demographic indicators throw light on one other area of familial change: the shape of the family cycle. Past falls in the age at marriage, the diminution of fertility at later ages and at longer marriage durations, and the *likely* fall in completed family size (which can only be calculated for women past childbearing ages), suggest that families at present in the nuclear phase will experience a longer gap between the cessation of procreation and rearing and the marriage of the first child, and a longer postparental phase. However central childbearing is to marriage both normatively and practically, and recent studies suggest it continues to be central (see, for example, Busfield and Paddon, 1977), childbearing and rearing will occupy a smaller part of the life course of a contemporary marriage than ever before in history. Moreover, low levels of mortality at middle age mean that marriages are highly unlikely to be broken by the death of one of the spouses. Hence, persons marrying in their early twenties may expect to spend only thirteen years with a child under 11 in their household and only eighteen years with a child under 16. In other words, in the period before the onset of old age an enduring marriage will involve the couples spending as much time without children in the household as with them, and probably as much time again as senior citizens. In the nineteenth century high rates of mortality at younger ages combined with a large completed family size entailed that in practice, as well as at the normative level, marriage was chiefly a childbearing and rearing partnership. Today this is no longer the case. For the greater part of the course of most marriages, their positive function will be that of providing a stable social and sexual relationship rather than the procreation and rearing of children. For this reason, if for no other, there must be a movement away from the institutional to the personal in the social definition of marriage. Moreover, were this shift *not* to take place, were marriages to continue to be defined in the traditional way, the result would be not a decrease, but an increase in the rate of marital breakdown, at that point in the course of the marriage when the child-centred *raison d'être* of the marriage disappeared.

The length of the postrearing and postparental phases of contemporary marriage means that the spouses will not be occupied with childrearing for a majority of their married life. However childraising is arranged between them, therefore, both spouses are going to require an occupation in addition to domestic work. This implies that for much of the marriage both spouses will be free to engage in paid work. As we said in Chapter 5, however, where both spouses are employed they are likely to develop different networks of acquaintances with different norms and values, and are subject to different rates of occupational mobility. Moreover the longer both are in paid work, the greater are the chances of the spouses becoming differentiated and the greater that differentiation is likely to be. The result of social differentiation may be to erode the shared values, attitudes and expectations upon which the marriage is based and increase the chances of its breakdown. Demographic changes, by changing the shape of the family, may therefore significantly affect the level of marital breakdown and dissolution at longer marriage durations.

However, it would be a mistake to regard demographic factors and the economic activity of both spouses as independent influences on marriage. It is likely that the postponement of childbearing is related to the fact that childbearing entails not only extra expenditure, but loss of the wife's income, since a large number of wives continue to work after marriage. This raises the gross cost of childbearing (that is, extra expenditure plus loss of income), unless the mother is entitled to paid maternity leave and can pay for or arrange for child care while she is at work, and this must affect the timing and duration of family building.

The proportion of married women working increased throughout the 1970s from 49 per cent in 1971 to 52 per cent in 1978. The proportion of women (married or not) with dependent children also increased over the same period from 41 to 52 per cent. However, this increase was entirely due to increases in part-time employment, the proportion of such women working full-time remaining around 16 per cent. Nearly half of all women without dependent children worked full-time in 1978 and a further 18 per cent part-time. It is however probable that the figures for 1980 and 1981, when available, will show a decline in these proportions as a result of the recession (*General Household Survey, 1978*, tables 5.1 and 5.3).

THE HOUSEHOLD

The demographic changes we have described so far are reflected in the changing distribution of household types. Table 11.1 shows the distribution of households by type in 1961 and 1979. The first point to be noted is that among family households the proportion living in com-

Table 11.1   *Household Distribution, 1961 and 1979*

	1961			1979		
Elementary family – nuclear	68·5 } 73			69·5 } 74·5		
Lone parent – nuclear	4·5			5·0		
Elementary family – postnuclear	19·0 } 27			17·5 } 25·5		
Lone parent – postnuclear	8·0			8·0		
Households with children	100	100	54	100	100	46
Married couples with no children present		26			27	
Two or more families		3			1	
Single-person and non-family households		16			26	
		100			100	

Sources: Social Trends, 1981.

posite ('extended family') households is tiny and has decreased over the last twenty years. On the other hand, the proportion formed by single-person and non-family households has increased enormously. The total number of households increased over the period by 13 per cent. In contrast, the number of single and non-family households increased by 49 per cent. The obvious explanation is the increasing number of elderly people. However, although the number of households containing elderly people (in this category) did increase by over half, the number of households in this category containing no elderly person also increased by 40 per cent. There is, therefore, a trend away from 'family living' quite independently of the growth in the number of old people.

This trend is, of course, the result of a number of changes which we have already considered. The cessation of the decline in the age at marriage and the growth of cohabitation before marriage, and the increasing incidence of divorce in the postparental phase of marriage, are all factors likely to increase the number of 'extrafamilial' persons who constitute this category of households. It seems likely however that an increasing (if still small) number of young people are living independently of their families of origin prior to establishing their own nuclear families, and that this too contributes to the size of the extrafamilial category. If this assumption is correct, it constitutes a further move in the direction of a nuclear family system in the sense of the predominant form of domestic group containing parents and *dependent* children only. The 'extended family' *household* as a national phenomenon (however important in certain localities), would appear to be virtually extinct; and the elementary family household now also appears to be shrinking to its nuclear core.

CONTEMPORARY CHANGES IN HISTORICAL PERSPECTIVE

It is extremely difficult not to see the changes which demographic data suggest are currently taking place in family life in any way other than as a continuation of the movement of emphasis from the institutional to the personal, from the collective to the individual. Indeed, a Durkheimian perspective seems entirely appropriate here. Apologists for high failure rates in marriage have claimed that these are to be understood in terms of the much 'higher standards' of personal relationships expected nowadays. In so doing they are introducing an unnecessary value-element into a straightforwardly Durkheimian point, namely, that as the content of a social relationship or practice becomes less closely regulated by the *conscience collective*, so its actual character is more and more determined by the negotiation of those party to it. Where a relationship depends on the successful outcome of negotiation, its successful establishment is likely to be less frequent than when it is dependent on a tried, tested and culturally prescribed form. In Weberian terms relationships which involve *vergemeinschaftung* are likely to be more successful than those dependent on *vergesellschaftung*.

It is therefore necessary to make a distinction, usually ignored, between on the one hand marriage as an action (getting married) and a state, and on the other marriage as a relationship. Most of the evidence cited does not point towards any rapid deinstitutionalisation of *marrying* or the marital *state*. The evidence that points to movement away from traditional conceptions of marriage may amount to the deinstitutionalisation of the marriage *relationship*, in the sense of a diminution in the amount of the behaviour of spouses which is culturally prescribed. It would be a mistake however to infer that, if this is what is occurring, then increases in the rate of marital breakdowns are due to increasing marital anomie, in the simple sense of the *absence* of normative regulations.

It would be a mistake for the same reason as it would be to suppose that the useful *analytic* distinctions of the nineteenth-century social theorists can be used to provide an adequate descriptive *account* of the historical process. *Any* social change must involve the deinstitutionalisation of traditional practices and relationships and a period of confusion during which the content of the relationships arising out of associative action has to be negotiated by the parties. It does not follow, therefore, that the direction of any particular social change can be determined by characterising *all* the features of that change. Rather, it is necessary to distinguish features specific to the change considered from those common to all changes. Common to all periods of social change is not anomie, *deregulation* as such, but the coexistence of a plurality of regulative principles and ideologies which originated from earlier relations and practices and which are still applied with varying degrees of success to quite different, emergent practices and relations. Comte's term 'anarchy' seems more appropriate to this situation than Durkheim's 'anomie', for 'moral anarchy' meant for Comte the absence of any ruling moral ideas, not the absolute absence of any regulative principles.

It may be granted that spouses have to negotiate their marital relationships without the assistance of *universally accepted* social definitions of its content. But it is not true that 'society' leaves them to get on with their negotiation in peace. On the contrary, they are bombarded with a variety of moral injunctions and moral worldviews which are massively taken for granted by their proponents. These views are mediated to couples by parents, sibs, neighbours, peers, churches, voluntary associations and the media, and most of them call forth some moral response from an individual who has been successfully socialised into the culture from which they originate. This combination of voices, individually claiming moral absolutism but mutually relativising, necessarily complicates the negotiation and establishment of stable interpersonal relationships between spouses. The net result, if contemporary novelists and media commentators are to be believed, is the creation, particularly in wives, of a potent mixture of anger and guilt. These phenomena do not however indicate the direction of change, but are rather phenomena integral to the process of change itself. It would be premature to conclude, therefore, that the deinstitutionalisation of the marital *relationship* describes the direction of family change. It may be merely the inevitable accompaniment of change itself.

The same cannot be said in respect of the progressive nucleation of the family. The norm of the nuclear family household, the absence of any authority of parents over mature children, has never meant the extinction of the relationship between parents and children at marriage, and grandchildren have continued to remain of very considerable significance to grandparents. The grandparent–grandchild relationship has remained an under-researched and underdiscussed topic. Its importance derives from the crucial nature of this relationship in maintaining the relation between parents and their married children and the way it illuminates the significance of children. If, as Ariès has suggested, in the modern family parents seek to reproduce not their society/family/house/line, but themselves through their children, then grandchildren are seen as just as much a continuation of both the individual and social being of the grandparent as are children. The result is intense and often conflictual relationships between grandparents and their married children and between the two sets of grandparents. Intense relationships between the generations have constituted the backbone of extended kin relationships in modern industrial societies. The nuclear family then, though structurally isolated within the bilateral kinship system (that is, part of no other kin group), has remained integrated within the network of kin relationships created by the family process.

The evidence is by no means clear, but it is at least possible that young people are increasingly beginning to reside independently of their parents before marriage/cohabitation. This would signify a change in the nature of the parent–child relationship and, indeed, in the significance of familial status as a component of adult status. The young adult would no longer depend for the attainment of an adult status (fully independent of his parents) upon founding his/her own nuclear family. Rather, the foundation of a family is made possible by the prior emancipation of the young adult from parental control and the creation of a period early in adult life when the individual defines him/herself independently of their familial status. The children of previously independent parents may continue to signify a continuation of the individuality of the parents, but would be distanced in both time and space from their grandparents, whose ability to control their upbringing would be severely diminished. The autonomy of the young adults signifies that they are not just their parents' children, and that their offspring are primarily *their* children not their parents' *grand*children.

The rising age of marriage may signify, therefore, the emergence of a period of extrafamilial independence among young adults which, if continued over several generations, may markedly affect the character of the relations between parents and their adult children, weakening their intensity and hence the whole structure of kin relationships to which intergenerational relations are essential. This is however speculation, albeit prompted by the statistical evidence, but it does suggest a possible direction of familial change which deserves closer investigation. The progressive extinction of the customary rights of grandparents in their grandchildren would constitute the elimination of the last vestiges of 'the family' as a multigenerational configuration and would complete the process of family nucleation in the strict sense. Family life would become an experience encountered by the typical adult twice in the life course: as a child in his/her family of origin and, after a period of independence, as a parent in his/her family of marriage. Outside these periods the adult, while *having* parents/married children, would cease in any sense to be a member of a familial group. The question to be asked is: is this indeed coming about, and if so, what is the future of marriage during that not-inconsiderable part of the life course not constituted by the two periods of family membership? In other words, it is not what will happen to the family if marriage 'declines', but what will happen to marriage when 'family' occupies only part of the life course?

Chapter 12

The Sociology of the Elementary Family

CHANGING MARITAL RELATIONSHIPS

Invaluable as statistical indicators are, they are only indicators. Their interpretation involves speculation about the nature of the changes occurring in the activities and relationships of which they are signs. The only substitute for speculation of the kind engaged in in Chapter 11 is sociographic investigation. Unfortunately, the empirical studies which sociologists should have been doing to chart the basic changes in family life which the statistics reflect, have simply not been done in Britain in the last decade. We lack the family sociography provided by community studies, since they aren't done any more. The sociological studies that have been undertaken have focused on contemporary marriage and the changing character of marital relationships, and it is to this topic that we now turn.

The point of departure of the present debate about the nature of changes in marital relationships in contemporary Britain is Elizabeth Bott's work *Family and Social Network* (1957, revised 1971). In this work Bott distinguished between two polar types of *conjugal-role relationship*, 'segregated' and 'joint'. In the *segregated* case 'husband and wife have a clear differentiation of tasks and a considerable number of separate interests and activities'. In the *joint* case 'husband and wife carry out many activities together with a minimum of task differentiation and separation of interests. They not only plan their family together but also exchange many household tasks and spend much of their leisure time together' (ibid., pp. 53–4). Bott thus provided the analytic categories corresponding to the global distinction made by Burgess and Locke (1953) between the functions of the family as an 'institution', and a means of 'companionship'. In so doing, she removed the distinction from its association with different time periods and, hence, its evolutionary association. While denying that marital relationships are directly 'class'-determined, she reflects the tendency of much empirical sociology of that time (Bott, 1957, p. 64) to replace the dichotomy's historical associations, by association with the sets of strata popularly termed 'working' and 'middle class'. Bott was not primarily concerned with the degree of the division of tasks connected with household maintenance as between the spouses, that is, the extent to which one spouse was exclusively responsible for income-earning and another for domestic tasks involved in housekeeping and child care, except in so far as joint-role relationships implied that the wage-earner necessarily took part in some domestic activity. She notes, rather, that 'in all families there was a basic division of labour by which the husband was primarily responsible for supporting the family financially and the wife was primarily responsible for housework and child care'. Her study is concerned with the 'considerable variation in detail' on this basic theme (ibid., p. 54).

Like Bott, Young and Willmott (1957) take for granted the traditional work–husband/home–wife division of labour; unlike her's, their work has a strong temporal perspective. A chapter of the book is entitled 'Husbands and wives, past and present', and in it they trace the growth of 'a new kind of companionship between men and women, reflecting the rise in the status of the young wife and children which is one of the great transformations of our time'. To use Bott's terminology they are claiming that the first half of the twentieth century has witnessed a shift, even among the working class, from segregated to more joint types of conjugal-role relationship. If one then combines both associations, segregated-ancient/joint-modern and working class-segregated/middle class-joint, if follows that the twentieth century has witnessed the progressive assimilation of working-class to middle-class styles of marriage. Rosser and Harris (1965) confirm Young and Willmott's (1957) findings:

> The husband is expected to help with the household chores, to stay at home or go out for the evening with his wife, to help with the children, to push the pram ... to share the major family decisions ... Our case studies of young married couples ... confirmed this marked change in the conjugal relationship and the marked contrast (particularly of course in working class families) within the recent past. (Rosser and Harris, 1965, pp. 184–5).

If we then add another comment by these authors who note 'the vast majority of what have been called "home centred couples" among those we visited', the stage is then set to receive the image of the family which emerges from Goldthorpe and Lockwood's study of affluent workers in Luton.

In attempting to explain workers' industrial attitudes and behaviour Goldthorpe and Lockwood, in the first of their three volumes (1968), refer to ongoing changes in working-class life outside work,

> and most notably ... to changes within the family. In consequence of the conjugal family assuming a more 'companionate' or

partnership-like form, relations between parents and children would seem likely to become closer and more inherently rewarding. (ibid., p. 175)

The evidence for this is, however, extremely thin. It is that 16 per cent of their sample mentioned 'demands of home and family life, *leisure activities etc.*' (emphasis added) as a reason for not attending union meetings, which is really rather a small proportion given that respondents were married men aged 21–46. The other piece of evidence is that 70 per cent had been brought up outside Luton and that 35 per cent mentioned separation from kin and friends as a disadvantage. These data scarcely warrant statements about the changing character of marital relationships. The authors' claims are, however, given firmer evidential basis in the course of their discussion of 'the pattern of sociability' in their third affluent-worker volume (1969), but the evidence is of a circumstantial kind. In the chapter on 'Sociability' the authors establish that their respondents' families are very much (in the terms of the present book) 'closed domesticated nuclear families' in so far as married couples rarely entertain jointly 'home is a place reserved for kin and for very "particular" friends alone'. They had relatively few associational memberships and contacts outside the home were confined to workmates, kin (when available) and neighbours. A number of measures indicated that 'time outside work was devoted overwhelmingly to home and family life rather than to sociability of any more widely based kind' (ibid., p. 103). Goldthorpe and Lockwood conclude that

primacy was clearly given to the material well-being, the social cohesiveness and the autonomy of the conjugal family over and against the demands or attractions of wider kinship or community ties; and one could at least suggest that probably the one most important concomitant of this changed emphasis was the acceptance among these workers and their wives of the ideal of the 'companionate' marriage. (ibid., p. 108)

It is clear that the affluent-worker study does not, as the authors recognise (ibid., p. 108, n. 2), remedy the absence of studies of working-class marriage. The argument assumes that, to the extent that husbands and wives are increasingly home-centred, marriage, within the home, must be increasingly companionate. There is, however, a tension in the argument of this crucial chapter between the desire of the authors to claim to have discovered a 'new' working class with norms and behaviour different from that of the 'traditional' working class, while at the same time claiming that, though not traditional, the 'affluent' workers are still, culturally, distinctively working class. The more successfully the latter claim is established, and it *is* established, the less 'non-traditional' the affluent workers appear; and the more traditional they appear, the more doubtful the companionate marriage hypothesis becomes. For example, while four diary-type records presented in the text demonstrate how little leisure-time the spouses spend outside the home and with non-family members, they also show a pattern of activity which exhibits a substantial degree of conjugal-role segregation. The authors demonstrate how 'working class' is the pattern of sociability (kin/neighbours, workmates) but, in so doing, reveal that there is a marked tendency towards segregation of the spouses' networks along sex lines. Whereas in their first volume the willingness of affluent workers to move away from kin to well-paid jobs is stressed, in the third volume the authors note 'the quite large part that parents, siblings and inlaws still play in our respondent's lives' (ibid., p. 89). The authors paint a picture of working-class family life, which is recognisably similar to that painted by the studies of traditional communities to which they refer in their footnotes with three exceptions. The first is that emphasised by Rosser and Harris: geographical separation from extrafamilial kin. The second is the amount of time spent in the dwelling. The third is the participation of men in domestic tasks. Table 11 (ibid., p. 108) shows that a quarter of all husbands 'participated to some degree' in doing shopping, two-fifths in washing up and from almost half to 80 per cent in the more interesting sorts of child care. In other words, *privatisation* (attrition of external contact and activities) and home-centredness (the normative salience of 'home' as against other social ties) is accompanied by Young and Willmott's 'great transformation' and Rosser and Harris's 'marked change'.

What is this change, precisely? It is that the *rigid* sexual division of labour *within the household* has broken down. If one starts off from the assumption that historically and culturally the wife is identified with domestic labour and the man with wage labour, and that this yielded further segregation of activity within the domestic domain of the most rigid kind – and this within living memory – then the change indicated by the findings of these three studies is indeed marked. In calling it a 'great transformation', Young and Willmott do not show a functionalist bias or manifest a belief in the naturalness of the sexual division of labour. They merely reflect the astonishment of their elderly informants.

The defects of these studies lies, rather, in their failure to specify precisely in what this marked change consisted. The evidence warrants the claim that the traditional division of labour had become less rigid, not that it was in the process of being abolished, or that marital relationships were becoming more *equal*. In Durkheimian terms the *conscience collective* was becoming more general, more diffuse and less specific. As a result spouses were more free to adopt their own forms of domestic organisation. That is to say, they had the responsibility of negotiating their own particular form of marital-role relationship. It does not warrant the assumption that the pressure to conform to the general principles of the sexual division of labour was any less marked.

Some of the confusion which has surrounded this issue must be traced back to Bott, since Bott did not ask questions systematically of all her respondents, and her classification depends on her interpretation of the manner in which spouses understood the distribution of responsibilities: 'it was also necessary to take into account what the couple thought and felt about (the activity)' (1957, p. 240). Bott also refers elsewhere to the 'ethic of equality' associated with 'joint' relationships. The net result is that it is not possible to establish in respect of Bott's families a list of tasks and answer questions about how *many* each spouse performed, and how *much* of any activity one spouse performed, only that in the case of 'joint' families the majority of tasks were performed 'together' or 'shared'. 'Jointness', as Bott uses it, would seem to imply a *norm* of home-centredness combined with an absence of a *clear-cut* division of labour. Her accounts of her families make it quite clear that it does not imply any sort of quantitative *equality*.

It is, however, unjust to accuse Bott of originating the confusion which developed in the subsequent literature between the development of a less rigid division of labour within marriage and equality between the spouses. For Bott explicitly distinguishes, at one point, role segregation and male authority one aspect of marital inequality: 'Male authoritarianism is often confused with segregation of conjugal roles' (ibid., p. 64). The distinction between the degree and rigidity of the division of labour on the one hand, and the subordination of one party on the other, is a conceptual distinction of the first importance. The former does not logically imply the latter, but where both exist together, segregation must limit the extent of the control of the superior party.

The confusion between these two analytically distinct dimensions of conjugal-role relationships stems, in part, from a failure to keep distinct the concepts in which informants describe their relationships and the analytic concepts of the sociological observer. The former frequently serve to mystify and confuse both those who use them and those who seek to establish the character of relationships by their means. The evidence that the sexual division of labour is less rigid and spouses spend more time in each other's company is overwhelming. The spouses clearly conceptualise the direction of this change as being in the direction of 'equality', but it does not follow that it is legitimate so to conceptualise the change described. What is required is rather an examination of exactly who does what and to what degree, and an attempt to relate the pattern of activity thus disclosed to the conceptions of the spouses which must be seen as legitimating and contributing to the reproduction of that pattern. If it is the case that works like those of Young and Willmott (1957), Rosser and Harris (1965) and Gavron (1966) are ideological, then they have this character because they uncritically reflect the consciousness of their informants. In so doing, they provide invaluable data but are led into dubious sociological interpretations of its significance. Indeed, rereading the sociology of the 1960s one is impressed with the extent to which sociologists were infected with the spirit of the age, to the extent of taking expressions of that spirit at their face-value.

In marked contrast to these works was the Pahls' study (1971) of managers and their wives. It is impossible to do justice to this very interesting study here, but vital to consider briefly what they have to say in two chapters which most concern marriage, entitled 'The wife's world' and 'Attitudes to marriage'.

The Pahls begin by noting that their managers' wives 'had great difficulty in being objective about themselves and the roles they played'; indeed, the whole account of the wives conveys an impression of confusion on the wives' part about their social identity in marriage. It is clear that many of the wives experienced considerable dissatisfaction with their marital status and the roles they were forced to play and consequently lacked any clear sense of social identity. On the other hand, belonging to a relatively favoured stratum of the society, and having husbands that were very often (by social standards) considerate and helpful, they felt that they ought to be satisfied with their lot. To put this another way: felt difficulties and dissatisfaction with their lives could not be legitimately expressed, because of thier favourable position relative to the reference groups given by their social experience. Research which focuses on evaluative statements by respondents involving comparisons tells us more about how the collective consciousness of the society structures respondents' experiences than the experience itself. In this case the consciousness of respondents seems to have been so structured as to inhibit the articulation and analysis of felt dissatisfaction, which the Pahls sensitively probe and explore.

The Pahls concur with Klein's (1965) conclusion that

women's lives ... are dominated by their role as wives and mothers ... All other occupátions are subordinated to this central function. The ... increase in the 'extramural' activities of married women ... is a corollary of the reduction in domestic responsibilities.

The Pahls, in a reference to Myrdal and Klein's (1968) study entitled *Women's Two Roles* comment on the wives in their own sample that

a discussion about the conflict involved in 'women's two roles' would be a discussion about the wife and mother roles, and about the conflicts which may arise between being a good wife and a good mother. Even for those women who do hold jobs, their domestic roles take priority. (Pahl and Pahl, 1971, p. 130)

For the Pahls' respondents, the proper and conscientious performance of the roles of (house)wife and mother were essential ingredients of their self-esteem – necessary conditions of their personal integrity. But once the demands made upon them by those tasks diminished (with the maturation of the children, more domestic help as the family became more affluent), the fact that they had spare-time *and* weren't 'working' (domestic labour being not socially defined as work) combined to provide a negative self-image of themselves as useless layabouts. If however they sought to remedy this situation by 'going out to work', this undermined their confidence that they were properly performing their 'essential' roles. However, since these were managers' wives, they felt that if they remained at home they were deprived of any chance of 'success' which was in any way comparable with that enjoyed by their husbands. In fine, they felt constrained by their purely ancillary role: as the Pahls point out, they used the phrase 'man and wife' rather than 'husband and wife'. Marriage, that is to say, is conceived of as union between an autonomous social individual and his helpmeet, not between two autonomous individuals (man and woman) or two equally interdependent individuals (husband and wife).

It is not surprising that the Pahls' managers' wives were uncomfortable in this situation. Why were they so poor at analysing it? Because they too were conscious of 'the great transformation'. Modern marriages were held by them to be 'close', and they valued this closeness. 'Closeness' seemed to involve both psychological closeness and participation in common tasks (especially childrearing), and these two features were understood to be based on or imply an egalitarian relationship between the spouses. Time spent together and the absence of rigid sexual division of labour equals or flows from 'equality'. This theme runs through all the studies, from Bott onwards. But the Pahls don't accept it at its face-value: 'This did not seem to imply that the partners shared equally in all the household tasks and decision making ... the household tasks were divided between those which were the responsibility of the husband and those which were customarily done by the wife.' Indeed, in spite of the high occupational status of the husbands in the Pahls' sample, however much 'sharing' there may have been, there was a very marked sexual division of labour, which was necessitated in part by the very strong orientation to work of the husbands and the demands their work made upon them. This had two consequences. Though spouses subscribed to an ideology of closeness, this was difficult to achieve in practice, particularly as the children grew older and the demands of the husbands' jobs increased. Hence, wives were forced either to attempt to participate in the husbands' worklife to maintain closeness, to retreat into a segregated complementary domestic role, or to seek an independent role outside the family. None of these solutions was satisfactory. The second consequence was that, however much consultation there was between spouses, in major decisions the husband always had the final voice. This was not because of a belief in the superior rights attaching to the position 'husband'; nor was it due to a belief in the superiority of men *per se*. Indeed, a rejection of such attitudes was the basis of the spouses' perception of marital equality. It derived, rather, from the two dependency relations noted at the conclusion of Chapter 10. The Pahls put it thus:

> Many wives are in an ambiguous position, in that the relationship which is most salient to them is one in which they are the less powerful partner, and one in which their roles as wives are dependent on and determined by their husbands. Yet the husbands too are in the position of having their most salient role under the control of others; the competitive nature of their work situation means that they, and so indirectly their wives, must accept such constraints as frequent mobility and a commitment to work of most of their time and energy.

Within marriage, the subordinate position of women does not appear to derive from the authority of the husband, nor from an ideology legitimating male dominance. It would seem, rather, to be an adaptation to the demands made upon the domestic group by the occupational system. This adaptation is functional for the survival of the group in as much as it supports the occupational activity of the man upon which the prosperity of the group depends, but it is clearly dysfunctional in creating a stable and positive identity for the wife, and dysfunctional for the stability of the marriage both for that reason and because it comes into conflict with the ideology of 'closeness' and 'equality'. In other words, there is a contradiction between securing the prosperity of the domestic group, and the stability of the marriage upon which the domestic group also depends. While this contradiction results in tension between the spouses which affects them equally, the task of accommodating the contradiction falls mainly to the wife – not because the husband is more powerful *per se*, but rather because he is more constrained by the occupational system than the wife is by her domestic situation. The price paid by the wife to enable the husband to pursue occupational success, is guilt, anxiety, disorientation and anomie, resulting from a combination of adult responsibility without the correlative degree of autonomy.

We can now identify another defect of 1960s family sociology: British studies concerned with or touching on marital interaction, by taking for granted the principle of the sexual division of labour in the society as a whole, failed to understand what went on within marriage, in so far as they neglected its determination by the actual operation of that wider division of labour. On the basis of the evidence of the studies so far mentioned, inequality within marriage does not appear explicable in terms of the ideologies of the spouses. Inequalities in domestic activities and decisionmaking have to be understood as the resultants of the persistence of the closed domesticated nuclear family, characterised by intense emotional relationships which have become normatively expected, which entails a division of social life into public and private spheres associated with men and women respectively. There is no evidence that this division and association has become any weaker, though plenty of evidence that it has become less rigid.

Now, it was one of the great merits of Young and Willmott's *The Symmetrical Family* (1973) that it focused on the relation between the 'private' relations of spouses, and the relation between the private and the public. One of its great demerits was that it introduced yet another confusing term into the argument about the changing character of marriage. The authors nowhere define 'symmetry' rigorously, but there is one fairly succinct statement of what they mean. In their concluding chapter they write:

> By the next century – with the pioneers of 1970 already at the front of the column – society will have moved from (*a*) one demanding job for the wife and one for the husband, through (*b*) two demanding jobs for the wife and one for the husband, to (*c*) two demanding jobs for the wife and two for the husband. The symmetry will be complete. Instead of two jobs, there will be four.

The essence of the authors' argument is, I think, this: with the emergence of the closed domesticated nuclear family *marriages* were symmetrical: they consisted of two roles, one public and one private, played by the man and woman respectively. However, the roles of *each spouse* were not balanced as between the two spheres. The opposite of this initial case (*a*) is (*c*), where each spouse has a domestic and a public role. Here it is the case that both the marriage and the roles of each spouse are symmetrical as between the two domains.

The fact that wives increasingly work and that men are increasingly involved in child care and housework, does not merely constitute a blurring of the sexual division of labour within the domestic domain, 'within marriage'; it also constitutes a blurring of the division of labour which assigns the sexes to different social spheres. This is an extraordinarily important development, but it does not entail that the power of the husband is any the less or that the roles of the different sexes within the same domain demand the same effort or bring the same rewards. The essentially behavioural changes which Young and Willmott document are not inconsistent with the traditional division of responsibility at the normative level, and with persistent inequalities in contribution and reward at the material level.

It is doubtful, as a number of commentators on Young and Willmott's work (Oakley, 1974, for example) have pointed out, whether the evidence cited in *The Symmetrical Family* warrants the claims made by its authors concerning the extent and direction of contemporary change in marital relationships. The discussion of the domestic division of labour simply reiterates the themes of earlier studies: the man participates in domestic activities (the blurring of the sexual division of labour) and spends large proportions of his time at home (companionship, closeness, jointness, home-centredness). But then the authors don't claim that we have reached symmetricality – only that 'we're on our way'. Similar considerations apply to their discussion of women's work. They make no claim that we have already reached equality in work; only that female participation in paid work is increasing.

Those who have criticised Young and Willmott have missed the point, which is not that they make unsubstantiated claims about the early 1970s, but entertain extremely old-fashioned progressivist evolutionary *beliefs*; these combined with a 'trickle-down' theory of cultural diffusion, enables them to interpret a rather cautious account of the situation in the 1970s as a step on the way to the destination for which their more general framework makes them *believe* society to be headed. That direction is specified not in terms of equality/inequality, but in terms of increasing involvement in terms of both time and interest of men with the domestic domain and women with the public domain of work. It would be fair to say that this trend is seen by Young and Willmott to be likely to lead to changes in cultural expectations concerning the division of labour between the sexes in society and within the domestic sphere, rather than being the result of such changes. Their thesis is not, therefore, refuted by pointing either to persistent inequalities between spouses, or to the strength of traditional attitudes. Because these criticisms do not succeed in demolishing the authors' hypothesis, this does not of course entail that their hypothesis is correct.

There are two types of arguments which may be adduced to suggest that it may be mistaken, of which Young and Willmott are well aware. The first is economic. They make it quite clear that the movement of married women into paid work has depended crucially on economic conditions since the Second World War namely, buoyant demand for labour and the growth of opportunities for part-time work. Clearly, the rise in unemployment during the late 1970s and the high levels which are likely to persist throughout the 1980s cannot but have a major effect on the opportunities for paid work open to married women, though in precisely what way it is too early to say. They give no recognition, however, to the barrier imposed upon the extension of employment opportunities to married women by the concentration of women's work in the secondary sector of the labour market (Barron and Norris, 1976).

This consideration leads us to the second type of argument, which concerns the different situations of families in the higher and lower occupational strata. Young and Willmott note that there is evidence to suggest that, at the managerial level, hours of work have been increasing rather than decreasing, thus militating against managers of either sex having a demanding domestic role. They also note (as did the Pahls) that determination to work among managerial wives is strongly related to educational level. The implication of this is that in the lower income/educational strata wives do not work in order to enjoy a demanding public role, since they lack the educational qualifications to achieve one. They work to augment the family income. If wives lacking educational attainment from lower-income strata have married into higher-income strata, they are glad *not* to have to work. It is only those who do not *have* to work, but can find a demanding and stimulating work role, that seek a career outside the family. It follows from this that the growth in the number of 'dual-career' families at the top of the occupational pyramid cannot be expected to 'trickle down' through the strata in the same way as 'fashion' in family size and contraceptive usage have done, because being a lower-stratum member implies low income and lack of education likely to militate against a high involvement in the work role.

There are, therefore, good reasons in Young and Willmott's account for supposing that the dual-career pattern will neither diffuse among the upper nor trickle down to the lower strata, in which case it does not seem reasonable to discern a trend to symmetricality, let alone equality; and we are left with a retention but a blurring of the traditional division of labour and unequal participation by each sex in the domain traditionally associated with the other.

The dual-career family was the focus of attention by a number of studies during the 1970s (Fogarty *et al.*, 1971; Rapoport and Rapoport, 1971, 1976; Rapoport *et al.*, 1978). The proportion of marriages in which both spouses have careers (as opposed to jobs) is still small and the Rappoports's (1971, 1976) work is based on a small number of case studies. It would be out of place to provide a detailed discussion here. The significance of their work from the point of view of this chapter is the analysis of the difficulties faced by 'dual-career' families. They identify five sets of dilemmas facing couples of this kind. The first concerns the problem of household maintenance. Just how arduous and time-consuming domestic labour is is only revealed when both spouses are pursuing careers and neither have time to do it. This problem of 'overload' can be minimised but not eliminated. The second concerns normative conflicts between (chiefly) the woman and her role audience, whose members regard her behaviour as counter-normative and try to sanction her return to domesticity. This leads to the third difficulty: problems of identity for both spouses deriving from the contravention of gender norms, inconsistencies between the rewards from work obtained by each spouse and competitiveness between spouses. The fourth dilemma resulted from being unable to fulfil demands of network members due to the pressure of work, and the final set concerned schedulling the varying demands of work and family, so that they were out of phase and didn't peak at the same time.

Two chief points emerge from the Rapoports' accounts: first, that while the couples considered their pattern of marriage to have substantial benefits to the individual spouses, their children and to the marriage, very considerable skill on both sides was required if the five dilemmas were successfully to be resolved. The second point is that, in spite of their unconventionality (the data derives from the 1960s), the wife's work 'was seen primarily in terms of the benefit to her' and that she would 'take up any demands created by her wish to work': 'it was alright with [the husbands], so long as it did not interfere too much with their own needs' (Rapoport and Rapoport, 1976, p. 320).

The Rapoports' findings cast doubt on Young and Willmott's belief that 'the pioneers of 1970 at the head of the column' had reached symmetricality: on whether there is yet anything which can diffuse downwards to the rest of the population over the next 100 years. This is yet another reason for doubting what has been termed Young and Willmott's 'optimism' (though why having two demanding roles instead of one should be regarded as an improvement is obscure – at least to the present writer).

The issues raised by the studies so far discussed are important ones, but even when taken together the studies provide relatively little evidence about the changing patterns of marriage in Britain in the 1970s.

Some light is, however, thrown on the matter by the developing interest in housework as a topic of social investigation. The pioneer in this field has been Oakley (1974). What is pioneering about her studies is that they are the first to treat housework as work and as an occupation and, hence, a determinant of social identity. The picture she paints is of women of both the working and middle social strata as finding housework unpleasant and reporting more fragmentation, monotony and time-pressure than the male factory workers in the affluent-worker study of Goldthorpe, et al. The median working week for her sample was between seventy and seventy-nine hours. Not only does this mean that housewives work longer hours than their husbands; this inequality is exacerbated by the husband's refusal to accept that housework constitutes 'work'. This means that the housework does not earn any social reward, hence there is no external definition of standards. This is disastrous given the nature of housework tasks, which are unending. The need for psychic reward leads therefore to an escalation of standards, or to an imprisonment in routines. However, in spite of their dislike of the housework integral to the occupation 'housewife', that role was central to the identity of a majority of Oakley's informants, even though they negatively evaluated it as an occupation. The salience of the identity 'housewife' was a result of its close identification with gender conceptions. Rejection of the role would have involved a rejection of gender identity as well.

In her discussion of the household division of labour Oakley makes many of the points already made in the course of this chapter, and she confirms the conclusion we have drawn from other studies in the following words: 'In only a small number of marriages is the husband notably domesticated' and even then 'home and children are the woman's primary responsibility'.

Her conclusions are reinforced by a more recent study of middle-class couples by Edgell (1980). Edgell's data confirms the view that contemporary married life involves *variations* on the theme of the traditional sexual division of labour which has however not been significantly altered, and he is able to come to this conclusion by distinguishing rigorously between marital-role segregation and marital equality. He also distinguishes, most usefully, the sexual division of labour from the household division of labour, and both from the distribution of marital power. The pattern of sharing of household tasks is a distinct issue from that of the distribution of power, and the latter is rooted in the sexual division of labour. Edgell concludes that his sample was characterised by unequal marriages, and locates this inequality (as the Pahls did, and this chapter has done) in the dependence of the husband on his employment and the dependence of the household on the husband for financial support and, hence, the dependence of the wife on the husband: 'it is . . . the wife who tends to "accommodate" the husband who in turn has to "accommodate" to the occupational system.'

The sexual division of labour produces inequality in marriage, therefore, and this inequality is legitimated by gender ideologies which Edgell sees as a reflection of 'the structure of work and family roles and their interrelationship'. The most original type of data that Edgell's study provides is data on the normative compliance of the spouses in his sample with a highly traditional marital-role ideology. In Edgell's words, 'neither husbands nor wives apparently felt even the need to pay lip service to egalitarian ideas, but boldly expressed their respective domination and subordination', in a way which is all the more remarkable since Edgell's respondents were professional couples – just the sort of people from whom, according to Young and Willmott, symmetricality should be trickling down to the rest of us, and among whom 'progressive' ideas are supposed to be most prevalent.

Edgell's data dates from the early 1970s and is approximately contemporaneous with that of Young and Willmott's (1973) study. It, therefore, throws doubt once again on the 'optimistic' view that there was a steady movement towards equality during the late 1960s and early 1970s. In view of the recent shifts in social and political consciousness, it is highly unlikely that, since then, traditional attitudes have been significantly eroded. However, Edgell's data refers to only a small number of families and it may be that they are untypical of professional families in general, though the present author is inclined to believe Edgell rather than Young and Willmott.

It does not follow, however, that the thesis that change is occurring in marital ideology is wrong. Those writers who have sought to disprove it have paid little attention to the mechanisms of the reproduction and transformation of family ideologies within the family, and have certainly underestimated the time required for ideological change to take place. A remark of one of Edgell's informants is highly significant in this respect. A wife says of her husband: 'He was always able to come home and his mother was there and he wants his children to be the same.' Another wife says: 'I remember when I was young, getting home and my mother being there.' In an earlier article Edgell (1970) emphasised a basic distinction between normative and behavioural conformity. This distinction may be applied to intergenerational change in this way. Generation one believe that 'a woman's place is in the home' and act accordingly. Generation two no longer believe this but feel they ought to give their children what they themselves had, but lacking any coherent belief, fail to transmit the idea that this behavioural pattern has any normative force. As a consequence generation three doesn't feel the same constraint towards behavioural conformity because they don't accept that conformity necessarily bestows a benefit on the children.

Edgell's sample had a median age of 36–40. Their childhood experiences, therefore, took place in the 1940s, when the sexual division of labour was virtually unquestioned. If the three-generational model has any substance, it is highly unlikely that significant normative or behavioural changes would be found in Edgell's sample, only a *weakening* of normative conformity. Behavioural change probably wouldn't occur until the next generation, who will themselves not be 35–40 until the end of the century. It is, therefore, a little naïve of Edgell to write: 'Despite de Beauvoir [1949, 1972] and other polemicists of her day, and the recrudescence of an extensive feminist and women's liberationist literature, public debate and agitation in recent years, little change was evident in the consciousness of the couples studied.' It may even be, given the nature of their beliefs, that Edgell's sample itself belongs to generation 'one', and that the effect of the intellectual movements he cites will make no normative impact until the end of the century and no behavioural impact until the 2020s.

Instead of regarding intellectual movements as causes of normative and behavioural change, they should instead be regarded as signs of more fundamental changes that give rise to them. The obvious candidate is that decrease in rigid role definition and increased 'sharing' which all the studies agree is taking place. Given male dominance in marriage, that dominance will be more acutely felt the less it is the case that both spouses have separate and independent spheres. When it ceases to be unthinkable that men should do housework, it becomes a matter of complaint that the husband only does the washing up. Whereas it was once unthinkable that a woman should go out to work (in the middle classes), staying at home now has to be explained in terms of the *husband's* wishes. Viewed even in quite a short historical perspective, Edgell's data suggest a very significant shift in the way people conceptualise the sexual and household divisions of labour.

This is not to argue that there is an empirical trend or a developmental process at work which will inevitably result in the character of marital relationships changing in any particular way. It is to argue that the old certainties which constituted 'traditional' marriage, itself probably only 100 years old, are now being relativised and questioned. These signs may be seen as presaging future fundamental changes in marriage as an institution. Unless, however, one sees history as embodying an immanent movement in the direction of a more specialised division of labour (like Herbet Spencer and Talcott Parsons) or moving ineluctably towards freedom and equality (like Goode, some feminists and other heirs of the Enlightenment tradition), it is much too early to descry the nature, let alone direction, of these changes.

PARENT-CHILD RELATIONS

If there has been a great change in marital relations in the direction of 'closeness' and a de-emphasis of the authority of the husband, such empirical studies as we have emphasise the same transformation in parent–child relations. The Newsons in the publications resulting from their longitudinal study (Newson and Newson, 1963, 1968, 1976), which contain a wealth of descriptive information, reveal that their informants perceive a shift as between their own and their children's childhoods in the direction of affectivity and psychological closeness. In their first book about 1-year-old children (1963) they conclude with a chapter which is the counterpart of the 'Husband and wives' chapter in Young and Willmott's first study (1957). In it they report parental perceptions of improved living standards, greater domestic convenience and, in the working class, smaller family size. These factors informants see as being responsible for less strictness on the part of parents and greater freedom for the children. They also perceive a greater openness in communication between parents and children, a greater sharing of interests and a shift from parental to quasi-friendship relationships.

The stress on closeness and affectivity, splendidly illustrated by quotation in the Newsons' (1976) study of 7-year-olds, chapter 8 of which is entitled 'With love and kisses', is in tension with the equally important stress on parental responsibility and, hence, control. The 'Love and kisses' chapter is, therefore, balanced by two further chapters, entitled 'Coming to blows' and 'Artillery of words'. In the first we learn something we would never have guessed from the 'Love and kisses' chapter, that for three-quarters of the sample being struck by an implement is 'at least within the bounds of conscious possibility' (ibid., pp. 324–5). Twenty-two per cent had actually been punished in this way and the remainder threatened with such punishment. Parental control for a significant majority is based, in the last resort, on the threat of force. Now, clearly this is a consequence of the growing autonomy and power of the child whose ability to affect others in the household, by the age of 7, is very considerable, but whose ability to foresee the consequences of action and to control his/her own impulses is still not fully developed. Resolving conflicts by use or threat of physical force is for many parents counternormative, and in conflict with their emotional involvement with the child and the desire for friendship and closeness. Hence, there are strong sanctions within the parent against physical punishment, and the Newsons' informants reported emotional disturbance in themselves after administering it. Its use in the majority of cases appears to be less principled than pragmatic. However, punishment is not merely resorted to as a means of resolving intense and immediate practical difficulties. It is also concerned with the long-term effects on the child of letting it get its own way: 'what will he be like later if I let him get away with things now?' (ibid., pp. 314 ff.); 'Clashes ... between parents and children may become testing times, when parents suspect that their long term ability to influence their child's behaviour ... could be irretrievably diminished if they are seen to lose' (ibid., p. 330).

The Newsons' chapter on the artillery of words goes into considerable detail about the way in which parents seek to avoid physical punishment by verbal manipulation of the child's consciousness. The effectivity of this method derives on the one hand from the parents' control of resources, and on the other from the psychic needs of the child: 'the child's wish to be worthy of love, approbation and attention is the prime force in his own socialisation' (ibid., p. 370). The authors remark: 'the reader may have found the catalogue of violence and other sanctions depressing; but one might ask whether the more equal battle of today is not more healthy than the earlier spectacle of the righteous parent with God (and later Truby King) firmly on her side.' The Newsons' picture of socialisation at 7 years old and their remarks are worthy of some comment.

First, in opposition to the Parsonian view of the family and socialisation, parent–child interaction is presented by the Newsons as rooted in conflict, involving the active participation of children as well as parents. Instead of the child learning to perform culturally prescribed familial roles, the parent and child roles appear in the Newsons' account as always open to negotiation, to be the subject of bargaining supported by threats, for the child rapidly acquires its own ammunition in the artillery of words and becomes adept at responding to the parental fusillade with its own barrage of cajolery and moral blackmail.

Secondly, the Newsons make no attempt to explain explicitly how the collapse of parental authority within the household has come about, and refer the reader only to changes in childrearing fashions ('Truby King'). This is inadequate, since while childrearing manuals may have legitimated the exercise of parental authority to the *parent*, they scarcely legitimated the compliance of the child.

Two considerations are important here. The first is that changes in 'scientific' beliefs about childrearing have played an important part in creating the ideology of closeness, friendship and equality between parents and children, which if acted upon by the parent reduces the social distance between the two to an extent which makes the enforcement of unquestioning obedience impossible, and opens the way to a reliance on verbal exchanges as a means of control.

The second, which the Newsons very clearly show, but emphasise too little, is the conflict between parents and teachers, and parents and peer groups. The Newsons' data clearly show the difficulty experienced by parents when confronted by a child who challenges their authority with reference to what teacher said and other parents let their children do. This returns us to a recurrent theme of the present book: the articulation of the family with other social institutions, people and relations outside the household.

If it is correct to suppose that there has been a movement from the seventeenth century onwards towards the creating of boundaries around the domestic unit, and towards a growth of intensity in the relationships found within it, and that this movement is reaching its apogee in our own time with the privatisation and nucleation of the domestic group, then that movement constitutes what Parsons would term its 'structural isolation'. However, the structural isolation of the domestic group no more implies that its members have no relationships outside it, than the structural isolation of the nuclear family means that strong relationships do not exist between its members and extrafamilial kin. The closure, the boundedness of the group is analytically distinct from the degree of participation of its members in contexts outside it.

Now, there may have been a moment, towards the end of the last century, at which for the middle classes the domestic group was not only bounded, but its children confined within it. That reality was at once the basis of notions of the empirical (as opposed to normative) importance of parents in determining the eventual character of their children and was the condition of the implementation of normative doctrines of childrearing. It may be argued that, since that time, though closure and domesticity have become more *widespread*, children have been decreasingly confined to the closed domestic group. This is due chiefly to the coming of universal education, but also to changes in childrearing ideologies which by delegitimising strict parental control, make it impossible for parents to confine the child to the domestic group. Clearly, the greater the time the child spends outside the household and the more alternative reference groups it has, the less effective will be parental attempts to mould its character.

It might be thought that these changes would have had the effect of destroying the accepted view that parents are responsible for the way that their children 'turn out'. However the Newsons' data indicate very clearly that this has not happened. The notion that parents' behaviour towards their children is decisive in forming their children's characters would seem to be deeply entrenched in social consciousness, and to affect members of all social strata. The reason for this would appear to be that the doctrine of the responsibility of parents is seen to be scientifically grounded and absolute rather than conditional on social circumstances. The term 'responsible' nicely combines the notions of both causal efficacy and moral responsibility. One of the characteristics of twentieth-century family culture is that, whereas in the past a bad child was seen as a misfortune and the parent deserving of sympathy, it now symbolises a character defect on the part of the parent ('I don't know where we went wrong'). This perspective constitutes a 'domain assumption' of childrearing ideology which both survives the swings of fashion and affects the attitudes and behaviour of those whose approach to childrearing is unaffected by those fashions.

This places the parent in a dilemma. Parents are socially regarded as responsible for their children's characters but, at the same time, are deprived of the ability to control their children which the attribution of responsibility *tacitly* assumes. The shift in the emphases of childrearing ideology (see Newson and Newson, 1974) from strictness to permissiveness, rationality to affectivity and authority to freedom compounds this dilemma. The net result is to affect profoundly the emotional relationships within the family as the Newsons splendidly show in the final chapter of their study of 7-year-olds:

> Parents are in fact chronically on the defensive over their parental role because the responsibility laid on them is not only limitless but supremely personal. Our children are a walking testimonial or advertisement for the sort of people we are; doubly so, since they advertise both their heredity and their environment [*sic*]. (Newson and Newson, 1976, p. 400).

> In the end criticism of the upbringing of a young child is still primarily aimed at the mother. If the children are aggressive mother will be blamed by the neighbours for not controlling them better; if they are namby-pamby . . . it is her fault for being over protective. (ibid., p. 401)

> The baby with severe colic, for instance, who will not be comforted, may arouse in his mother feelings of anger and inadequacy for her failure in her basic mothering role of comforter . . . young mothers

are often ill prepared for the violence of their own feelings which stems from the threat to their own sense of worth from the very person who would make them feel most needed. (ibid.)

Let us point up this, the *central dilemma* of modern parenthood, even more. If the parent is seen to be socially responsible for the character of the child; if the child's behaviour is regarded as a measure of the moral and personal worth of the parent, then the power of the child becomes enormous. By its behaviour it can determine the respect accorded to its parents by their significant others and the self-image of the parents themselves. But if the child has so much power, then it can use that power effectively to diminish the area of parental control. Quite apart from the influence of others on the child, and quite apart from the content of the dominant childrearing ideology, the domain assumption of modern childrearing: parents are responsible for the characters of their children, itself effectively deprives them of the degree of control over their children which they need if they are to discharge that responsibility.

It is not surprising that the Newsons quote with approval a remark made by the authors of an American child-psychology text (Johnson and Medinnus, 1965) that the modern mother's 'feelings of inadequacy are matched only by her undying efforts' and then go on to point out that what makes it worse is that parents are supposed to enjoy parenthood. In Wolfenstein's phrase: 'Fun has become not only permissible but *required*' (Mead and Wolfenstein, 1955, quoted in Newson and Newson, 1976, p. 399).

At the cultural level what is being described is the intrusion into the domestic domain of the values and attitudes characteristic of the public domain in industrial societies. Childraising is a technical task, judged by the effects it achieves. Parents, like other producers, are judged by the quality of their products. Hierarchy, tradition, authority and control are, however, archaic features of preindustrial society, and must be replaced by spontaneity, equality and liberty. Set free from the constraints imposed by the past, family life should be fun, and failure to achieve that culturally defined goal once again suggests personal inadequacy on the part of the parents.

This cultural intrusion into the private domain in respect of childrearing practices exactly parallels the same intrusion with regard to marriage and sexuality. *Failure* to *achieve* mutual orgasm is seen as both technical incompetence and moral failure, because morality has become so closely identified with technical competence. We live under the shadow of a stern moral injunction to make sexual relationships fun. Happiness has ceased to be a gift, a blessing, a benison, a grace, and become instead a moral duty. But whereas, in marriage, democracy and equality are enjoined but rendered difficult if not impossible, in the sphere of parent–child relations it is responsibility that is enjoined and simultaneously made impossible, and these contradictions themselves make the achievement of that other culturally prescribed goal, 'happiness', even more difficult.

To refer as we have done to the central dilemma of parenthood, which is compounded by these cultural intrusions, is to refer to a relation between 'family' and 'society', to a particular mode of articulation of the private with the public domain which has profound consequences for the emotional interior of the family. The Newsons concentrate on the intensity of these emotions in parents, but thus far in their series of publications they have neglected the emotional consequences for the children. If parenthood is a dilemma for parents, so must childhood be for children.

These consequences may be seen to be of two kinds. In the first place the greater power of the parent and the imperative need to control the child results in *de facto* control, which is not rendered *de jure* by any ideology of parental authority. Hence, the child will perceive the inevitable restrictions on its freedom as unwarranted and illegitimate and they will engender feelings of frustration and anger towards the parents long after the preverbal stage has passed. In adolescence these feelings may be given intellectual form in terms of accusations of parental hypocrisy.

The second consequence may be even more serious from the point of view of the child. To give the child the power to determine the self and social esteem of its parents, particularly its mother, is rather like giving a 5-year-old a loaded revolver. The damage it can do to others is out of all proportion to its capacity to control the implement or its understanding of its effects. It is unthinkable that, if child behaviour generates in parents emotions of the intensity that the Newsons claim, the child itself does not respond emotionally to those parental feelings. That is to say, it will become aware that its actions engender violent and disfavoured emotions in its parents for reasons it cannot understand. The result is likely to be the addition of guilt to the anger it already feels as a result of parental attempts at control, and further anger that it should be made to feel guilty.

Anger and guilt were, we suggested earlier in the chapter, the predominant emotions experienced by women in their capacity as wives. If that supposition is correct, this complex of emotions would appear to be associated with the subordinate members of both of the two relationships which constitute the family (husband–wife and parent–child). The causes, however, are not the same in each case. The wife's guilt derives from her domination by a traditional ideology, while the child's guilt arises from the unintended consequences of its exercise of socially constituted power. The anger felt by both parties is, however, the result of frustration but the child's *sense* of frustration derives from the absence of any legitimation of parental control, while the wife's derives from the blurring of the boundaries of the traditional division of labour. If we now relate these two sets of relations and their associated emotions, it is possible to infer that in so far as the allocation of the domestic role to the wife is culturally legitimated with reference to her role as mother, then the woman's anger at domestic confinement may be triggered by the children whom she is culturally expected to love and for whom she is held responsible by others. This resentment towards the children by the mother then exacerbates their sense of guilt deriving from their exercise of power.

Let us now extend this web of conflicting and intense emotions by taking into account the husband. If his absence from the household absolves him from much of the tasks of parental control, and his involvement with his children is confined to gratifying them rather than frustrating them, this may increase his wife's sense of anxiety about her own capacities, as he achieves 'fun' where she fails. This increases her unarticulated resentment of her husband who is not confined to the domestic sphere, wherein she is held morally responsible for the children's defects: it's the dads what gets the pleasure and the mums what gets the blame. His wife's increasing anxiety and hostility will be incomprehensible to the husband, who regards his working life as the discharge of an onerous responsibility to his family, and his contribution to child care a meritorious act of supererogation.

This configuration of anger, guilt, anxiety and resentment is not however the same the whole world over, though certainly a bloomin' shame! It is the result of a very particular historical and cultural conjunction. It would only be possible in a society with on the one hand the cultural characteristics of post Enlightenment Europe, and on the other a capitalist mode of production. It is not, however, general throughout the class of such societies. This pattern may be regarded as the dominant pattern throughout contemporary British society in the sense that variations between regions and strata may be understood on variations on this theme.

If this somewhat rash assertion is found to be correct, it is because, first, the progressive development of capitalism has led to the proletarianisation of practically everyone and to the continued encapsulation of women in the secondary labour market. These two elements ensure the dependence of the wife on the husband and the husband on the labour market. Secondly, it will be because of the extension of the hegemony of bourgeois culture to the working class, which may be in turn understood in terms of the erosion of the basis of a distinctive working-class culture on the one hand, and the homogenising effects of the mass media on the other. To make the assertion of the existence of a single predominant pattern is not to deny the existence of inter-strata differences. Indeed, one of the most fascinating aspects of the Newsons' work is their demonstration of just such differences. But these differences seem to the present writer to be primarily differences of emphasis rather than indications of the existence of different sub-cultures. This is not to deny the existence of sharp differences in political and social attitudes, thought structures and communicative behaviour between strata. It is merely to claim that the family form, mode of articulation and emotional structure of families in different strata may be understood as variations on the pattern that has been described.

To regard both the form and character of family life as determined by its articulation and by shifts in the collective consciousness could be seen as grounded in the assumption that 'the family' is merely a product of processes going on elsewhere, determined not determining. There is a sense in which this is true. The family is not the site of the elaboration and formulation of ideologies nor, as we have noted, has there been any development of the forces of reproduction sufficiently fundamental to have transformed the relations of reproduction. It is, however, still the chief 'primary group' within society. It is the group which is primary in forming the moral character of the individual. Hence, changes in this group cannot but have profound consequences for the conduct of individuals in all other social spheres. The family is not the site of the elaboration and formulation of ideologies, but it does constitute one of the most important spheres of experience which ideologies reflect. The family does not, in any significant sense, determine either the basic economic structure of capitalist societies, nor even the social institutions which have grown up on that basis, but it does, by determining the consciousness and feelings of individuals, determine how those institutions operate. A generation reared in groups having the emotional structure that has been outlined are likely to behave, in all walks of life, in a manner very different from a generation reared in families having quite different emotional structures.

It is not possible, for a number of reasons, to discuss the implications for behaviour in general, but it is appropriate and necessary to refer briefly to the consequences of the arrival of the type of family described for relationships between parents and adult children. This relationship between parents and young adult children is one of the themes explored by Leonard's (1980) study of courtship and marriage in Swansea. Though there is nothing in her account which supports the view that the emotional structure of the nuclear family responds to the model put forward above, she does bring out the importance of children, even when adult, in determining the status of parents in the community as 'good parents'. More importantly, she emphasises the way parents 'spoil' their children:

> the indulgence described ... lasts through babyhood, childhood, adolescence, and into adulthood and continues after marriage. It could be claimed that all parents 'spoil' their children ... and that this is always a mechanism for keeping the children in contact with their parents and psychologically dependent. (ibid., pp. 62–3)

What Leonard so carefully describes, however, is not the continued *psychological* dependence of the young adult on the parent, but their continued material dependence, which is carefully contrived by the parent. Because the transfer of resources which creates this dependence benefits the child and lies outside the sphere of socially defined parental obligation, it creates (according to Leonard) 'the basis for the establishment of an *obligation* by the child to "keep close"' (ibid., p. 63, emphasis added). If there is psychological dependence, it would appear to lie more on the side of the parent than the child. The picture Leonard paints is, then, one of material 'spoiling' which functions to create a moral obligation in the child to stay close and thereby satisfy the parents' social and emotional needs.

This picture is in conformity with the childrearing pattern described by the Newsons as interpreted here. If the doctrine of parental responsibility confers power on the child and diminishes parental control and inhibits the exercise of authority, then parental control can only be made effective by an appeal to the child's self-interest. If the basis of the child's power is its ability (deriving from its function as an advertisement for its parents) to reward or deprive them emotionally, then childrearing will create the sort of emotional dependence in the *parent* conventionally associated with children. If spoiling results in rewarding behaviour on the part of the child, the parent will be motivated to persist in spoiling in order to ensure such behaviour, and will use it to keep the child close enough for the parent to benefit.

It will surprise no one to learn that the parent who bears the chief costs of the spoiling is the mother. This may be related both to the sexual division of labour in society which assigns the domestic role to women, and the household division of labour where by the husband's participation in domestic activities is minimised. In this situation the only power possessed by the mother/wife derives from her control and employment of the resources necessary to the exercise of her domestic functions, her time, labour, skill and money. It follows that she acquiesces in her own exploitation (to use Leonard's term) in order to preserve the continued exercise of her power to control her children. But as Leonard points out, 'her husband reaps with her such returns as there may be'.

From the children's standpoint, what keeps them close is their sense of their own advantage – that is to say, the material rewards are perceived as much greater than the costs of being within range of parental interference and control, and it is this sense of net advantage which, as Leonard points out, serves to legitimate that interference and control. Because compliance with parental control is seen as reciprocation on the child's part for the parents' spoiling, the parent–child relationship is not characterised by guilt. The child's staying close is a witness that the parties are good parents and good children. The Swansea system (if it may be so termed) constitutes a solution to the emotional problems created by the type of structure which, it has been suggested, characterises the contemporary British family. Its success depends on very specific cultural, social and material conditions, which, while not confined to Swansea, are by no means universal. It must also be remembered that the date of the Swansea material is 1969 and refers to an age group significantly earlier than the 7-year-olds reported on by the Newsons.

If the Swansea system can be correctly viewed as a response to the emotional structure we have described, there may clearly be a range of responses which require exploration. The emotional structure we have described does not, therefore, constitute an empirical hypothesis which encompasses the character of contemporary family life. Rather, it is an attempt to delineate the contemporary cultural and historical predicament of family members. Concrete family types will be constituted by the responses of those placed in the predicament whose delineation has been attempted here. That predicament arises out of the attempt to perform domestic and reproductive activities under specific conditions.

If families constitute specific responses to cultural and historical predicaments; if not only family form, family activity, family functioning, but also the emotional interior of the family is highly variable, then it is questionable whether the term 'family' itself should be dispensed with, thus rendering both terms of the title of the present work unacceptable; neither 'the family' nor 'industrial society' referring to rigorous theoretically constituted phenomena. 'Industrial society' may be saved as the name of an empirically delimitable class of societies but 'family' would appear to refer neither to a specific empirical type, nor be a theoretical type in the sense of theoretically constituted model of a phenomenon. The answer to those who question the continued deployment of the term 'family' is to point out that it is not a 'type' at all, but an analytic category, and that is the way it has been employed in Chapter 3. It is an essential tool in analysing the groups and relations that grow up around the universal human activities of procreation and rearing. Chapter 3 lists a bewildering variety of other activities that may be associated with such groups. Chief of these are domestic activities: the provision of food, clothing and shelter.

By the employment of the terms 'family' and 'domestic group' it is possible to specify a very real defect in 'traditional' family sociology which has focused either on kinship or child care, and occasionally on both. We may say that the analysis of the relationships between members of residential groups, has proceeded by viewing them as family relationships rather than as domestic relationships.

The domestic has been taken for granted and subsumed under the category 'family'. It has taken the work of historians to make us see the identity of the domestic and the familial as a distinctive historical conjunction. By focusing on women rather than mothers, feminist writers have likewise made us see that residential groups must be analysed in terms of their domestic activities, as well as their reproductive biological functions.

If historical work has directed our attention to the changing articulation of nuclear family groups with its social environment, feminist analyses have taught us to attend to the relation of the household to its environment, and Marxist theorists have taught us to regard the household as an economic entity and posed the question of its relation to the capitalist mode of production. Whatever its obscurities, this last perspective enables us to see the members of the nuclear family as typically constituting a household which is an essential link between two markets: the market for wage goods and the market for wage labour. Because it is a family group and not merely a household, it also functions as the agency of generational reproduction. This task it shares with other institutions, notably the educational system, and is increasingly subject to state intervention and control. These issues are only just beginning to receive the attention they deserve. (See, for example, David, 1980, on the 'family-education' couple, and Land in Harris, et al., 1979, on the family and the state.) If family members struggle to ensure the maintenance and survival of their household, the state attempts to regulate and direct the process of social reproduction which occurs within it, and to ensure its congruence with that other agency of social reproduction, the school.

It should be remembered that the meeting between the infant and the teacher is the first public occasion on which children constitute advertisements for their parents. This encounter may now be seen to have a deeper significance: it is the first test of the parents' capacities as agents of social reproduction. The rhetoric of responsibility also takes on a new significance. The anxiety about declining standards of parental responsibility may be seen as to be associated closely with the recognition of the centrality of social reproduction in maintaining political stability coupled with the inability effectively to control it. The pressures on parents are not merely those deriving from a child-rearing ideology, but stem also from a situation in which social stability depends on the reproduction of the hegemony of the dominant ideology.

If this perspective is correct, however, what people do matters. But what people do is not merely determined by their socialisation into the dominant culture pattern, it also depends on their personalities in the emotional sense, and the production of personality is one of the unintended consequences of the multiple forces which play upon families.

It would be absurd to conclude by singling out any one of the perspectives involved or any one set of relations constituting the articulation of the family. For what is required, if the place of the family in industrial societies is to be better understood, is that a new generation of studies comes into existence which examines the pattern of relations between the private and public domains and regards the household as the site of their articulation.

Bibliography

Althusser, L. (1971), *Lenin and Philosophy and Other Essays* (London: New Left Books).

Anderson, M. (1971), *Family Structure in Nineteenth Century Lancashire* (Cambridge: Cambridge University Press).

Anderson, M. (1976), 'Sociological history and the working class family: Smelser revisited', *Social History*, vol. 1, no. 3, pp. 317–34.

Anderson, M. (1979), 'The relevance of family history', in C. C. Harris, M. Anderson, D. M. Leonard and D. J. H. Morgan (eds), *The Sociology of the Family*, Sociological Review Monograph No. 28 (Keele: University of Keele), pp. 49–73.

Anderson, M. (1980), *Approaches to the History of the Western Family, 1500–1914* (London: Macmillan).

Anderson, M. (ed.) (1980), *Sociology of the Family* (Harmondsworth: Penguin).

Anthias, F. (1980), 'Women and the reserve army of labour: a critique of Veronica Beechey', *Capital and Class*, no. 10 (Spring), pp. 50–63.

Arensberg, C. M., and Kimball, S. T. (1940), *Family and Community in Ireland* (London: P. Smith).

Ariès, P. (1962), *Centuries of Childhood* (London: Cape; Harmondsworth: Penguin, 1973).

Barron, R. D., and Norris, G. M. (1976), 'Sexual divisions and the labour market', in D. L. Barker and S. Allen (eds), *Dependence and Exploitation in Work and Marriage* (London: Longman), pp. 47–69.

de Beauvoir, S. (1949), *The Second Sex* (Harmondsworth: Penguin).

Beechey, V. (1977), 'Some notes on female wage labour in capitalist production', *Capital and Class*, no. 3, (Autumn), pp. 45–66.

Beechey, V. (1978), 'Women and production: a critical analysis of some sociological theories of women's work', in A. Kuhn and A.-M. Wolfe (eds), *Feminism and Materialism* (London: Routledge & Kegan Paul), pp. 155–97.

Bell, C. R. (1968), *Middle Class Families* (London: Routledge & Kegan Paul).

Berkner, L. K. (1972), 'The stem family and the development cycle of the peasant household', *American Historical Review*, vol. 77, no. 2, pp. 398–418.

Berkner, K. K. (1975), 'The use and misuse of Census data for the historical analysis of family structure', *Journal of Interdisciplinary History*, vol. 14, no. 5, pp. 721–38.

Bilton, T., Bonnett, K., Jones, P., Stanworth, M., Sheard, K., and Webster, A. (1981), *Introductory Sociology* (London: Macmillan).

Blum, J. (1978), *The End of the Old Order in Rural Europe* (Princeton, NJ: Princeton University Press).

Bott, E. (1957), *Family and Social Network* (London: Tavistock; rev. edn, 1971).

Bronfenbrenner, U. (1970), *The Two Worlds of Childhood* (London: Allen & Unwin).

Brown, A., and Kiernan, K. (1981), 'Cohabitation in Great Britain', *Popula-

tion Trends, no. 25 (Autumn), pp. 4–10.

Brown, J. S. (1952), 'The conjugal family and the extended family group', *American Sociological Review*, vol. 17, no. 3, pp. 297–306.

Brown, J. S., *et al.* (1963), 'Kentucky mountain migration and the stem family', *Rural Sociology*, vol. 28, no. 1, pp. 48–69.

Brunner, O. (1968), *Neue Wege der Verfassungus- und Sozialgeschichte*, 2nd edn (Göttingen).

Bulmer, M. (1975), *Working Class Images of Society* (London: Routledge & Kegan Paul).

Burgess, E. W., and Locke, H. J. (1953), *The Family from Institution to Companionship* (New York: American Book Co.).

Busfield, J., and Paddon, M. (1977), *Thinking about Children* (Cambridge: Cambridge University Press).

Campbell, J. K. (1963), 'The kindred in a Greek island community', in J. Pitt-Rivers (ed.), *Mediterranean Countrymen* (The Hague: Mouton), pp. 73–96.

Cartwright, A. (1978), *Recent Trends in Family Building and Contraception*, Studies in Medical and Population Subjects No. 34, (London: HMSO).

Chayanov, A. V. (ed., D. Thorner, R. E. F. Smith and B. Kerblay) (1966), *The Theory of Peasant Economy* (Homewood, Ill.: Irwin).

Coleman, D. C. (1955–6), 'Labour in the English economy of the 17th century', *Economic History Review*, 2nd ser., vol. 8, no. 3, pp. 280–95.

[*Report of*] *Committee on One Parent Families* (1974), Cmnd 5629 (London: HMSO).

Cooley, C. H. (1962), *Social Organization* (New York: Schocken Books).

Davis, K. (1948), *Human Society* (London: Macmillan).

Demographic Review, 1977 (1978) (London: HMSO).

Demos, J. (1970), *A Little Commonwealth* (London: Oxford University Press).

Draper, H. (1970), 'Marx, Engels and women's liberation', *International Socialism*, July–August, pp. 20–9.

Dunnell, K. (OPCS) (1979), *Family Formation, 1976* (London: HMSO).

Durkheim, E. (1964), *The Division of Social Labour* (New York: Collier Macmillan).

Edgell, S. R. (1970), 'Spiralists: their careers and family lives', *British Journal of Sociology*, vol. 21, no. 3, pp. 314–23.

Edgell, S. R. (1980), *Middle Class Couples* (London: Allen & Unwin).

Eisenstadt, S. N. (1956), *From Generation to Generation* (London: Routledge & Kegan Paul).

Eldridge, J. E. T. (1980), *Recent British Sociology* (London: Macmillan).

Flandrin, J.-L. (1979), *Families in Former Times* (Cambridge: Cambridge University Press).

Fletcher, R. (1973), *The Family and Marriage in Britain*, rev. edn (Harmondsworth: Penguin; 2nd edn, 1966).

Fogarty, M., Rapoport, R., and Rapoport, R. N. (PEP) (1971), *Sex, Career and Family* (London: Allen & Unwin).

Fortes, M. (1950), 'Kinship and marriage among the Ashanti', in A. R. Radcliffe-Brown and D. Forde (eds), *African Systems of Kinship and Marriage* (London: Oxford University Press), pp. 252–84.

Fortes, M. (1953), 'The structure of unilineal descent groups', *American Anthropologist*, vol. 55, no. 1, pp. 17–41.

Foster, J. (1974), *Class Struggle and the Industrial Revolution* (London:

Weidenfeld & Nicolson).

Fromm, E. (1942), *The Fear of Freedom* (London: Routledge & Kegan Paul).

Gavron, H. (1966), *The Captive Wife* (Harmondsworth: Penguin).

Geertz, C. (1963), *Agricultural Involution: The Processes of Ecological Change in Indonesia* (Berkeley, Calif./Los Angeles: University of California Press).

General Household Survey, 1978 (OPCS) (London: HMSO).

Gerstein, I. (1973), 'Domestic work and capitalism', *Radical America,* vol. 7, nos 4, 5, pp. 101–28.

Giner, S. (1976), *Mass Society* (London: Robertson).

Goldshmidt, W. (1966), *Comparative Functionalism* (Berkeley, Calif./Los Angeles: University of California Press).

Goldthorpe, J. H., Lockwood, D., Bechhoffer, F., and Platt, J. (1968), *The Affluent Worker: Industrial Attitudes and Behaviour* (Cambridge: Cambridge University Press).

Goldthorpe, J. H., Lockwood, D., Bechhoffer, F., and Platt, J. (1969), *The Affluent Worker in the Class Structure* (Cambridge: Cambridge University Press).

Goode, W. J. (1963a), *Word Revolution and Family Patterns* (New York: Collier Macmillan).

Goode, W. J. (1963b), 'Industrialisation and family change', in B. F. Hoselitz and W. E. Moore (eds), *Industrialisation and Society* (The Hague: Mouton/Unesco), pp. 237–55.

Goody, J., Thirsk, J., and Thompson, E. (1979), *Family and Inheritance* (Cambridge: Cambridge University Press).

Gouldner, A. W. (1970), *The Coming Crisis of Western Sociology* (London: Routledge & Kegan Paul).

Green, E. R. R. (1944), 'The cotton handloom weavers in the northeast of Ireland', *Ulster Journal of Archeology,* vol. 7, pp. 30–41.

Habbakuk, H. J. (1955), 'Family structure and economic change in nineteenth century Europe', *Journal of Economic History,* vol. 15, no. 1, pp. 1–12; also in N. W. Bell and E. P. Vogel (eds), *The Family* (New York: The Free Press, 1960), pp. 163–72.

Hajnal, J. (1965), 'European marriage patterns in perspective', in D. V. Glass and D. E. C. Eversley (eds), *Population in History* (London: Edward Arnold), pp. 101–43.

Handel, G. (1968), *The Psycho-Social Interior of the Family* (London: Allen & Unwin).

Harris, C. C. (1969), *The Family: An Introduction* (London: Allen & Unwin).

Harris, C. C. (1980), *Fundamental Concepts and the Sociological Enterprise* (London: Croom Helm).

Harris, C. C., Anderson, M., Leonard, D. M., and Morgan, D. J. H. (1979), *The Sociology of the Family,* Sociological Review Monograph No. 28 (Keele: University of Keele), pp. 49–73.

Harrison, J. (1973), 'Political economy of housework', *Conference of Socialist Economists' Bulletin,* (Winter), pp. 35–52.

Hart, N. (1976), *When Marriage Ends: A Study in Status Passage* (London: Tavistock).

Hartman, H. I. (1979), 'The unhappy marriage of Marxism and feminism', *Capital and Class,* no. 8 (Summer), pp. 1–33.

Homans, G. C. (1941), *English Villagers of the Thirteenth Century* (Cambridge, Mass.: Harvard University Press).

Howell, C. (1975), 'Stability and change, 1300–1700: the socio-economic content of the self-perpetuating family farm in England', *Journal of Peasant Studies*, vol. 2, no. 4, pp. 468–82.

Hunt, D. (1970), *Parents and Children in History* (New York: Basic Books).

James, M. E. (1974), *Family, Lineage and Civil Society* (London: Oxford University Press).

Johnson, R. (1979), 'Three problematics: elements of a theory of working class culture', in J. Clarke, C. Critcher and R. Johnson (eds), *Working Class Culture* (London: Hutchinson), pp. 201–37.

Johnson, R. and Medinnus, G. R. (1965), *Child Psychology: Behaviour and Development* (New York: Wiley).

Joyce, P. (1980), *Work, Society and Politics* (Hassocks: Harvester Press).

Kenny, M. (1956), *A Spanish Tapestry* (London: Cohen & West).

Klein, J. (1965), *Samples from English Culture* (London: Routledge & Kegan Paul), Vol. 1.

Klein, V. (1965), *British Married Women Workers* (London: Routledge & Kegan Paul).

Kuhn, A. (1978), 'Structures of patriarchy and capital in the family', in A. Kuhn and A.-M. Wolfe (eds), *Feminism and Materialism* (London: Routledge & Kegan Paul), pp. 42–67.

Laing, R. D. (1971), *Politics and the Family* (London: Tavistock).

Landes, D. S. (1966), *The Rise of Capitalism* (London: Macmillan).

Laslett, P. (1969), 'Size and structure of the household in England over three centuries', *Population Studies*, vol. 23, pt 2, pp. 199–223.

Laslett, P. (1971), *The World We Have Lost*, 2nd edn (Cambridge: Cambridge University Press).

Laslett, P. (1972), 'Mean household size in England since the sixteenth century' (revision of Laslett, 1969), in P. Laslett and R. Wall (eds), *Household and Family in Past Time* (Cambridge: Cambridge University Press), pp. 125–58.

Laslett, P. (1977), *Family Life and Illicit Love in Earlier Generations* (Cambridge: Cambridge University Press).

Leach, E. (1967), *A Runaway World* (London: Oxford University Press).

Lebowitz, M. A. (1976), 'The political economy of housework', *Conference of Socialist Economists' Bulletin*, vol. 5, no. 1.

Leete, R. (1978), 'One parent families: numbers and characteristics', *Population Trends*, no. 13 (Autumn), pp. 4–9.

Leete, R. (OPCS) (1979), *Changing Patterns of Family Formation and Dissolution in England and Wales, 1964–76*, Studies in Medical and Population Subjects No. 39 (London: HMSO).

Leete, R., and Anthony, S. (1979), 'Divorce and remarriage', *Population Trends*, no. 16 (Summer), pp. 5–11.

Leonard, D. (1980), *Sex and Generation* (London: Tavistock).

Le Roy Ladurie, E. (1978), *Montaillou* (London: Scolar Press).

Levine, D. (1977), *Family Formation in an Age of Nascent Capitalism* (London: Academic Press).

Levy, M. J. (1965), 'Aspects of the analysis of family structure', in A. J. Coale (ed.), *Aspects of the Analysis of Family Structure* (Princeton, NJ: Princeton University Press), pp. 1–67.

Lieberman, S. (1981), *Transgenerational Family Therapy* (London: Croom Helm).

Lis, C., and Soly, H. (1979), *Poverty and Capitalism* (Hassocks: Harvester Press).

Litwak, E. (1960a), 'Occupational mobility and extended family cohesion', *American Sociological Review*, vol. 25, no. 1, pp. 9–12.

Litwak, E. (1960b), 'Geographic mobility and extended family cohesion', *American Sociological Review*, vol. 25, no. 3, pp. 385–94.

Litwak, E. (1965), 'Extended kin relations in an industrial democratic society', in E. Shanas and G. Streib (eds), *Social Structure and the Family* (Englewood Cliffs, NJ: Prentice-Hall), pp. 290–323.

Lockwood, D. (1966), 'Sources of variation in working-class images of society', *Sociological Review*, vol. 14, no. 3, pp. 249–67.

Lukes, S. (1973), *Individualism* (Oxford: Blackwell).

Macfarlane, A. (1978), *The Origins of English Individualism* (Oxford: Blackwell).

Macintyre, S. (1976), ' "Who wants babies?" The social construction of "instincts" ', in D. L. Barker and S. Allen (eds), *Sexual Divisions and Society: Process and Change* (London: Tavistock), pp. 150–73.

McIver, R. M., and Page, C. N. (1957), *Society* (London: Macmillan).

Malinowski, B. (1930), 'Kinship', *Man*, vol. 30 (February), item no. 17, pp. 19–29.

de Mause, L. (ed.) (1976), *The History of Childhood* (London: Souvenir Press).

Mead, G. H. (1934), *Mind, Self and Society* (Chicago: Chicago University Press).

Medick, H. (1976), 'The proto-industrial family economy', *Social History*, vol. 1, no. 3, pp. 291–315.

Mendels, F. F. (1972), 'Proto-industrialisation: the first phase of the industrialisation process', *Journal of Economic History*, vol. 32, no. 1, pp. 241–61.

Millar, J. R. (1969), 'A reformulation of A. V. Chayanov's theory of the peasant economy', *Economic Development and Cultural Change*, vol. 18, no. 2, pp. 219–29.

Moore, W. E. (1963), 'Industrialisation and social change', in B. F. Hoselitz and W. E. Moore (eds), *Industrialisation and Society* (The Hague: Mouton/Unesco), pp. 299–359.

Morgan, D. H. J. (1975), *Social Theory and the Family* (London: Routledge & Kegan Paul).

Morgan, D. H. J. (1979), 'New directions in family research and theory', in C. C. Harris, M. Anderson, D. M. Leonard and D. J. H. Morgan (eds), *The Sociology of the Family*, Sociological Review Monograph No. 28 (Keele: University of Keele), pp. 3–18.

Morgan, E. (1966), *The Puritan Family* (New York: Harper).

Murdock, G. P. (1949), *Social Structure* (London: Macmillan).

Myrdal, A., and Klein, V. (1968), *Women's Two Roles* (London: Routledge & Kegan Paul).

Neumann, S. (1965), *Permanent Revolution* (New York: Praeger).

Newby, H., Bell, C., Rose, D., and Saunders, P. (1978), *Property, Paternalism and Power* (London: Hutchinson).

Newson, J., and Newson, E. (1963), *Patterns of Infant Care* (Harmondsworth: Penguin).

Newson, J., and Newson, E. (1968), *Four Years Old in an Urban Community* (London: Allen & Unwin).

Newson, J., and Newson, E. (1974), 'Cultural aspects of child rearing in the English-speaking world', in M. P. M. Richards (ed.), *The Integration of a Child into a Social World* (Cambridge: Cambridge University Press), pp. 53–82.

Newson, J., and Newson, E. (1976), *Seven Years Old in the Home Environment* (London: Allen & Unwin).

Nimkoff, M. F., and Middleton R. (1960), 'Types of family and types of economy', *American Journal of Sociology*, vol. 66, no. 3, p. 215.

Nisbet, R. (1967), *The Sociological Tradition* (London: Heinemann).

Oakley, A. (1974), *The Sociology of Housework* (London: Robertson).

Oakley, A. (1976), *Housewife* (Harmondsworth: Penguin).

Ogburn, W. F. (1938), 'The changing functions of the family', in R. F. Winch, R. McGuinnis and H. R. Barringer (eds), *Selected Studies in Marriage and the Family* (New York: Holt, Rinehart, 1962), pp. 157–63.

Pahl, J. M., and Pahl, R. E. (1971), *Managers and Their Wives* (London: Allen Lane).

Park, G. K. (1962), 'Sons and lovers', *Ethnology,* vol. 1, no. 4, p. 412.

Parsons, T. (1942), 'Age and sex in the social structure of the United States', in Parsons (ed.), *Essays in Sociological Theory* (New York: The Free Press, 1964), pp. 89–103.

Parsons, T. (1943), 'The kinship system of the contemporary United States', in Parsons (ed.), *Essays in Sociological Theory* (New York: The Free Press), pp. 177–96.

Parsons, T. (1949), 'The social structure of the family', in R. N. Anshen (ed.), *The Family: Its Function and Destiny* (New York: Hayner, 1959), pp. 241–74.

Parsons, T. (1952), *The Social System* (Glencoe, Ill.: The Free Press).

Parsons, T. (1956), *Family, Socialisation and Interaction Process* (London: Routledge & Kegan Paul).

Parsons, T. (1970), 'Reply to his critics', in M. Anderson (ed.), *The Sociology of the Family* (Harmondsworth: Penguin), pp. 120–1.

Pearce, D., and Farid, S. (1977), 'Illegitimate births: changing patterns', *Population Trends*, no. 9 (Autumn), pp. 20–3.

Pinchbeck, I. (1954), 'Social attitudes to the problem of illegitimacy', *British Journal of Sociology*, vol. 5, no. 4, pp. 309–23.

Pitts, J. R. (1964), 'The structural-functional approach', in H. T. Christensen (ed.), *Handbook of Marriage and the Family* (Chicago: Rand McNally), pp. 88–90.

Population Trends, 2 (1981) (London: OPCS/HMSO).

Poster, M. (1978), *The Critical Theory of the Family* (London: Pluto Press).

Rapoport, R., and Rapoport, R. N. (1971), *Dual Career Families* (London: Robertson).

Rapoport, R., and Rapoport, R. N. (1976), *Dual Career Families Re-Examined* (London: Robertson).

Rapoport, R. N., Rapoport, R., and Bumstead, J. (eds) (1978), *Working Couples* (London: Routledge & Kegan Paul).

Redfield, R. (1953), *The Primitive World and its Transformations* (Ithaca, NY: Cornell University Press).

Redfield, R. (1956), *Peasant Society and Culture* (Chicago: Chicago University Press).

Rees, A. D. (1950), *Life in a Welsh Countryside* (Cardiff: University of Wales Press).

Rex, J., and Moore, R. (1967), *Race, Community and Conflict* (Oxford: Oxford University Press).

Riasonovsky, N. (1953), 'Fourierism in Russia', *American Slavonic and East European Review*, vol. 12, pp. 295–6.

Richter, H.-E. (1973), 'Pathogenic constellation in family dynamics', in A. P. Dreitzel (ed.), *Childhood and Socialisation* (New York: Collier Macmillan), pp. 85–110.

Rosenberg, C. (ed.) (1975), *The Family in History* (Philadelphia, Pa: University of Pennsylvania Press).

Rosser, K. C., and Harris, C. C. (1965), *The Family and Social Change* (London: Routledge & Kegan Paul).

Schochet, G. J. (1975), *Patriarchalism in Political Thought* (Oxford: Blackwell).

Schuecking, L. (1969), *The Puritan Family* (London: Routledge & Kegan Paul).

Schwarzweller, H. K. (1964), 'Parental family ties and social integration of rural-urban migrants', *Journal of Marriage and the Family*, vol. 26, no. 4, p. 410.

Scott, J. W., and Tilly, L. A. (1975), 'Women's work and the family in nineteenth century Europe', *Comparative Studies in Society and History*, vol. 17, no. 1, pp. 36–64.

Seccombe, W. (1974), 'The housewife and her labour under capitalism', *New Left Review*, no. 83, pp. 3–74.

Seccombe, W. (1975), 'Domestic labour: a reply to critics', *New Left Review*, no. 94, pp. 84–96.

Selznick, P. (1960), *The Organisational Weapon* (New York: The Free Press).

Sennett, R. (1970a), *Families against the City* (Cambridge, Mass.: Harvard University Press).

Sennett, R. (1970b), *The Uses of Disorder* (New York: Knopf, 1970; London: Allen Lane, 1971).

Sennett, R. (1974), *The Fall of Public Man* (Cambridge: Cambridge University Press).

Sennett, R., and Cobb, J. (1972), *The Hidden Injuries of Class* (New York: Knopf, 1972; Cambridge: Cambridge University Press, 1977).

Shanin, T. (1971), 'Peasantry as a political factor', in T. Shanin (ed.), *Peasants and peasant Societies* (Harmondsworth: Penguin, 1971), pp. 238–63.

Shanin, T. (1972), *The Awkward Class* (Oxford: Clarendon Press).

Smelser, N. J. (1959), *Social Change and the Industrial Revolution* (London: Routledge & Kegan Paul).

Social Trends, 1981 (London: HMSO).

Stehower, J. (1965), 'Relations between the generations and the three generational household in Denmark', in E. Shanas and G. Streib (eds), *Social Structure and the Family* (Englewood Cliffs, NJ: Prentice-Hall, 1965), pp. 142–62.

Stone, L. (1961), 'Marriage among the English nobility in the sixteenth and seventeenth centuries', *Comparative Studies in Society and History*, vol. 3, no. 2, pp. 182–206.

Stone, L. (1975), 'The rise of the nuclear family in early modern England', in C. E. Rosenberg (ed.), *The Family in History* (Philadelphia, Pa: University of Pennsylvania Press), pp. 13–57.

Stone, L. (1977), *Family, Sex and Marriage in England, 1500–1800* (London: Weidenfeld & Nicolson).

Stuckert, R. P. (1963), 'Occupational mobility and family relations', *Social Forces*, vol. 41, no. 3, pp. 301–7.

Sussman, M. B. (1959), 'Isolated nuclear family: fact or fiction', *Social*

Problems, vol. 6, pp. 333–40.

Sussman, M. B. (1965), 'Relationships of adult children with their parents', in E. Shanas and G. Streib (eds), *Social Structure and the Family* (Englewood Cliffs, NJ: Prentice-Hall, 1965), pp. 62–92.

Sussman, M. B., and Burchinal, I. G. (1966a), 'Parental aid to married children: implications for family functioning', in B. Faber (ed.), *Kinship and Family Organisation* (New York: Wiley), pp. 240–54.

Sussman, M. B., and Burchinal, I. G. (1966b), 'Kin family network: unheralded structure in current conceptualisations of family functioning', in B. Faber (ed.), *Kinship and Family Organisation* (New York: Wiley), pp. 123–33.

Thirsk, J. (ed.) (1967), *The Agrarian History of England and Wales* (Cambridge: Cambridge University Press), Vol. 4.

Thorner, D. (1971), 'Peasant economy as a category in economic history', in T. Shanin (ed.), *Peasants and Peasant Studies* (Harmondsworth: Penguin, 1971), pp. 202–17.

Thornes, B., and Collard, C. (1979), *Who Divorces?* (London: Routledge & Kegan Paul).

Tilly, L. A., Scott, J. W., and Cohen, M. (1976), 'Women's work and European fertility patterns', *Journal of Interdisciplinary History*, vol. 6, no. 3, pp. 447–76.

Titmuss, R. (1958), *Essays on the Welfare State* (London: Allen & Unwin).

de Tocqueville, A. (1968), *Democracy in America* (London: Collins).

Toennies, F. (1955), *Community and Society* (London: Routledge & Kegan Paul).

Trumbach, R. (1978), *The Rise of the Egalitarian Family* (London: Academic Press).

Veevers, J. E. (1980), *Childless by Choice* (London: Butterworths).

Vincent, D. (1979), Review of A. S. Wohl, *The Victorian Family, Social History*, vol. 4, no. 3, pp. 541–3.

Wallerstein, I. (1974), *The Modern World System* (London: Academic Press).

Walrond-Skinner, S. (ed.) (1979), *Family and Marital Psychotherapy* (London: Routledge & Kegan Paul).

Weber, M. (1930), *The Protestant Ethic and the Spirit of Capitalism*, trans. T. Parsons (London: Allen & Unwin).

Weber, M. (ed., T. Parsons) (1964), *The Theory of Social and Economic Organization* (New York: Collier Macmillan).

Williams, W. M. (1956), *The Sociology of an English Village* (London: Routledge & Kegan Paul).

Williams, W. M. (1963), *Ashworthy* (London: Routledge & Kegan Paul).

Wolfenstein, M. (1955), 'Fun morality: an analysis of recent American child-training literature', in M. Mead and M. Wolfenstein (eds), *Childhood in Contemporary Cultures* (Chicago: University of Chicago Press), pp. 168–78.

Wrigley, A. (1968), 'Mortality in pre-industrial England: the example of Colyton, Devon over three centuries', *Daedalus*, vol. 97, no. 2, pp. 546–80.

Wrigley, A. (1969), *Population and History* (London: Weidenfeld & Nicolson).

Young, M., and Willmott, P. (1957), *Family and Kinship in East London* (London: Routledge & Kegan Paul).

Young, M., and Willmott, P. (1973), *The Symmetrical Family* (London: Routledge & Kegan Paul).

Zaretsky, E. (1976), *Capitalism, the Family and Personal Life* (London: Pluto Press).

Name Index

Subject Index